Meditations on a Loving God

Leslie F. Brandt

Meditations on a Loving God

Daily Readings Through the Church Year

Publishing House
St. Louis

Copyright © 1983 Concordia Publishing House,
3558 South Jefferson Avenue, St. Louis, MO 63118

Manufactured in the United States of America

Library of Congress Cataloging in Publication Data

Brandt, Leslie F.
  Meditations on a loving God.

  Includes index.
  1. Church year meditations. I. Title
BV30.B67   1983   242'.2   82-14472
ISBN 0-570-03858-8

1 2 3 4 5 6 7 8 9 10   WP   92 91 90 89 88 87 86 85 84 83

To my wife Edith,
who lovingly rounds off some of the rough edges
of both the author and his writings, and with whom
he, enduring and rejoicing, has shared life for over forty years.

Contents

Preface

I remember how important a book of daily meditations was to me during my college days. It was Oswald Chambers' *My Utmost for His Highest*. While that particular book seldom meets my needs today, I have often longed for a day-by-day book of meditations that would. Not being able to find any, I have attempted to write my own. It is not written for small children or even families in general, but is designed for Christ's followers, high-school age and above, who sincerely want to be His disciples in our kind of world.

In order to select Scriptural texts that depict the "whole counsel of God," I decided to follow the traditional Three-Year Lectionary readings, which follow the Church Year calendar. Members of liturgical churches will be familiar with them and may find it beneficial to follow through the Church Year rather than day-by-day meditations on a Roman calendar basis. It should be noted that the length of the Epiphany and Pentecost seasons differs each year and readings will be carried out accordingly. Nonliturgical readers may find and keep pace in these meditations by finding the Festival Sunday readings, such as Christmas, Easter, Pentecost, and go from there. According to the Church Year calendar, the year begins, as does this volume, with the First Sunday in Advent—four Sundays before Christmas.

If these daily meditations are to be meaningful, they must be read in conjunction with the reading of the Scripture lesson assigned to each day. Read the Scripture; meditate with me; conclude with prayer; have a good day!

Leslie F. Brandt

First Sunday in Advent
Matthew 24:37–44 (A)

Later than You Think

"Heaven and earth will pass away . . ." announced Jesus in a verse just before this Gospel lesson. And all the rioting, flag-waving, dissenting, and politicizing in the world will not stop this predicted and unprecedented event which guarantees that life as we know it, the pleasures that pamper, the comforts that cuddle, the toys we tinker with, will not be ours forever.

Jesus refers to Noah and the flood to get His point across: "For as in those days before the flood they were eating and drinking, marrying and giving in marriage, until the day when Noah entered the ark." There is no mention of wife-swapping, drug addiction, nudie bars, or sexploitation films. As unsavory and degenerate as these things are, they were not the things that brought on world destruction. What provoked God's anger in Noah's day was not the various outer symptoms of sin that disturb us today, but the self-centeredness, which is really unbelief, of people who felt they didn't need God or anybody else outside of their selfish circles. God apparently could take their egotism and arrogance no longer. He simply turned on the water.

Whether or not it is the wickedness of God's children that will bring on the end of the world as we know it, Jesus uses the Old Testament event to illustrate the suddenness and unexpectedness of His final appearance. Irrespective of the numerous would-be prophets and their predictions, "the Son of man is coming at an hour you do not expect." Escape from that judgment is possible only by faith in Him who stayed the hand of God from utterly destroying the rebellious world.

Monday   *Romans 13:11–14 (A)*

Time to Get Up

It is time to get up and "put on the Lord Jesus Christ." "The night is far gone, the day is at hand," wrote Paul, and that is as close as he comes to making any predictions in respect to Christ's coming and the final gathering together of God's children into His eternal kingdom. While Paul warned against date-setting and even reprimanded some of his readers for giving up their jobs and daily duties to ready themselves for Christ's promised return, he was filled with anticipation and expectation concerning that great and ultimate event.

There is, nonetheless, something we can do as we anticipate that incomprehensible happening. It is to "put on the Lord Jesus Christ," to emulate Jesus, to walk with God as He has been revealed through Christ. This most certainly means a daily "dying" to those things within our natures and our world that come between us and God—and between us and our fellow beings. It means, as well, that we work as servants and ministers of the kingdom to which we already belong. As God came to us through Christ, so Christ seeks to reach our brothers and sisters in the human family through us.

We are to live and act as if the kingdom has already been revealed, the sun already risen, for even while there is much darkness about us, Christ *has* come, the kingdom of God *is* here. We are to "cast off the works of darkness" and live and love, minister and serve, as God's sons and daughters are destined to do. It is as we do this that the coming dawn dispells all fear and fills our beings with joy and excitement.

Tuesday   *Mark 13:33–37 (B)*

Be Alert—and Responsible

While self-appointed prophets continue to gather followers with enthusiastic proclamations concerning the imminent end of our world and the second coming of Christ, our Lord states emphatically that the day and hour of this fantastic event is not known even to Himself. Paul asserts that "salvation is nearer to us now than when we first believed" (Romans 13:11). It is certainly nearer to this day in which we live a couple of millenniums after Paul. "But of that day or that hour no one knows" (v. 32).

The response of many Christians to the predictions of Christ's impending return to this planet is non-involvement in this world's affairs, a running away from the reality of this earth's gross tragedies, walling themselves in away from the atrocities that fall upon the human family. Rather than being ministers and servants of the invisible but ever-present Lord and Savior, they are frightened, cowering creatures, seeking to be taken away from it all.

We are, indeed, to be alert, to "watch"; for our Lord and Master may return at any moment. We are likewise to be responsible, obedient, trustworthy, in the task He has laid upon us. It is not important that we be physically alive to greet and celebrate His visible return to this

12

world. It is important that we be faithful to our calling and, in our love for and service to God's creatures about us, enlarge and nourish the kingdom of God that is among us.

Wednesday   *1 Corinthians 1:3–9 (B)*

Amazing Grace

It is the very grace of God that makes us capable of being and doing what He would have us to be and do. By His grace we were received into God's family through Christ's redeeming love. By His grace we are made guiltless and will be sustained and kept to and beyond the end of this world. Because of His grace we are gifted—enriched with all the provision and power needed to carry out His plans for us in this life and within this world. Paul insists that we are "not lacking in any spiritual gift" as we work and wait "for the revealing of our Lord Jesus Christ."

This is amazing, astounding—almost unbelievable! Yet it is true. We need not bemoan our inadequacies nor envy our colleagues who appear to be better endowed than we. We are redeemed, forgiven, ordained for service in God's kingdom, and empowered to carry out our assignment as God's messengers and ministers.

Something we must do, however, as the dawn of the new kingdom turns into the full light of day, is to act on our assignment, to utilize God's gracious gifts for the benefit of others. We must renew our commitment to God and His purposes and yield our bodies and beings to His control. God is faithful; we must walk in faith and serve in loving obedience as His responsible servants within His eternal kingdom.

Thursday   *Luke 21:25–36 (C)*

Living in the Shadows

Thomas Campbell, a poet of the last century, once penned these words: "Tis the sunset of life gives mystical lore, and coming events cast their shadows before." We are living in the shadows. The gaiety, the buying and selling activity, the sensuality and superficiality about us do not succeed in obliterating these shadows.

There are shadows flitting across our paths that are both ominous and exhilarating. We may not see much happening "in sun and moon and stars," but the things that transpire about us, the wild commotions

13

and calamities that engulf the nations of the earth, the fears and forebodings that afflict the hearts of men and women, may indeed indicate that our "redemption is drawing near." While people wonder what the world is coming to, we are wondering what is coming to our world. Whatever the event these shadows portend, it is time that we "take heed" to ourselves, to make preparations, not in fear of the things to come, but by faith in the God who has come, who is here, and who at any moment may consummate His purposes for this planet on which we live.

It is time that we discover or rediscover God's order and orbit for our lives. It is time that we cease shadow-boxing with God, get off the fence, and begin making some genuine decisions in respect to our relationship with Him. It is time that we who claim to follow Christ begin to act like the Christ we follow. It is time that we desist from our competitive, profit-and-gain aspirations, recognize the human family as our family, and dedicate our lives and means to God and His purposes and share our abundance with our brothers and sisters throughout the world. It is time that we who are God's children begin to recognize who we are and demonstrate the joy of that relationship to our fellow beings about us. It is time that we wake up and look up, for "the kingdom of God is near."

Friday   *1 Thessalonians 3:9–13 (C)*

Ready for His Coming

As we contemplate "the coming of our Lord Jesus with all His saints," we are lovingly concerned about our dear friends, our brothers and sisters in the Lord, who are faithfully laboring and serving in the various arenas in which God through call or circumstance has placed them.

We are grateful for them. They are our colleagues in kingdom service and, whether their station be high or low, out front or behind the scenes, their contributions are vital to the purposes of our Father.

We must remember them in our prayers—these brothers and sisters of ours. We sincerely hope they remember us in their meditations before God.

God grant that our love for one another is increased and enriched as we work within His kingdom and anticipate the coming of our Lord Jesus Christ to consummate our labors upon this earth. It is such love, our love for one another, through which our God strengthens and sustains us in those difficult hours when our efforts appear to bear so little fruit.

Of this we can be sure: As we individually and mutually lay claim to God's righteousness as revealed and made available through Jesus Christ and abound in our love for one another and thereby become effective vehicles of His love to others about us, our hearts will be "unblamable in holiness before our God and Father, at the coming of our Lord Jesus with all His saints."

Saturday   *Jeremiah 33:14–16 (C)*

Promises, Promises

The pages of the Old Testament—along with its portrayal of many conflicts and struggles—are permeated with bright flashes of divine light. They revealed, through inspired prophets such as Jeremiah, the plan of God to execute righteousness amidst this world's darkness.

We live in the day of promise-fulfillment. God has visited this planet. This is what Christmas is all about. Through Jesus Christ, God-incarnate, His righteousness has been manifested and made available to this world's inhabitants, and the Judah and Jerusalem that Jeremiah referred to becomes the church that embraces the blessed recipients of this divinely imparted righteousness.

Inherent in Jeremiah's prophecy is the great event that is still to come—the final revelation and gathering-together of God's kingdom of righteousness that will become the new and eternal Judah and Jerusalem. It is a part of Jeremiah's prophecy; it is an integral part of what is even now being fulfilled. We are citizens of that promised kingdom. We are servants of God who are working by His grace and indwelling Spirit towards its fulfillment. We look forward with anticipation and joy to its consummation.

Promises, promises. We live even now amongst fulfilled promises. The ultimate fulfillment is not yet, but when it happens we will be a part of it even as we are now observers and participants in the prophet's proclamations and promises.

Second Sunday in Advent
Matthew 3:1-12 (A)

The Need for a Changed Heart

"Repent, for the kingdom of heaven is at hand," was John the Baptist's message to those who gathered to hear him in the Judean wilderness. He was preparing the way for Jesus' entrance into His public ministry. "You must change your hearts," John cried, "for God's kingdom has arrived."

It means that we must tear down, by the grace God grants, those obstructions that stand between us and our God—the deceit, the hypocrisy, the pride and self-sufficiency, the inordinate affection for the things of this world. They must be stripped from us as if they were plague-infested garments, for they come between us and the Christ of Christmas, between us and Christmas joy, between us and eternal life.

John the Baptist didn't stop there—though we often do. "Bear fruit that befits repentance," he challenged. "Go and do something to show that your hearts are really changed," he says in essence. It is this second half of the Gospel that we tend to ignore. John said it and Jesus reiterated it, that the tree, or the life, "that does not bear good fruit is cut down and thrown into the fire." We cherish Christ's invitation to "come" unto Him; God grant that we hear and obey His command to "go" with Him—into the dark places of this world to channel His life and power into the hearts and lives of hungry, oppressed, unregenerate people.

Monday   *Romans 15:4-13 (A)*

Abounding in Hope

We would like to begin each day with a smattering of ecstasy—rising to our feet with happiness in our hearts and hallelujahs on our lips. There are those days, however, when we have to settle for hope. Spiritual ecstasies may be few and far between, but hope abounds forever. Even the dark days of our lives are pregnant with hope. Behind the heavy clouds that threaten is the sun that will eventually burn them away and flood dull lives with light and joy. Thus there is hope; always there is hope.

The Scriptures encourage us and give us hope—as do the lives of those suffering saints before us. God loves us; Christ has come to declare and demonstrate that love. We may not always *feel* this to be true, but it is true nonetheless, and this is the source of the everlasting joy that overcomes our bouts with depression and undergirds our lives with that incomprehensible peace that is not obliterated by the tempests of this daily existence.

We can begin each day with praises on our lips—no matter how heavy the heart. Indeed, as we praise God for the facts concerning our redemption and adoption as His children, for His eternal and unchanging love as our heavenly Father, the heart's burdens are lifted, the sun breaks through the clouds, and we continue, by the power of the Holy Spirit, to "abound in hope."

Tuesday   *Mark 1:1–8 (B)*

This Is It!

Advent is the beginning of the Church Year. We begin all over again to read and rejoice in God's story. The first Gospel that was ever written was probably the Gospel according to Mark. He was a realist. He doesn't take the time to philosophize or conjecture. His Gospel is the shortest of all the Gospels—and the bluntest—a sort of these-are-the-facts approach to the story of God and the presentation of Christ as God's fullest revelation of Himself and His purposes for His created world.

Mark does not even begin with the birth of Jesus as do Matthew and Luke. "Here begins the Gospel of Jesus Christ, the Son of God," he starts off, and in only eight verses is already deep into the Biblical drama.

What Mark is saying, in effect, is that "this is it!" This is what God has been preparing His creatures for throughout the centuries; this is what the prophets were dimly predicting as their minds slowly opened to God's eternal truth. "This is it." This One, Jesus Christ, God's Son, is the answer to the aching longings of men and women throughout the ages, the healing and the cure for the twisted and distorted lives of God's human creatures, the canceling out of the debt of sin that has impregnated the lives of all people since the beginning of time, the way back to God's order and orbit, wherein alone there is peace and joy even in the midst of this life's fractures and failures.

"This is it," the purpose of our lives, the reason for our existence—and it is this that will restore us to that purpose and objective. This is the One who has come, who is here, and who confronts us today with the promise, as we embrace Him as our Savior and Lord, to enthrone Himself in our hearts through His Spirit and to make us His children and servants forever.

Wednesday   *2 Peter 3:8–14 (B)*

Waiting—Patiently and Faithfully

While scoffers treat the promise of Christ's return as sheer nonsense, the children of God are often impatiently awaiting that great event. They ought to regard the fact that He is "slow about His promise" with joy, suggested Peter. His immediate return would indeed deliver us from a multitude of trials and temptations that frustrate us and from atrocities that frighten and threaten to destroy us, but might also seal the fate of scores of our friends and relatives—our brothers and sisters in the human family—who have not as yet surrendered to His redeeming love and servanthood. God is still waiting for His created children to separate themselves from the degradation of this planet and return to His plan and orbit for their lives. The desire of His loving heart is that they, too, will be ready to greet the Christ when He returns.

In the meantime, we are to wait patiently and serve faithfully. We do not know the day or the hour, not even the year or the century, of His coming. We only know that we belong to Him, and as long as we continue committedly and joyfully to labor within His purposes, we are ready for the fulfillment of His promised return.

In obediently and lovingly serving Him and our fellow beings, we may even bring closer that Day of His final and ultimate revelation.

Thursday   *Luke 3:1–6 (C)*

Getting Ready for God

As John the Baptist was sent by the Spirit to ready the people for God-revealed-through-Christ's ministry, so we must be a part of preparing the way for Christ's entrance into and ministry through our lives. Christ's initial coming was demonstrated in the Christmas event and the manger scene. His coming into His public ministry was signaled by John the Baptist. As with Isaiah's picture of the preparation necessary to make possible the journey of an ancient monarch, so the

18

Spirit of God must make possible God's march and manifestation through us.

The Spirit of Christ has to *fill up the valleys* in our lives. This refers to the elimination of those gaping holes that become monumental evidences of our vain efforts and endeavors to find meaning and purpose in life apart from Christ. We have dug great excavations in our frenzied attempts to find soul peace and divine order and have found fool's gold instead. "Every valley shall be filled," wrote Isaiah, and this is what happens when Christ has His way in and through us.

God's Spirit must *tear down the mountains and hills,* the obstructions and obstacles that stand in His way. The smallest molehill may be the greatest mountain as long as it stands between us and God. The removal of these molehills or mountains will take place only if we, enlightened and inspired by the Spirit of God, obediently *will* that they be crumbled and done away with.

The Spirit of God must *straighten out the crooked paths and make the rough ways smooth.* It means that all irregularities, hindrances, distortions, all that is shady and sinful, must be brought out of the dark corners of our inner beings and submitted to the judgment and forgiveness of a loving God.

Christ came at Christmas; He invisibly indwelt our hearts and lives at our baptism. He will carry out His mission through us as long as we permit Him to fill the emptiness, tear down the obstacles, straighten the crooked paths, and through us reach out to touch others around us with His loving grace.

Friday   *Philippians 1:3–11 (C)*

Keep On Loving

In view of Christ's eventual second advent to this planet, it is Paul's prayer that the love of his Christian brothers and sisters will continue to increase and to abound—along with the gifts of knowledge and discernment. And this in order that they may be "filled with the fruits of righteousness which come through Jesus Christ."

Paul's injunction is to keep on loving—loving God and loving one another. We need, in these precarious days, not only the everflowing grace of God which comes to us through His Spirit by way of Word and Sacrament, but the strength and encouragement that comes through loving relationships with one another.

We can be as certain as Paul that God, who adopted us as His children and gifted us with His Spirit, will complete this great thing He has done for us "at the day of Jesus Christ." Let us pray as Paul prayed that we may be "filled with the fruits of righteousness which come through Jesus Christ" and that our lives today and always may be lived "to the glory and praise of God."

Thus, whatever the difficulties this day and this life hold for us, we must keep on loving. Whether or not others reciprocate and respond to our love, we must keep on loving—our family, friends, adversaries, especially our fellow laborers within the kingdom of God. This is God's role for us in our world today.

God help us to keep on loving!

Saturday   *Isaiah 40:1–11 (B)*

A Comforting God

The Old Testament seems, at times, to be overweighed with frightening visions and prophecies of God as the One who would enforce justice upon this world—a sort of warring God who would lead heavenly armies against the enemies of righteousness and destroy idol-worshipers and wicked rulers and all those people and things that stand between Him and His purposes for this world and its creatures. Every now and then, however, prophets and poets saw or envisioned something of the Almighty's loving concern for His created children. They beheld Him not only as a God of justice and righteousness, but as One who seeks to comfort His children within an unjust, atrocity-ridden world.

"He will feed His flock like a shepherd," announces Isaiah. "The Lord is my shepherd, I shall not want," said the psalmist. God will come— indeed He has come—not only to judge, to rule, and ultimately to destroy all that stands in the way of His kingdom, but to comfort His people, to "gather the lambs in His arms" and "carry them in His bosom."

It is this facet of God that is revealed through God-Incarnate, Jesus Christ. Now we know that God loves us, cares about us, and comforts us as we strive to serve Him in our kind of world. And this is the good news we are assigned to share with our suffering, struggling colleagues on this planet. This makes each day a joyful and significant one.

Third Sunday in Advent
Matthew 11:2–11 (A)

John's Question—Christ's Response

John the Baptist's blunt and courageous tongue soon talked him into jail and execution, but not before he baptized a plain, simple son-of-a-carpenter called Jesus and received a sign from God that this man was God's Son who was sent to establish and build His Father's kingdom. While marking time in Herod's prison, John was anticipating and assuming that this Jesus, whom he had announced and introduced to the crowds that followed him, would be uniting Israel to resist Herod and Rome and reign over a rebellious world as God's chosen people. This obviously was not happening, and so John asked his comrades to go out and see what Jesus was doing—to find out if this man was truly the Christ, the Messiah, who was to come. "Are you He who is to come, or shall we look for another?" they asked Him.

Jesus, who dearly loved and deeply respected John, did not respond directly to their inquiry. He simply stated: "Go and tell John what you hear and see: the blind receive their sight and the lame walk, lepers are cleansed and the deaf hear, and the dead are raised up, and the poor have good news preached to them."

Jesus was sending a message back to John the Baptist. Perhaps His words to these questioning friends of John have something to say to us as well. What He may be saying is that some churches—and Christians—are more authentic than others. Where one sees these things happening—the sick being healed, the dying given new life, the poor offered eternal hope, men and women being restored to God and His purposes—therein is revealed Christ working and therein are seen churches and Christians carrying out the objectives of God.

Salvation is by faith, not works. While it is essential to proclaim this, it must be dramatized by going where Jesus goes, doing what He does—out there in the world—relating to God's creatures in love, drawing them to God's eternal love and grace through acts of sacrificial service, healing, helping, sharing, communicating God's divine power to humanity about us. This is what it means to be, in Luther's words, "a little Christ" in our world today.

God Will Intervene

Whereas we may not be riddled by fear in the midst of the ugly, atrocious things that transpire in the world about us, we are often uneasy, frustrated, and sometimes very angry. Almost every newscast violates our sensibilities and we inwardly call out for divine intervention in this planet's sad state of affairs. The world is well on its way to self-annihilation and the children of God are apparently helpless and incapable of arresting its mad rush to destruction. We sometimes wish the world would stop and let us get off—sincerely feeling that we cannot put up with it any longer.

Neither James nor any other of the apostles held any high hopes for the world as such. Their hopes and their faith were in the promises and purposes of God as revealed through Jesus Christ. God will intervene; the Lord will come, they insisted. Their message was needed in their day; it is needed as much or more in our day. "Be patient"—as were the ancient prophets—shore up your failing hearts; "the coming of the Lord is at hand."

Peter even dared to suggest that Christians would actually hasten Christ's coming by actively serving in the kingdom that is about them—seeking to advance that kingdom as God's ministers and servants in this world. They certainly would not accomplish anything for God by fretting about this world's conditions or focusing their energies on praying for His immediate return. It is important that we recognize the Christ who came at Christmas, who sent His Spirit at Pentecost, and who is here even now indwelling His redeemed brothers and sisters, the sons and daughters of God, and that we dedicate our lives to carrying on toward fulfillment the objectives of our heavenly Father.

He will come; "the coming of the Lord is at hand." We must be patient, obedient, and faithful.

One Whom You Do Not Know

John may not have realized the full significance of his classic statement to the priests and Levites, but it has characterized humankind in its relationship to God from the very beginning of history. "Among you stands One whom you do not know." It was true of the ancient Jews during the period of the judges, the fall of the kingdom of Israel, the Babylonian Exile. Even as multitudes were being converted under John's fiery preaching and were baptized at the river Jordan, "among them stood One whom they did not know." He remained unknown to most of the people before whom He appeared and preached—even to His very disciples who followed Him during His earthly ministry. For three years He walked among them and with them, taught, performed miracles, and set in motion a movement that was to rock the world with its impact and influence. Yet He stood among them as unknown and unrecognized.

Even to this day when the birthday of Christ is celebrated throughout the world and honored throughout the churches where the Gospel is repeatedly proclaimed, men and women still do not know Him and the masses give only slight acknowledgment of Him.

How can Christmas mean what it is designed to mean to us this year? John gives the answer: "Behold, the Lamb of God, who takes away the sin of the world!" There is no other way to discover the true meaning of Christmas. God has come to this planet; God has made Himself available—revealing Himself in such a way that His creatures might know and love and worship and serve Him.

It is when we are willing to accept and follow Jesus Christ as our Savior, Lord, and King that we will truly know the Christ who came at Christmas.

Wednesday   *1 Thessalonians 5:16–24 (B)*

In All Circumstances—Give Thanks

"Rejoice always, pray constantly, give thanks in all circumstances." Paul sounds like a fanatic. In view of the pain and misery that circumvent this world, how can one rejoice at all? In the midst of the fast-paced living and the innumerable, unreasonable demands that plague us today, how is it possible to be continuously engaged in prayer? And to "give thanks in all circumstances"? It sounds like a person who is possessed or obsessed; it is utterly unrealistic. Yet Paul defines this as "the will of God" for His children.

Paul did not have rocks in his head—he had Christ in his heart—and he found that it was possible to be joyful and thankful even in the face of the dire circumstances that afflict this planet and its inhabitants.

Paradoxical as it may appear, it is only when a person does find joy and peace—acknowledged with gratitude—in a redeeming and reconciling relationship with God that he or she can stand firm amidst this world's tempests and effectively relate to people in the midst of its distortions and dissipations. Whereas God's children cannot be grateful for the ugly things that happen to them or about them, they can be joyful and grateful in the assurance that God is not the author of such things and is indeed pained by them and promises to keep His own spiritually secure irrespective of the horrendous things that afflict this earth.

"God's will" for His children is not the ugly circumstances they confront; it is the kind of abiding in Him and relationship of love and trust to Him that is demonstrated in rejoicing, prayer, and thanksgiving despite the conditions and circumstances of the world. The amazing consequence of such trust and abiding—and this is beyond human comprehension—is the way God can turn many of these difficult circumstances into a means of accomplishing His divine purposes in and through His beloved children and servants.

Thursday   *Luke 3:7–18 (C)*

Sharing One's Shirts

We sometimes have difficulty in accepting John the Baptist as the forerunner or introducer of Christ, as the one who was to bring down mountains and smooth out rough roads for that One who was to follow him. It certainly was not a very popular ministry—though by his strange appearance and fiery proclamations he brought back nostalgic and nervous memories to the crowds gathered to hear him speak.

He looked and sounded like a prophet out of the ancient past. He spoke a language they could understand and to which they could respond. But it was a far cry from the let-Jesus-come-into-your-heart injunctions we have been subjected to throughout our lives. He came on like a bulldozer, blasting away the foolish facades that people hide behind, driving his listeners to their knees in recognition of the spiritual poverty and the emptiness of their lives.

"What then shall we do?" they cried. John's reply was simple and to the point: "The man with two shirts must share with him who has none" (NEB).

We are tempted to relegate the do-or-die message of John the Baptist to the realm of Old Testament obscurity. We like the words of Jesus better—those words, at least, that appear to carry little threat to our awesome indifference to the needs of the masses about us or our apathy in the face of the inhumanity perpetrated upon those masses. We have

24

"let Jesus come into our hearts." We make regular visits to our religious shrines. We assume that this puts us in solid with God.

But every now and then we are brought up short with the possibility that this "shirt-sharing" demand is as relevant to our theology as is the Apostles' Creed. It is that aspect of the Christian life we assume we can cheat on without threatening our relationship to God. After all, Jesus never suggested that we could buy our way into His favor by participating in social welfare projects. We are made the children of God by virtue of Christ's sacrifice on the cross.

Yet Jesus repeatedly underlines the proclamation of John and makes it abundantly clear that authentic Christianity must resolve in "shirt-sharing." We cannot help but wonder, at times, if the number of shirts in our closet, our middle-class prosperity over against the vast multitudes of deprived and dispossessed, does not point up a fatal weakness in our faith.

Friday   *Philippians 4:4–7 (C)*

Rejoice Always?

A letter from my English authoress friend jolted me out of my mid-winter malaise: "Paul encouraged the Philippians to 'rejoice in the Lord always,' and he himself exemplified an inner state of permanent happiness," she wrote. "It was as if joy was completely independent of or able to transcend the situation in which he and his fellow believers found themselves. 'That's all very well,' we may say, 'life is far more complicated now. How can modern Christians possibly rejoice always in this corrupt society?' We can if we open ourselves to the same Spirit of the Christ that filled the early church. That has not changed nor ever will."

Paul then follows with another fantastic injunction: "Have no anxiety about anything. . . ." We might understand if he had written this letter after a huge Las Vegas jackpot winning, but he probably wrote it in some Roman jail. Yet he who experienced both sorrow and anxiety in his day of persecution was able to charge his readers in Philippi to "rejoice in the Lord always" and "have no anxiety about anything."

As long as we are on this planet there will be, of course, both sorrows and anxieties to contend with. Some of them are a very necessary part of our experience—and may even contribute to our development as God's children and servants. Most of our bouts with depression and anxiety are unnecessary and possibly destructive to our health and our attempts to serve God and fellow beings. My friend in England is right;

we can rid ourselves of these debilitating periods of doubt, fear, worry, and despair "if we open ourselves to the same Spirit of the Christ that filled the early church."

Saturday   *Isaiah 61:1–3 (B)*

Christ for Everyone

One reason this lesson out of the Old Testament has become a most important and memorable piece of literature is because it was the Scripture lesson Jesus read and commented on in what may have been the first sermon He ever preached. The scene of His "baptism by fire" in respect to His preaching ministry was His hometown, Nazareth, where He lived in His youth. His listeners thought well of His choice of Scripture and were quite impressed by His interpretation and application of these words of Isaiah.

Not for long, however. When Jesus attempted to place before His listeners the real challenge of Isaiah's words—what they really meant or ought to mean to these synagogue-goers, they became very provoked and proceeded to evict Him from their place of worship and their city.

Jesus obviously saw elements of truth behind Isaiah's prophecy that those worshipers were not able or willing to embrace and which Isaiah himself may not have fully understood. Isaiah, whether he realized it or not, was proclaiming the positive message that God's love is for the world and all men and women, Jew or Gentile, white or black, and was revealing God's honest desire to minister such love and grace to the physical hurts as well as the spiritual needs of every human being.

Isaiah is saying, in effect, that the challenge of social service, the plea for human justice and dignity, the endeavor to lovingly and sacrificially reach out to our debased, oppressed, disenfranchised brothers and sisters about us, is a necessary fruit of the same Gospel that offers the forgiveness and acceptance and grace and love of God. This is God's commission to every one of us—what He empowers us for and expects us to do.

Fourth Sunday in Advent
Matthew 1:18–25 (A)

A Significant Happening

The Bible reports and interprets significant happenings. Whereas all of them are significant, the most important to our faith are those which relate to Jesus Christ, God-incarnate. They are not abstractions or theories or pantheistic generalities, but concrete, actual events localized in time and space. Long before Christmas, even with creation itself, God revealed Himself in omnipotent action. At Christmas, through the Christ of Christmas, He became visible before humankind and began to relate to people in redeeming love.

It means that Christians don't have to go about telling tales about some doctrine of "salvation," but in proclaiming Christ may present a living, personal salvation for individual men and women about them. "Faith in Jesus Christ," wrote Emil Brunner, "is not an interpretation of the world, but it is participation in an event, in something which has happened, and which is going to happen." In other words, either in Christ God the Creator and Redeemer came right into human life or else the gospels are the record of some conspired fallacy. Either God was born in a manger, God ascended the cross, God bore our sins on our behalf and arose from the dead, or else Christmas—and Easter—are a gigantic farce.

This is the central miracle of Christianity—the Incarnation. Every other true miracle prepares for this, or exhibits this, or results from this. It was towards this, the Incarnation, that everything moved until its accomplishment, finding therein fulfillment and explanation. It is from this, the Incarnation, that all subsequent movements have proceeded, depending upon it for direction and dynamics. "Blessed is she who believed," said Elizabeth concerning Mary, who was to be the mother of God-Incarnate. "Blessed are those who have not seen and yet believe," is our Lord's word to us who live a couple of thousand years on this side of the great Christmas, Easter, and Pentecost happenings. As Christians we believe, by the grace of God, that these happenings are more significant than anything else in life.

27

Debts and Obligations

The apostle Paul introduces himself to the church at Rome as one who is set apart for God and His purposes. He thus speaks on behalf of all God's children and servants. The Good News was first promised and proclaimed through the prophets in the ancient Scriptures and has now been revealed through the resurrected Christ, God's Son and our Lord and Master. It is through Christ that we have been commissioned and empowered to communicate this Gospel, the Good News of God's saving love, to the human family throughout the world.

This is something to really celebrate. The blessed Word of God has been enfleshed in us. And while we celebrate we need, as well, to continually remind one another of this splendid truth and encourage one another to be faithful to our adoption as God's children and our appointment as His servants.

Paul goes on to say that because of our great deliverance we are obligated and indebted to every man, woman, and child. Our assignment is to love them into God's kingdom, to demonstrate in our lives and living, to proclaim in our speaking and writing, to reflect in our concern and caring our great God's love for His human creatures.

God Is with Us

It is true! God has visited our planet! He broke through into our dimension of existence. We may never comprehend just how or why, but God, Eternal, All-Glorious, Infinite Spirit, has come to us—as a baby.

As incredible as it is, it was to a young Jewish girl, very poor, who held no position or prominence among her peers, that God sent the angel Gabriel with the earthshaking announcement that she was chosen by God to be the mother of the Messiah, the Lord Jesus Christ. Thus it happened as it was announced, and this poor, insignificant girl was destined to become the most significant and heralded woman in the civilized world.

Her significance is, of course, because of the magnificence of Christ, to whom she gave birth. Jesus Christ was the One about whom the prophets had spoken and whom the children of Israel had anticipated throughout the centuries. It was this One, God-incarnate, the Word made flesh, who would draw God's human creatures back into His loving orbit for their lives and bring joy and peace and significance back into the lives of the poor, the oppressed, the despairing inhabitants of this distorted world.

It is God's act through the virgin Mary and God's coming to us through the birth of Jesus that makes not only that Jewish teenager, Mary, but every one of us significant as God's children and as His servants and disciples.

"Here am I," said Mary to the angel. "I am the Lord's servant; as you have spoken, so be it" (NEB). This must be our daily prayer to God, who is now with us. It is this that makes each one of us truly significant as God's children and ministers in our world today.

Wednesday   *Romans 16:25–27 (B)*

He Is Able

"To Him who is able to strengthen you," wrote Paul in the final paragraph of his letter to the church at Rome, "according to my Gospel and the preaching of Jesus Christ, according to the revelation of the mystery which was kept secret for long ages but is now disclosed and through the prophetic writings is made known . . . according to the command of the eternal God. . . ."

It means that we have a lot going for us—we who are, through faith in Christ's atoning death, the adopted and redeemed sons and daughters of God and who work and serve in the "obedience of faith." We have a God who came to us. This is what we celebrate at Christmas—and every day of the year. We have a God who goes with us into busy streets and high-pressure jobs, through difficult days and dark, lonely nights, and crises and conflicts, depression and despair. Christmas means that we need not face any of these things alone. God is with us—and He is able to strengthen and secure us whatever the consternations and circumstances that come our way.

It is no wonder that Paul concludes his remarkable letter to the persecuted church of Rome with praise: "to the only wise God be glory for evermore through Jesus Christ! Amen."

Blessed Are Those Who Believe

"With God nothing will be impossible," said the angel to Mary. Mary indeed discovered this to be true. Not only was it declared by a heavenly creature that she would give birth to the Son of God, but her kinswoman, Elizabeth, who was old and considered to be barren, conceived—and upon hearing Mary's greeting felt her baby move within her. Elizabeth's real joy, however, was in the touch of God's Spirit upon her, revealing that Mary was chosen by God to give birth to the Christ. It was probably this visit with Elizabeth—and what transpired there—that fully assured Mary that all that was said to her by the angel was true. She was really to be the mother of God's Son, to give birth to the Messiah, the Christ. Her heart rises in gratitude as her lips form the words of praise, the beautiful Magnificat.

Some things are untouchable and ought not be subjected to critical interpretation. One of them is the response of Mary to God's choice of her to give birth to His Son. It is an ecstatic song, flooded with praises to God and full of confidence in God's promise to accomplish His purposes through this humble handmaiden of the Lord. Yet it is a song that we, too, can sing. As it was with Mary and her very special appointment and subsequent contribution as God's servant, so all of us are redeemed, adopted, and appointed to be God's children and servants in this world He has created. In an amazing way God is also born in us and through His Spirit reaches out through us to accomplish His purposes in the world around us.

"Our souls magnify the Lord and our spirits rejoice in God our Savior. . . . For He who is mighty has done great things for us, and holy is His name."

The Purpose of Christmas

"Lo, I have come to do Thy will, O God."

These were the very words of Christ according to the author of the Letter to the Hebrews. This was the purpose of His coming, of His first Advent, which we celebrate this Christmas—to carry out the purposes and objectives of His Father. The day of sacrifices and burnt offerings had passed. The law of God as revealed through the Old Testament was incapable of reconciling men and women to God. It had, nonetheless, prepared the way for the next order of events, whereby God Himself would come to His human creatures through Jesus Christ and through the single sacrifice of His Son make it possible for the inhabitants of this world to be redeemed and reconciled to their Creator.

This would happen—and did happen—because Jesus, God-incarnate, came to this planet and carried out God's will even to the point of offering up His own body on the cross as the one, single sacrifice sufficient to atone for all the sins of the human family.

Now God's redeemed creatures are drawn into the blessed, loving will of God. They are, in a sense, Christ-incarnate, appointed and destined to offer up their lives in the course of carrying out the Father's purposes in this world. They present their bodies and beings as living sacrifices—offered up to God on the altar of their neighbor's need.

The words of Christ, who carried out the will of His Father, are now flung out to each of us. While Jesus presented the all-sufficient sacrifice on our behalf, there is a sacrifice for us to offer, a cross for us to carry—not to secure our salvation, but to proclaim and demonstrate the Good News of God's saving love to our fellow-beings.

"Lo, we are here to do Thy will, O God."

Christmas Day   *Luke 2:1–20 (A, B, C)*

Christmas—It Really Happened!

Christmas—it really happened! God has visited our planet! He broke through into our dimension of existence. We may never comprehend just how or even why, but the fact is He came by way of the Bethlehem manger. God, Creator, eternal, all-glorious, infinite Spirit, came to us—as a baby. This great One who astounded the masses with His out-of-this-world feats and amazed people with His out-of-this-world teachings, whom no one is really able to ignore, who drew men's thoughts to Himself with a mysterious power, who rises in stature above all even as He was nailed on a cross by those who hated Him, and who conquered over death itself as He arose from the grave—He came to us by way of the manger!

It's a true story! The people around this fantastic event are real: Caesar Augustus, Cyrenius, Mary, Joseph, and the Christ Child. It is a story that needs to be told again and again. Catching the world with its head in the emptiness of outer space or the dumps of existential despair, Christmas proclaims what our world desperately needs to hear and to take to heart. Christmas really happened; God has visited our planet. Perhaps this manger-happening is the only way God could come to us. We could never approach the Holy and All-Righteous God, any more than we can draw near to the sun that blazes in our sky. Thus God condescended to come to us—by way of the manger. Christmas really happened, and because it happened we are assured of God's love for and acceptance of us. We are loved and accepted not simply as a part of humanity's masses but as individual entities and personalities. It means that there is meaning and purpose to our lives, that we are truly significant no matter what the level or our IQs or the size of our bank accounts, and no matter how numerous or depressing our failures. It means that we can be extricated from the pitfalls of our lives, reconciled to God, and restored to effectiveness and productivity once more.

Christmas really happened. It is continuing to happen through God's sons and daughters who embrace the Christ of Christmas and demonstrate His love and power in their interpersonal relationships. God grant that it may happen even through each of us, that we may be able to make Christmas vital and significant in our world and thereby convince others that Christmas really happened.

First Sunday After Christmas

Matthew 2:13–15 19-23 (A)

God's Intervention

It is a beautiful story—God's care and concern for His Son, the Christ child. It was His miraculous intervention and guidance that spared the child a terrible fate that was not spared scores of other babies that died at the cruel hands of Herod and his reaction to the birth of Jesus.

It raises some agonizing questions. Where was God during the Holocaust when millions of human beings were slaughtered, or when almost a thousand died by their own hands at the command of a demented cult leader in the jungle of Guyana? Where was God when we yielded to temptation and had to suffer the consequences, or when, through no fault of our own, we had to traverse the dark corridors of pain and suffering?

It appears at times that God's power is limited in respect to the calamities and atrocities that fall upon our world and affect our lives, that it isn't His policy to intervene and come between His children and the ugly things that often happen to them, that He chose powerlessness in order that He may grant to us the power to choose. And yet He did intervene in the circumstances of the Christ child—leading His parents to bring Him to Nazareth where He "increased in wisdom and in stature, and in favor with God and man" (Luke 2:52). He did intervene in this world's hell-bent course when He came to this planet through the Christ. This is what Christmas is all about—God's great intervention. While we are aware of the times when God did not shield us from tragedy or trouble, we could hardly know of those times when He did intervene. In fact, our health and well-being in this hour may well be the result of the many divine interventions of our heavenly Father.

We do not have the answers to many of life's agonizing, nagging questions, but we do have a loving God and the gift of eternal life, and these free us from the absolute need for such answers. We have, as well, God's commission and empowerment to be the instruments and vehicles of His grace, to be His interveners in the suffering of those who cross our path and thereby bring the healing touch of a loving God to people in need.

We Are God's Children

The time has come. The long-promised Messiah has arrived. Redemption has taken place. God's salvation is available. We are now the sons and daughters of God.

It is difficult to believe—to keep on believing—in this astounding intervention and activity of God, but it is true! We have been restored to the family of God. It began with Christmas; it culminated in the cross and the resurrection. "Beloved, we are God's children now . . ." wrote John (1 John 3:2). And to make this amazing fact an everlasting conviction in the lives of true believers, "God has sent the Spirit of His Son into our hearts. . . ."

If we had to rely on our worth or status or any ability of ours to make this come to pass, it would never happen. But it is God's doing. He came to us. He adopted us. We have within us the very Spirit of Christ.

God forbid that this incredible restoration to Himself should ever become commonplace or mundane. May it always be exciting, enriching, renewing, and result in a joyful abandonment of all that we are and have to God and His eternal purposes.

The Christmas Aftermath

It is the Christmas aftermath—and it is something of a letdown. What we spent weeks building up to is now reflected in trash cans overburdened with ribbons and wrappings, trees looking about as spent as we feel, and probably overdrawn checking accounts.

There should, of course, be a Christmas aftermath. But it should *not* be one of depression, apathy, or inactivity. There was no Christmas letdown for Simeon or a prophetess named Anna. Simeon, on seeing the baby Jesus, exploded in a beautiful song of praise. He knew that something vastly significant happened in the birth of the Christ child. Anna, the prophetess, turned from praying to praising after seeing this little one who was to be the Redemption of Israel. Armed with new confidence and courage, our visit to the Bethlehem manger should resolve in spiritual progress and growth in our lives. We have once more seen and commemorated the birthday of our King. We heard the thrilling message in word and song, visualized it in symbol and pageantry, felt it in the spirit of Christmas about us.

Now we are about to turn the page and face the new year—with all of its dark uncertainties as well as its bright possibilities—with an eager determination to work within God's purposes and extend His kingdom in scorn of consequences. "Lord, now lettest Thou Thy servant depart in peace, according to Thy Word," prayed Simeon, "for mine eyes have seen Thy salvation." This was not a cry of defeat; it was an exuberant song of victory. He had met the Christmas Christ. Now he was ready for the aftermath—whatever it might be.

We may live between a rock and a hard place. The painful circumstances that surround us may at times be more than we can bear. There may be hours of physical pain, of economic need, of loneliness and frustration. There may be deep, hidden weaknesses or conflicts that we must continually confront and can seldom overcome. But whatever the circumstances before us or the uncertainties about us, the designed aftermath of Christmas and the challenge of the new year is that we, empowered by divine grace, be the children and ministers of God right where we are, "for [our] eyes have seen Thy salvation which Thou hast prepared in the presence of all peoples."

Wednesday   *Colossians 3:12–17 (B)*

Response to God's Coming

We have been adopted as the very children of God; we *are* His beloved children. In response to His redemption and our adoption and the gift of the Holy Spirit, we are empowered and expected to reflect the qualities and attributes of the family of God.

It doesn't' come naturally. The mind and body of mortal man and woman are still earthbound and subject to temptations that afflict and are difficult to resist. A total dedication to God and His purposes and a determination to live as He would have us live is necessary in the daily struggle to allow the Spirit to work out in and through us the attributes and objectives of the heavenly Father.

Above all is the high goal and challenge of loving. It is because of God's love that we are His children forever. It is by means of His love through us that others about us may be introduced to His saving grace. This, therefore, must be our response to the events of Christmas, Good Friday, and Easter. Having embraced His saving love, we are to love others even as Christ loved us. The word of Christ and the Word who is Christ dwell within us and are revealed through us. We, the children, are to become more and more like the Parent. God provides the grace and enablement to do this. We must provide the fertile field in which His sown seeds of grace may bring forth fruit.

Thursday   *Luke 2:41–52 (C)*

The Matter of Priorities

We might conjecture whether or not the boy Jesus was yet aware of the circumstances of His birth or His divinity as the very Son of God. His parents soon realized that He was very special. The teachers at the temple were astounded at His youthful wisdom and insights concerning the revered writings of the prophets and the hand of God in the history of His people. When Jesus responded to His parent's inquiry as to the reason for His remaining at the temple when they returned to their home, they were surprised at His reference to the temple as "[His] Father's house." His mother appears to have recognized some significance in this episode in the life of her son.

It is obvious, whatever Jesus' comprehension of His identity and eventual ministry at this point, that God and His purposes were more important to Him than anything else. Even at a very early age He had His priorities in order. He began even then a life of commitment and dedication to His God and Father, a life that was to be of greater value and significance to His world and our world than that of any other human being from the beginning of time until now.

What are our priorities, our values, our life-styles? Whatever they are, they will never be what they ought to be unless we begin to see the importance of our "Father's house" and commit ourselves to God and His purposes for our lives.

Friday   *Hebrews 2:10–18 (C)*

He Is Our Brother

It happened on that first Christmas. We could not come to God, so He came to us through Jesus Christ—identifying Himself with our earthbound natures—in order that He might take upon Himself the consequences of our sins and release us forever from their bondage. This makes us the brothers and sisters of Jesus Christ, God's Son, and therefore the very children of the heavenly Father.

36

I can't comprehend it; I can only accept it and rejoice in it. He is my Lord; He is also my Brother. As my Brother He identifies with me in my human weaknesses, shares with me my sorrows and conflicts, helps me with life's heavy burdens, and through His Spirit accompanies me through the dry, heat-stricken deserts as well as over the green hills and snowcapped mountains of my day-by-day existence.

He is with each of us today—Jesus, our Lord, our Brother. Thus we can push forward without fear, knowing that He cares about us and will help us to confront and overcome whatever obstacles lie in the sometimes torturous course that stretches out ahead.

Saturday *Isaiah 45:22–25 (B)*

Turn . . . Turn . . . Turn

"Turn to me and be saved," is God's word through the prophet. "To me every knee shall bow. . . ." Turning toward God, His life and purposes, is what repentance is all about.

I have discovered that such "turning" does not end with my initial embrace of faith that assured me of God's saving grace and His gift of everlasting life. While I need not, and must not, grovel in and struggle with the guilt of past sins and errors for which I have been forgiven, I need again and again to turn from the temptations that harass, from self-centeredness and the self-serving instincts that cause me to stumble, and face up to God's love and purposes.

We are God's children and servants, and yet each day offers the opportunity and very often the necessity of turning toward Him. This includes, as well, renewal and recommitment to what God wants us to be and to do as His beloved and appointed ministers in our world today.

We need not worry about falling from God's grace today—any more than an adopted child of loving parents need worry about his daily status in his human family. We do need to place ourselves at God's disposal day by day—to "turn" toward His love and grace and His assignments for us in our broken world.

Second Sunday After Christmas

John 1:1–18 (A, B, C)

The Power to Become Persons

By all appearances, the common denominator of life today is not goodness or beauty or truth, but power. Man's primary quest, in spite of our idealists, is not the quest for peace of mind; it is the reach for power—probably with the assumption that this will ultimately bring peace of mind.

One of the significant contributions of Christmas is that it celebrates the gift of true power and points the way to its creative, life-giving use in our disjointed world. "He came to His own home," wrote John, "and His own people received Him not. But to all who received Him, who believed in His name, He gave *power* to become children of God." The key to happy, creative, life-giving, authentic power for this life and the next is God's gift of power—the power to become the children of God, sons and daughters of the heavenly Father—the power to become persons.

If one could sift all the reasons for mental illness, for the feeling of low-worth and invalidity, for the hours of depression, for the frightful distortions that often result in violent assaults upon others or even in self-destruction, one might find in the residue the inability to recognize or to accept one's own identity. Man and woman, created in the spiritual image of God, lost this sense of identity or personhood in giving way to sin and disobedience. Ever since that time the human creature has been trying to find personhood once more—often in the most bizarre and atrocious ways—in a false sense of power over others through wealth or position, or through competition, material success, ambition, or just honest-to-goodness hard work.

The Christmas event declares once and for all that identity and personhood was restored to the fractured, failure-fraught creatures of this earth by God Himself when He, in the Person of His Son, broke through into our world of sin, our dimension of humanity, by becoming one of us, identifying Himself with our sin-ridden natures, and paying the supreme penalty in our stead, in order that He might restore us to God's life and purposes once more. He thereby offered to His creatures, lost and estranged, the power to become His sons and daughters through faith in Him, the power to be reunited with His family, reconciled to His kingdom. Our great God is the giver of many gifts, but the greatest gift of all is the gift of personhood and identity. This was God's Christmas gift to each of us.

Monday   *Ephesians 1:3–6, 15–18 (A, B, C)*

The Wealth of a Christian

Truly, we have much to celebrate as the sons and daughters of God. We have, through this Christ who came at Christmas, become the recipients of God's whole treasure house of spiritual gifts. Even before man and woman and the world itself were created, we were destined to be His children.

Christ's death on the cross set us free from the Law's demands. All charges against us were blotted out. Our sins were forgiven. Reconciled to the divine family, we are now an integral part of God's plan to reconcile the whole world to Himself. It is not something we can comprehend, but God created us and chose us to be His people, and this was God's purpose and plan from the very beginning. It was made known to us and made possible for us through Jesus Christ. Through this Christ and His indwelling Spirit the brand of God's ownership was burned indelibly into our hearts. With the gracious gifts of His Spirit is the guarantee that all of these gifts, though at present unseen and little understood, are already ours and will be revealed to us in God's own time.

God grant that His Spirit will break through the numbness of our small thinking and reveal to us something of who we are and what we have become through Christ. He is Lord over all, and we are His church, His body, the extension of this Christ in this world to which we are assigned.

How immeasurably and infinitely blessed we are!

Tuesday   *Isaiah 61:10–62:3 (A, B, C)*

A Time to Rejoice

The ancient prophet didn't fully know it, but with remarkable insight he was rejoicing in the same gift of God as we have this Christmas season. It is God coming into our world through Christ that made possible all that Isaiah stated in his prophecy. With Christ came our

39

salvation; with Him and through Him we were made righteous. Because of Christmas we were made the sons and daughters of God forever.

It truly is a time for rejoicing—even in the midst of the holocausts that afflict this world and its inhabitants. "Righteousness and praise" *have* sprung forth "before all the nations." Because we are the objects of God's saving love, we are compelled to echo that praise and adoration of the Christ who came at Christmas.

The Epiphany of Our Lord
Matthew 2:1–12 (A, B, C)

They Walked a New Path

When it is dark enough, one can see the stars. It has been dark enough for us to see the Star again this Christmas season—a Star pointing to the one remaining hope for ourselves and our faltering world. There were several Wise Men, it is reported, who saw that first Star of Christmas. These men from the east were convinced that it would lead to something or someone significant and set out to follow its directing rays.

They met Christ. "And going into the house they saw the child with Mary His mother, and they fell down and worshiped Him." God's Christmas gift to the world, the Lord Jesus Christ, makes available to every person the peace of sin forgiven, the love and acceptance of a righteous God, the promise of life eternal. Whatever the particular star that leads a person to Christ, he or she must individually and personally meet this Christ. Without this meeting, Christmas is little more than a pagan festival.

They gave Him gifts. "Then, opening their treasures, they offered Him gifts. . . ." We are aware of the high cost of living; we still have much to learn about the high cost of loving. "God so loved the world that He gave His only Son. . . ." It is this kind of love that we are enjoined to demonstrate in response to God's love for us. This is the meaning of worship—the giving of ourselves to God and to others on God's behalf. This ought to be the consequence of Christmas in our lives.

They walked a new path. "They departed to their own country by another way." Their response to this meeting with Christ symbolizes what ought to happen in response to our meeting with Him. If we plunge into the new year continuing to walk in the old paths of selfishness, deceit, sensualism, fear, anxiety, despair, it indicates that Christmas has done little for us, that we have scarcely met or genuinely worshiped the Christ of Christmas or, having met Him, are not consistently following Him. A new life means a new walk, a new path—and new goals, attitudes, motivations. God grant that we may walk in the paths that Christ sets before us.

41

First Sunday After the Epiphany

Matthew 3:13–17 (A)

The Baptism of Christ

Jesus, the sinless One, God's beloved Son, requested and received baptism by water under the hands of John. Whatever it may have meant to Christ, it is most often regarded as His "ordination" into His public ministry. If we had any doubts about the identity of Jesus as God's Son following His manger birth, the event of Christ's baptism accompanied by the special revelation of the Holy Spirit and the voice of God out of heaven should eliminate those doubts once and for all. This is truly the Christ—the Christ who gave Himself into death for us, the Christ in whose name we were baptized and to whom we have surrendered our lives.

Perhaps the most significant thing about this event is "the Spirit of God descending like a dove" and the voice from heaven saying, "This is My beloved Son, with whom I am well pleased." It is this, along with many further revelations, that ought to assure us that our commitment is valid. He is not a remarkable teacher, a radical revolutionary, or a sainted guru to whom we are signing over our lives—though He may be some of those things as well—He is the Son of God. All other leaders, as gifted and qualified as they appear to be, may lead us down some primrose path to darkness and emptiness, but not Jesus, God's beloved Son, "with whom [He is] well pleased."

We can follow Christ today, His teachings and example, without fear, and with the conviction that we are thereby within our Creator's design and destiny for our lives.

Monday   *Mark 1:4–11 (B)*

Jesus Christ—God Revealed

We live in a day of confusion and confoundment. Our world abounds with false shepherds and bizarre cults. There are "messiahs" of all sorts attempting to control the lives of lonely, unhappy people. There are millions of God's human creatures who continue to create God in their own image—or latch on to some false concoction of a divinity that appears to meet their superficial needs. God has come and revealed Himself through Jesus Christ and through this Christ became fully incarnate, relating Himself through His Bethlehem birth, and now in His baptism by John the Baptist, with the human family about Him. He did this that men and women might be found by God and restored to His purpose for their lives.

The significance of this event is in its identification of Jesus as the true Messiah—as God revealed. While our baptism in the name and Spirit of Jesus Christ differs considerably from Christ's baptism, it once and for all identifies us as the sons and daughters of God-revealed-in-Christ and the very brothers and sisters of this Christ who was baptized by John. Jesus was God's Son before this world was created; He was revealed as such at His baptismal event. It is our baptism into Christ that unites us with and adopts us into the Holy Family and makes us the very children of God.

It is through Christ that we can know the true God. It is in following this Christ that we follow the true Shepherd who embraces us in love and restores us to our Creator and His purposes for our lives.

Tuesday   *Luke 3:15–17, 21–22 (C)*

Christ's Baptism and Mine

There is a difference between Christ's baptism and mine. Jesus Christ, God's beloved Son, was through His baptism identified and introduced to His human and divine ministry among us sinful beings. My baptism made me God's child, reclaimed me from sin's bondage, and restored me to His eternal kingdom.

My baptism, in some respects, was also similar to Christ's. It was that event in which I was commissioned and empowered to be His servant. I was made to be God's child at my baptism. The Holy Spirit entered my life at my baptism. As God's work in and through Christ began with His baptism, so my baptism unites me with the saving presence of Christ and initiates the work of God and Christ in and through me. As the baptism of Christ identified Him as the Servant and as a part of the servant-people that had been prophesied and promised in the ancient Scriptures, so my baptism makes me a part of that servant-people.

The baptism of Christ ultimately led to the cross and the resurrection. My baptism makes the death and resurrection of Christ applicable to my life. It also sets my feet upon a narrow path that leads through

43

struggle and conflict and that promises a cross for me to carry on behalf of others. It is a life of joy and peace—in the midst of sorrows and strivings. It is a life that I must often reclaim and return to when the siren voices of this world tempt me to go astray. The dramatic and momentous event of my baptism was the most important event of my life. It united me to God through Christ and identified me as God's child and servant forever.

Wednesday   *Acts 10:34–38 (A, B, C)*

God for the World

The Old Testament prophets occasionally expressed insights concerning the God of Israel as indeed the God of all people. Elijah and Elisha performed miracles of healing, in the name of their God, upon individuals outside of the family of Israel. Jesus certainly gave evidence that God is a universal God even though His own three-year mission was directed primarily to ministering among the Jews.

Peter, in his postresurrection ministry, was beginning to realize the implications of Jesus' death and resurrection—and his own response to them—finally acknowledging and timidly obeying the charge of his Lord to communicate the saving message of God-incarnate to the Gentiles as well as the Jews.

Christ's first disciples were fallible creatures who had to grow in the faith as do all Christians. As with us, so their vision—and their responsibility—had to be enlarged until it embraced the whole human family.

As children of God, disciples of Christ, and the brothers and sisters of Peter, we will either grow in our understanding of Christ's ultimate mission initiated by His baptism or we will stagnate. The mission of God was and is to all the world. While our immediate parishes or arenas of service may be very small, our vision must encircle the world; our love and concern must be available to every human creature.

Thursday   *Isaiah 42:1–7 (A, B, C)*

He Is Here

"Behold, My Servant, whom I uphold, My Chosen, in whom My soul delights; I have put My Spirit upon Him. . . ."

These glorious, insightful words are a reference to God-incarnate,

44

Jesus Christ. We truly live in the day of prophecy fulfilled. Jesus has come; He was initiated, through John's baptism and the infilling of the Spirit of His Father, into His ministry to and among the human creatures of God on this planet. "This is the One," our God would say to us. "Hear Him, accept Him, follow Him, for I have sent Him."

Now we are the ones, redeemed and reconciled to our Creator by this Christ and filled with His Spirit, who have become the servants of God and are charged with the enormous task of being "a light to the nations, to open the eyes that are blind, to bring out the prisoners from the dungeon, from the prison those who sit in darkness."

Whatever may be our avocation—the things we do to feed and clothe our bodies and support those who are dependent upon us—our primary vocation is to serve God, to be His servants in our fractured world. We are to emulate Jesus Christ and through proclamation and daily demonstration, through witness in word and deed, bring God through Christ to people about us, to communicate His love and grace to those who cross our paths. This ought to be the consequence of our baptism into the Christ who was baptized by John, and this by the grace of that God who has "taken [us] by the hand and kept [us]" and "given [us] as a covenant to the people."

Second Sunday After the Epiphany
John 1:29–41 (A)

This Is the One

Whatever John the Baptist may have comprehended about the Christ, his proclamations about this Christ were obviously inspired. In two brief, remarkable statements John summarized what Christ's ministry was to be in the following months. These statements declared who this man Jesus Christ was and, at the same time, what He had come to accomplish in His short sojourn on this planet.

"Behold, the Lamb of God, who takes away the sin of the world," proclaimed John. He may not have fully understood what he said, no more than the prophets before him could have grasped the full significance of their amazing pronouncements. Nevertheless, he said it, and it must have sounded audacious and incredulous to his hearers.

"This is He who baptizes with the Holy Spirit," continued John. The sacrifice of the Lamb for the sins of the world and the baptism of the Holy Spirit—these were the two central truths in John's preaching that day. They are inseparable. And this is precisely what Jesus accomplished in His earthly ministry. He not only bore our sins on the cross, but we were filled with His Spirit. It is this that was gifted to us in our baptism into this Christ. Setting us free from sin's guilt and power and eternal consequences through the sacrifice of the Lamb, Jesus Christ, and incorporating us into His divine family, He has also given us His Spirit.

God grant that John's proclamation—and God's eternal truths—may become a perpetual experience in our lives!

Monday   *1 Corinthians 1:1–9 (A)*

Let Us Give Thanks

There is no better way to begin this day—or any day. We can do this even if the sun refuses to break through the cloud cover, or if the conflicts we must face in the coming hours appear foreboding and unsolvable. It is our privilege and our need to begin this day with thankfulness.

Our reason for gratitude? It is, of course, "because of the grace of God which was given [us] in Christ Jesus." Because of that grace we are forgiven sinners and God will keep us—guiltless—to the very end of our lives. Because of that grace we are constantly in fellowship with God's Son, Jesus Christ. Because of that grace we are enriched in every way "so that [we] are not lacking in any spiritual gift, as [we] wait for the revealing of our Lord Jesus Christ."

We are equipped to step boldly into the activity of this day as God's children and His ministers, with the assurance that the grace He has given us will enable us to face any circumstances, to confront violence with courage and hatred with love, and to reflect the joy of our relationship with God in the darkest and most difficult hours that come our way.

Let us give thanks!

Tuesday   *John 1:43–51 (B)*

"Come and See"

"Come and see." Jesus gave this response to the two disciples who inquired as to where He was staying. Philip gave this same response to Nathanael, who listened to his testimony about the discovery of the One "of whom Moses . . . wrote" and asked, "Can anything good come out of Nazareth?"

"Come and see." Most people in our community have heard the message of John the Baptist: "Behold, the Lamb of God, who takes away the sin of the world!" What a message to proclaim to a sin-ridden, broken world! The problem is that the majority of the people in most communities have never accepted this message or submitted to its Christ in repentance and faith.

While there are various reasons for this—pride, self-sufficiency, blindness to true values—we need to consider the possibility that there may be something wrong with or lacking in the methods the church uses to broadcast this message to the world at large. Well-meaning Christians have attempted to supplement the institution's efforts with "Jesus Saves" and "Jesus Is the One" bumper stickers, but such endeavors probably do little to advance God's kingdom.

Perhaps the key lies in the interpersonal, eyeball-to-eyeball approach of those first followers of Christ, as exemplified by Philip, who invited Nathanael to "come and see." We are all ministers of the Gospel. We all have our little parishes or arenas of service. We can't coerce people to come to Christ. We certainly can't convert people; that is the task of the Holy Spirit. We can, all of us, in one way or another invite people

47

to "come and see." They ought to be able to see something of God's love and saving power in our lives—the things we say and do—and if we are authentically loving and concerned about them, we may be able, as was Philip, to lead such people to the Lamb of God "who takes away the sin of the world."

Wednesday   *1 Corinthians 6:12–20 (B)*

Free to Be

Through the atoning word of Christ we are free to be—what God wants us to be, what He has created and destined us to be. We are set free from manmade laws and regulations, traditions and dogmas, free to live, as enabled by God's grace, in accordance with His plan and design for our lives. We are freed from sin and self-idolization, from our assumed need to satiate the desires and demands of the flesh, free to belong to God and to live and move within His purposes for our lives.

True freedom, however, is discovered only in recognition of God's reign over our life and in commitment to His order and will for us. It means that we are no longer the captain of our soul or the master of our fate. We are the children of God, created in and restored to His image, and have become the vessels and vehicles of His indwelling Spirit. Our very beings become the members of Christ and the means through which the invisible Christ carries out His purposes throughout our world.

We are free—free from the manmade moralities of past and present generations, free from the need for material wealth, free from ancient prejudices, free from the need for self-assertion through bigotry or racism or bizarre activities, free from the fear of death, free to risk our reputations and even our lives in pursuit of divine purposes and of justice and equality for every human creature.

We are free to be what our Creator and Redeemer wants us to be. May this happen in and through each of us.

Thursday   *John 2:1–11 (C)*

Consecrating the Commonplace

In this day when people are so impressed by big things, large numbers, extravaganzas, wealth and power, fame and fortune, and so oppressed by great problems like war, racism, world poverty, and the

48

national economy, it is paradoxically significant and particularly refreshing that Jesus' first demonstration of divine power took place at the rather commonplace, humdrum circumstances of a wedding party. This same Christ who refused to turn stones into bread to satiate His own hunger did not hesitate to convert water into wine to further the enjoyment of a crowd of merrymaking guests.

This happening in the life and ministry of Jesus says some important things to us. For one thing, it reveals that the glory and splendor, the power and might of our Father in heaven is available and applicable within the ordinary, commonplace, mundane circumstances of everyday living. "So whether you eat or drink, or whatever you do, do all to the glory of God," wrote Paul (1 Cor. 10:31). "I can do all things in Him who strengthens me. . . . And my God will supply every need of yours according to His riches in glory in Christ Jesus," he said in another epistle (Philippians 4:13, 19). It means that the Christ who came at Christmas has come to manifest His presence and glory in even the most commonplace events of daily life. It means, as well, that the commonplace task need no longer be common or mundane. Whether it be within the realm of tedious housework or the equally drab duty of selling merchandise or running an office or working in a factory or teaching a group of rowdy children, the presence of Christ blesses and clothes it with prestige and purpose. He is able and willing to work miracles in our most ordinary circumstances, thereby transforming the day's drudgery and routine into a vehicle of blessing and abundance for us and for others about us.

The Christ who, without pomp or ceremony, created the best wine of the feast after the natural, ordinary supply was consumed, will give to us, if we will but receive it, a fountain of living water or wine which will supply our needs long after our natural and human resources have been exhausted.

Friday   *1 Corinthians 12:1–11 (C)*

God-Incarnate—in Us

Pentecost was a great deal more than wind and fire, or even the utterance of strange languages by uneducated tongues. God, incarnate in Christ, is also incarnate in the body of His church, His sons and daughters commissioned to carry out His purposes upon this planet. With the gift of the Holy Spirit are made available the great spiritual gifts—the equipment we need to accomplish His objectives in those arenas of service in which He has placed us.

The gifts of the Spirit differ. The Spirit, however, is one and the same, and makes every one of us of equal value and importance to God. We are all credentialed and equipped to be and to do what God would have us to be and to do.

Some of the gifts imparted to God's children are more popular than others—gifts of preaching or healing or intelligence or insight, making money or making music. Other gifts, equally important but less visible, may be little recognized or appreciated. The more popular and visible gifts do not indicate a greater measure of spiritual power or the Spirit's presence.

The most important gifts are available to all of us who will allow the Spirit total access to our bodies and beings. Above all is the grace to love one another, to share with one another, and to help one another in the way of our Lord and Savior Jesus Christ. That gift comes to us by way of God's love. We need daily to exercise it and utilize it as we grow together in our Christian faith.

Saturday   *Isaiah 49:1–6 (A)*

God's People for God's Purposes

Some readers may assume that the author was speaking about himself and his task as God's prophet to the people of Israel. Others will insist that Israel, as God's chosen people, was God's servant to the nations. As we read these words in the light of New Testament revelation, we see Christ projected through this remarkable prophecy—an amazing picture of the Messiah whom God was to send to His people.

He truly was sent by God: "The Lord called [Him] from the womb." He experienced periods of great sorrow when His message and ministry were rejected: "I have labored in vain. . . ." He revealed to Israel that He was to be "a light to the nations, that [God's] salvation may reach to the end of the earth."

The message of the prophet, as presumptuous as it sounds, could also be applied to each of us. We, too, are called from the womb. We are His servants. We will often meet with defeat in our efforts to communicate God's Word to others. We are, nonetheless, to persist in being "the light of the world" in the dark corners of our planet.

We may not, as with Jesus, see much success in our endeavors to carry out God's purposes in our communities and our world, but we are commanded to keep the faith, to keep witnessing to the faith, and to leave the consequences in God's hands.

Third Sunday
After the Epiphany
Matthew 4:12–23 (A)

His Ministry Our Ministry

Jesus had been baptized by John the Baptist and was thereby identified with the human race as the human Christ and initiated into His public ministry. He had been tried by fire in the wilderness and had passed every test. Now was the time to begin the task He had been sent to accomplish. He was made responsible for establishing God's kingdom on this planet, a kingdom, beginning with the Israelites, that would spread out over all the world and draw through its portals men and women of every race and clime.

Jesus took off from where John's ministry had concluded: "Repent, for the kingdom of heaven is at hand." The foundation had to be laid; hearts had to be prepared. John's cry for repentance was well-timed, and Jesus confirmed it. There would be no spiritual kingdom apart from repentance.

He began His selection of men who would learn from Him and continue building the announced kingdom after His own ministry was terminated. "Follow Me, and I will make you fishers of men." Along with His reaching and teaching was His miracle-working ministry of healing "every disease and every infirmity among the people."

Proclamation, gathering together those who will follow the Christ and serve in His kingdom, communicating God's grace and power to the infirm bodies as well as the impoverished spirits of people—is this not our ministry as God's sons and daughters, ministers and servants in our world today?

Monday   *1 Corinthians 1:10–17 (A)*

Be Aware of Whom You Follow

It is unfortunate how many Christians latch on to powerful and charismatic personalities that impress them as God's very special saints and leaders and structure their faith in accordance with their precepts and pronouncements. Whereas God may speak through such, there is a great risk in this; their fans or followers may end up with some human concoction about God and His will for their lives.

However such leaders may interpret it, God reveals His love and redeeming power through Christ and His cross. When self-appointed interpreters attempt to go beyond proclamation into some rational or human explanation, to subdue or dilute its offensiveness or dissect its mystery, they come off as confusers rather than articulators and confound rather than clarify the purposes of God.

The fact is clear: Christ died for our sins. We are reconciled to our loving God through this Christ. Nonsensical to some, offensive to others, it remains for us proof positive of our relationship to a living God and our perpetual and eternal acceptance as His sons and daughters. It is because of what Christ has done on our behalf that we can meet this day and every day with the utmost confidence that we are encircled by His love and indwelt with His Spirit.

Tuesday   *Mark 1:14–20 (B)*

"Follow Me!"

"Stop the world; I want to get off!" It is what some of us are saying, audibly or otherwise, as we are bombarded daily by the tragic, complex, violent events that explode all about us. The storm warnings are out, and people, frustrated and fearful, are running for their lives in search of security or serenity that will blot out the disturbing threats to their well-being.

Those of us who are older tend to reach back into some past generation and try to hang on to those forms and traditions we once felt secure with, to set the clock back—at least to those postdepression or postwar days that in spite of our forgotten tragedies and problems seem in retrospect so happy and secure. There are many who crawl further back into the womb of the church and cling desperately to the "horns of the altar" as a sanctuary from life's vicious storms. Or they may latch on to those movements that feature religious ecstasy, the get-ready-for-heaven gospel or the Christ-is-coming-soon emphasis in response to the convulsions of our world today.

The message of our Lord is not always comfortable, but this is His message to us in this hour: "Follow Me and I will make you become fishers of men" He does not give us permission to "get off" this calamitous ball of clay we call our world; He invites us—commands us—to follow Him into it, to serve Him and our fellow persons within it, knowing full well, as Christ did, the possible consequences of our obedience to Him. The strange and wondrous thing is that it is precisely in such obedience, which results in loving commitment to people about us, that one discovers an out-of-this-world joy and security that cannot be eradicated by those tragic, complex, violent events that explode all about us.

Endtime Christianity

We don't know the year or the day, but we are nearer to the end of this dispensation and the time of Christ's return than we have ever been before. It is time to consider our priorities. While we are not expected to leave our families or our jobs—or even to discontinue making arrangements for our postretirement years—we had better be aware that earthly relationships and matters are not to have priority over the matters of the Spirit, the kingdom matters for which God has made each of us responsible.

Our relationship to God has first priority. Proceeding from this, our relationship, as His children and servants, to our fellow beings is of vital importance. Whether we are happy or sad, rich or poor, prominent or inconsequential in respect to this world, is not ultimately significant. Our primary concern must be our relationship to God, to "seek first His kingdom and His righteousness."

It is admittedly difficult to be what Jesus—and Paul—exhort us to be. It is not even very rational or reasonable in our kind of society and culture. Our faith has not yet reached the pinnacle that looks down over this world as something that has no eternal significance whatsoever. God's gift of eternal life, and our inclusion in His eternal kingdom, is not comprehensible to our earthbound minds. But we had better, by His grace, work at it—ever reaching toward the glorious freedom that enables us to soar over and above the entanglements that hold us so close to this planet. We have been created and redeemed for far better things.

Communicating Christ

Advent and Christmas introduced us to the glorious truth that what man, fallible as he is, could not do, God in His love for His wayward creatures did do. He found a way to get through to and communicate with us. It is impossible for us to comprehend and even difficult for us to accept, but God broke through into our conflicts and confusion in the person of His Son, Jesus Christ. We could not come to Him, so He came to us.

What methods did the Son of God, this humble figure from Nazareth, use to accomplish this end? They hardly seem very dramatic in our day of space travel and moon landings. He did not call down legions of angelic hosts to sweep the world clean of its evil and ugliness. He did not organize and set up a power block or corporation of influential and wealthy men. He never picked up a pen, much less a sword, to assist Him in His purposes. And yet He, more than any person this world has ever known, succeeded in communicating to billions of human creatures the will and purposes of the loving and eternal God.

For one thing, He did it by *proclamation*. "The Spirit of the Lord is upon me, because he has anointed me to preach good news to the poor." What a seemingly naive and insignificant weapon against the fearsome powers of evil and darkness that abounded throughout the world! He chose disciples and they preached, and those who followed in their wake continued to preach. It was out of such preaching that reformations and crusades were launched, revivals born, tidal waves of wickedness checked, lands garrisoned with churches, institutions of mercy inaugurated, slaves set free, the sacredness of life established.

He did it through *demonstration*. He came "to set at liberty those who were oppressed," to give "release to the captives" and "sight to the blind." This is what evangelism ought to mean to us. It must include, but is not confined to, preaching. In our day and within our circumstances when the proclaimed Gospel is so available—and so ignored—it may be even more important at times that we demonstrate God's love to our world by channeling it to people through concern for their bodily as well as their spiritual needs.

God has come to us; may He in His love and grace come to others through us!

Many Members—One Body

Whether we refer to the local congregation, the national synod, or to Christians of every denomination and sect scattered over our world, we are all members of one body. Our baptism made us members not only of our particular congregation, but of the church at large, the body of Christ. This does not disavow divisions and disagreements, or the necessity to defend the truth of God's Word with its saving Gospel, but it emphatically declares God's pattern and design for His children and servants on this planet.

While we, with tongue in cheek, may agree to this, we seldom act as if we really believe it. It is difficult enough to carry out this divine concept in local churches; it isn't likely that, while we need constantly and obediently to reach for it, we will ever attain to Paul's vision of unity and well-being as the Christian church in a broken world.

If the church is to be what it is gifted and designed to be—Christ-incarnate among the inhabitants of this planet—we must begin to recognize and apply this concept within the group with which we are affiliated. We are all members of the same body. For every mouth to proclaim the good news of God's redeeming love, there are two ears to listen to the joys and sorrows of others, two eyes to see the needs of people about them, two feet to take one into the hard places of human existence, two hands to help bear another's burdens.

We are not all mouths to speak or feet to run. All parts are to be honored and respected and encouraged to perform their various functions. And "if one member suffers, all suffer together; if one member is honored, all rejoice together."

Hope for All

What makes this selection from the prophet Isaiah especially significant is that it was the text from which Jesus preached in what is considered to be His very first sermon. He said to those synagogue listeners that He, Jesus, was the fulfillment of this ancient prophecy.

The Spirit of the Lord was upon Him. He was sent by His Father-God "to bring good tidings to the afflicted . . . to bind up the brokenhearted, to proclaim liberty to the captives . . . to comfort all who mourn."

Those in attendance at that synagogue service listened to Jesus only to the point in His sermon where He attempted to apply the tremendous hope expressed in Isaiah's message to God's creatures outside the confines of God's ancient people.

There is salvation for all, hope for all. Jesus brought it to pass in the lives He touched in His earthly ministry. And He brings such hope to the lives He is able to touch through each of us. While Isaiah was prophesying the eventual restoration of Israel as the people of God, Jesus makes that restoration a very present and personal act in the life of every person who embraces His saving grace. And we, to extrapolate the prophet's words, are "the priests of the Lord" and "the ministers of our God" assigned to be the conveyers and communicators of that divine hope to those who cross our paths.

Fourth Sunday After the Epiphany

Matthew 5:1–12 (A)

Life-Style of a Christian

Mahatma Gandhi praised it; Nietzsche cursed it. Many people sentimentalize over it. Most of us just bow politely to its beautiful thoughts and respectfully put it into cold storage. But always it leaps to life again to provoke and disturb us. And well it should, for it is the Sermon on the Mount, a collection of Jesus' most profound and best-remembered words.

For non-Christians this sermon is a frustrating, impossible sort of thing, a picture of life totally contrary to everything that is human in our kind of world; yet even they wistfully return to it, half persuaded that somewhere in its hundred-odd verses is the cure for human ills.

For the Christian it is something else again. It is designed to be his or her style of life—not something attained or accomplished, but something to reach for, to aim at, to become the goal of Christian living.

The Sermon on the Mount does not lead to salvation—except to drive a person to the need for God's grace. It is something which, by that grace, ought increasingly to come out of an authentic Christian. It ought to be the portrait of a saint and to result in the kind of life that will communicate God's healing and power to the lives of sick, lonely, oppressed, broken, unhappy people in our world and the community about us.

This sermon is meant to be a sort of agenda for our daily activities. It won't win us God's favor; that has already been bestowed upon us through Jesus and His cross. It is, however, the life-style of the family of God—a life-style we are empowered and expected to grow into as the adopted members of that family.

Monday   *1 Corinthians 1:26–31 (A)*

I Am Eligible

I certainly am not wise—according to worldly standards. I have no power over the lives of others—and very little in terms of managing my own life. I have not inherited any sort of nobility, even if many of my ancestors were rugged, noble people. I do not possess the charisma that attracts followers or initiates fan clubs.

Perhaps this serves to make me, according to Paul, eligible for servanthood in respect to the kingdom of God. The fact is, while God may use, even speak through, the very gifted personalities about me, the powerful and influential, the very bright and talented people who pull down the spotlights upon themselves while they occupy the great pulpits and stages of our world, history bears witness that God has more often revealed His purposes through men and women who were rejected, despised, imprisoned, even martyred by the communities in which they lived.

Whatever the world may think about us, or even if few people ever have occasion or reason to think about us at all, God chose us, however weak or foolish or failure-fraught. He has, through Christ, set us free from sin, even from our subjective feelings about ourselves, to be His children and servants forever.

Tuesday   *Mark 1:21–28 (B)*

Jesus and the Heckler

The ministry of Jesus was on its way. It was when He began teaching in the synagogue at Capernaum that some of the listeners realized that this ordinary-appearing young man, the son of a carpenter, was someone quite extraordinary. "They were astonished at His teaching, for He taught them as one who had authority, and not as the scribes." It was a demented heckler, however, who marked Him for who He really was. "I know who You are, the Holy One of God," he shrieked. It was at this point that Jesus revealed something of His true origin and present mission. He rebuked the evil spirit within this man and commanded it to come out of him.

What the synagogue audience witnessed was the touch of God upon a demon-possessed man—through this ordinary looking itinerant preacher. This and the several astounding confrontations Jesus had following this incident indicated that He was indeed someone very special.

Mark, the Gospel writer, is building up a strong case for Christ as that One sent by God to touch with divine, out-of-this-world power the lives of those who crossed His path. It is this One, this Jesus, who now abides in our hearts and lives and who through us seeks to touch with divine power the lives of those who cross our paths.

The Ethics of a Christian

The Christian life is not lived by rules and regulations. Our salvation is a gift of God's grace and is not dependent upon conformity to the traditions of the past. There is, nonetheless, a limit to our freedom. It is revealed in that ancient absolute or principle spelled out by our God in the command to love Him with our whole being and our fellow persons as ourselves. It is further imposed and demonstrated by our Lord, who commanded us to love one another "as I have loved you" (John 15:12).

This injunction formulates our ethics and our agenda in terms of our everyday relationships. It means that, insofar as possible, we must be all things to all persons, that we become servants to our neighbors. Thus freedom becomes the enslavement of love to God and His human creatures—to spread the Gospel of God's saving love, to serve Him day by day in our vocation, and to demonstrate His love in our interpersonal relationships.

Our standards, as the children and servants of God, ought to be determined in each situation by what we understand to be the most loving thing to do, as Christ would. It is often ambiguous, and we must be sensitive to the enlightenment of history as well as the expectations and requirements of our culture, and open always to the promptings of God's Spirit and the guidance of His Word. This is our ultimate course, our inevitable goal, our day-by-day intention. This constitutes our ethics as "little Christ's," to use Luther's phrase, in a broken and disjointed world.

Would I Know Him if I Saw Him?

When Jesus began preaching his first sermon, the congregation was fascinated if not flabbergasted by the sheer audacity of this young man. Even when He announced that He was about to fulfill the ancient prophecy of Isaiah, they accepted His words as those of an enthusiastic young preacher. The moment, however, that He said something provocative—such as challenging their racist attitude by referring to God's concern for foreigners and through Elijah and Elisha ministering to a widow in Zarephath and Naaman the Syrian, "all in the synagogue were filled with wrath."

He was promptly and forceably dispatched from the synagogue and the city. They failed, of course, to recognize that He was Christ, the Son of God.

"If I had lived in His day," I used to think, "if I could have heard and seen and touched Him, how dearly I would have loved Him; how gladly I would have left all to follow Him!" That, of course, is nonsense. If I can't recognize Him in His Word or in the ministry of this century's prophets, or can't see Him in the lives of my mate, children, teachers, friends, parishioners and pastors, and perhaps even in some fanatics I instinctively dislike because they appear to threaten my comfortable assumptions, I would have been as blind as those synagogue-goers when Jesus preached His first sermon.

Jesus is here—and He is walking with us every day of our lives. He speaks—sometimes through the joys of young Christians caught up in the ecstasy of conversion, but also through the miseries of minority races, the hungry and oppressed crying out in pain, the ill and addicted, the masses who are in bondage, and even our next-door neighbors in deep despair. God grant that we may recognize Christ—and obey Him.

Friday   *1 Corinthians 12:27–13:13 (C)*

The Supreme Gift

God's greatest gift to us is His gift of eternal love revealed through Jesus Christ. This includes the gift of His own Spirit, who consequently indwells each of us and is the Giver of many other gifts to the members of Christ's body, the instruments of His purposes in our world. The most important fruit of this relationship to God is the grace to love one another. That grace is also a gift.

It is a fruit or a gift that most of us appear to possess in rather small measure. We have little difficulty in loving those who love us or in showing concern for those who will respond favorably to our investment in them. If the time and place are right, we are even capable of risking our lives and possessions on behalf of a brother or sister who is in trouble.

True lovers, however, are few and far between. Theirs is a selfless, truth-seeking, all-enduring love. They love in the measure that they acknowledge and experience God's love for them—and are empowered and motivated by divine love. They discover that their response to

God's love must be demonstrated in their relationship to humanity about them.

Love, authentic love, is eternal and propagates and perpetuates love. This ability to love is truly the supreme gift—the gift to which we all should aspire. It is only as we rest in God's love for us that we will learn how to respond in love to others.

Saturday   *Deuteronomy 18:15–20 (B)*

Presumptuous Prophets

There are prophets and there are prophets. There are those who are raised up by the Lord and impelled by His Spirit to become His mouthpiece to community, nation or world. But there are many who are guided by some other spirit and who unwittingly or purposely use God-language for self-aggrandizement and personal gain. Those who presume "to speak a word in [God's] name which [He has] not commanded [them] to speak, or who [speak] in the name of other gods," they shall die, says our God. In the meantime, they are leading unsuspecting people down paths that divide them from God's grace and will for their lives. If we listen to them, we do so at our peril. "Test the spirits [and the prophets] to see whether they are of God," exhorted John (1 John 4:1a).

There are those in our midst who do speak the Word of God. We are to listen to them and hear God speaking to us through them. In a strange and remarkable sense all of God's servants are called and empowered to prophesy—to proclaim God's Word of love and healing and salvation to a sin-ridden, broken world. We need to listen to one another, to speak in love and concern to each other. If our lives are submerged in God's love and grace, He speaks through us, for we are His prophets, the vehicles and transmitters of His love to others about us.

Fifth Sunday
After the Epiphany
Matthew 5:13–20 (A)

The Christian and the World

"You are the salt of the earth," said Jesus. In the midst of a decadent
and sin-permeated world He set up before His disciples the high task
His Father had assigned to Him and through Him to those who would
follow Him. It was as if He said: "You, a mere handful, are chosen and
imbued agents of God who are to keep this world from rotting and
decaying and destroying itself." Our Lord implies that human society,
without God's influence and grace, would become like a disintegrating
carcass. The faithful few before Him who would catch a vision of His
mission and a measure of His power were to be rubbed like salt into
the rotting mass in order to disinfect its wounds, to arrest its decompo-
sition, to give flavor to its insipidity, and to save it from total destruction.

Jesus Himself set the pace when He became salt amid the corrupted
religion of the scribes and Pharisees. It so antagonized them that they
rebelled to the point of participating in His execution. The disciples-
become-apostles became as salt in the degenerate worship of their day.
There were large numbers who found life and purpose in their contacts
with these men; others reacted in bitterness and persecuted them
severely. Luther and the other Reformers became salt in the sickness
of the church of the Middle Ages. Kai Munk of Denmark and Dietrich
Bonhoeffer of Germany acted as salt in the rotting wounds of the
20th-century German dictatorship.

Our Lord's injunction is now extended to us. If there ever was a day
in which a wild and wanton world needed salt, it is within the society
and culture of this present hour. We are "the salt of the earth" and "the
light of the world." Even as God and His salvation is our only hope in
the dark night before us, so we who have become His children and
servants are His only hope for reaching His human creatures in this
rapidly dissipating world.

Ministers or Misconstruers?

Whereas some are especially called or gifted to be preachers and proclaimers of God's Word, all of us are ministers of the Gospel. We are all called to bear witness, in word and deed, to God's forgiving and saving love as revealed through the crucified and resurrected Jesus Christ.

We need to be aware, however, that our task is not to impress people with our knowledge and experience. There is the danger of acquiring fans or followers by flaunting our personality or charm or using whatever gifts we have been endowed with to fortify our shaky egos with the plaudits or commendations of those who gather about us. This may very well result in polluting God's simple message of love, or obscuring the blessed Gospel as revealed in Christ, and thereby contributing to the destruction of people to whom we witness.

This frightening possibility should compel us to search our hearts and examine our feelings and our words in order to make sure that we are promulgating God's testimony and not some half-baked concepts of our own.

We are to proclaim Jesus Christ, to bear witness to His eternal love in the things we say and do. We have neither wisdom nor power of our own. We are vehicles of the indwelling Spirit of God. If we are to bear witness to that Reality who is Christ, we must be sure that we are rooted in that Reality. Only then can God bless and work through our witness in our relationship with others about us.

In Touch with God

This Gospel lesson is a graphic picture of the desperate need of the masses of God's creatures that inhabit this world—and of that One who is able to apply healing and fulfillment for those needs. What I continuously need to review and remember is that this same Christ also applies His divine touch to the ailments of the suffering people in and around me today. He knows all about the "demons" that afflict me—whether they take the form of some abominable habit or despicable weakness, or manifest themselves in some compulsion to hate or covet or lust or fear. He knows, and He stands ready to cleanse and cure—if only I will allow Him and trust Him to do just that.

The key to Christ's great power—and to the supernatural, abounding power of a Stephen or a Paul or all the unseen and unheralded saints of God who truly are the light of the world and the salt of the earth—is suggested in the practice of Jesus, who early in the predawn hours of the day "rose and went out to a lonely place, and there He prayed." Jesus Christ, and the scores who follow Him, are wells of water to the thirsty and life to the dying because they were constantly in touch with God. This is the solution to my problem, to my need for power and poise in everyday living, to stability and serenity in even the stormiest of waters: I must keep in touch with God.

How can we find the power, that inner joy and peace, the spiritual health that will keep us strong and motivated through the blue Mondays, the difficult Tuesdays, the unhappy Wednesdays of our lives? And how can we channel such power and peace and joy to difficult people and situations all about us? There is only one way: We must keep in touch with God and allow Him to keep in touch with us through Word and Sacrament, the means of grace. Then God will have His way with us and through us.

Wednesday   *1 Corinthians 9:16–23 (B)*

Blessed Enslavement

I am free to marry or not to marry, to eat and drink, laugh and cry, work and play. I am free from the "dos" and "don'ts" that become so important to many religious people. I am no longer irrevocably bound to the ancient law. My salvation is a gift of God's grace and not dependent upon conformity to the traditions of the past or the rules and restrictions set up by religious leaders, whatever may be their claim to divine insight.

Nevertheless, I am enslaved—a bondslave of love to a loving God and consequently committed to His plan and purposes for my life. Set free from the bondage of sin and self-will, I, by God's gracious enablement, freely choose this blessed enslavement and soon discover the faith-full life to be the quenching of my thirst, the satisfying of my heart-hunger, and the total answer to my deepest needs.

The practical consequences of this enslavement, this total commitment to God and His will and purposes, is a commitment to the real needs and best interests of my fellow persons. It means that I "become all things to all men" and women—in order that I may be God's instrument or means of channeling to them divine love and that they may become His redeemed children.

Thursday   *Luke 5:1–11 (C)*

Stunted Christianity

"We toiled all night and took nothing." This has often been our response to our Lord's commands—or what we assume to be His commands—as we follow Him. We have honestly tried to serve Him, to work within His purposes, to extend His kingdom within our little arenas of service. More often than not, we fall flat on our faces. We continue to be more like potted plants than forest giants, sort of stunted Christians that live off the surface roots of God's grace. I wonder if we have ever really discovered the profound, powerful depths of God's eternal love. Perhaps, like the disciples in their early relationship with Christ, we are still fishing in shallow waters.

"Put out into the deep," Jesus said to Peter. "Get out of the shallow waters of the apparent and the tangible," He is saying to us today, "and push out into the depths of My life and promises. You have only been dangling your toes at the shoreline of God's great sea of grace. Put out into the deep and let down your nets."

Shallow waters are necessary to our lives and experiences. We are incapable of plunging from shore to ocean depths without first passing through the shallows. But we need not remain within the shallow waters of human effort and ineffectiveness; we don't have to settle for a stunted Christianity. It is in the great, incomprehensible depths of God's life and promises that we will truly meet the supernatural. We must "put out into the deep." We must lay claim to and lay hold of all that God through Christ has done on our behalf—forgiveness, reconciliation to God, our adoption as His sons and daughters, our commission as His servants. We have, by virtue of God's promises and gifts, access to everything we need to be beautiful and bountiful human beings in the love and service of God. We need only to cash in on it, claim it, use it—and act as if it is so.

"Put out into the deep and let down your nets," said Jesus. It means that we get unpotted, that we untie the taproots of our lives and send them deep into the grace of God. Only then will we become effective in channeling the power and provision of God into the weakness and want of humanity.

Friday   *1 Corinthians 14:12b–20 (C)*

The Gifts That Build

Whereas a sign or symbol of the Spirit's presence and power may well take the form of strange, ecstatic sounds, and may even stimulate God's servants to more radical obedience, it is far better that I aspire to those gifts that build up the church—that will more emphatically proclaim God's love and reveal His concern for the human family.

While others may revel in the language of ecstasy, I covet the gift of speaking and writing lucidly in the language of my fellow beings. What I desire most of all is the quality of love that goes beyond verbal witness and proclamation to the dedication of my energies and talents, even my very life, to the bodily welfare and spiritual salvation of God's human creatures on this planet. I sincerely want this because when my loving falls short of this, it falls short of Jesus' requirements for obedient and effective discipleship.

God grant that we may mature in our thinking about spiritual matters and our understanding concerning spiritual values. The church needs the more mature gifts if it is to reach men and women with the message of God's love in Christ. While we need not and must not deny or demean the gifts or experience of others, we must concentrate on those things that will be meaningful and significant for our ministry to our fellow beings.

Saturday   *Isaiah 6:1–8 (C)*

The Call of God

Isaiah had his eyes, ears, and heart attuned to God. He heard his God calling for ministers and servants, and he responded in humble joy and obedience.

66

This is the blessed risk of being in the presence of God. We sense our own unworthiness. We are smitten with the enormity of our sin—our human condition. We are forgiven and redeemed by God's grace. We are called into ministry.

Our great God may not tap each of us on the shoulder and beckon us to specific tasks or arenas of service. If we are attuned to Him, however, if we abide daily in His presence, we can overhear Him calling out: "Whom shall I send, and who will go for us?" And we can be assured that He waits on us for our individual responses.

It is in response to His call and appointment that we step out into our world today. This is our arena of service, our place in the sun. God grant that we overhear His call and launch out in loving obedience.

"Here am I! Send me."

Sixth Sunday After the Epiphany

Matthew 5:20–37 (A)

Discipleship and Discipline

To be a disciple of Jesus demands a discipline which is far higher and more stringent than was the law of Moses. Such a discipline is not projected as a means of winning God's favor; it is or ought to be our joyful response to God's redeeming love.

The key or king-pin to the discipline of a Christian is the enthronement of God and His purposes over and above every other loyalty or responsibility in our lives. Our human relationships—even with our family, our personal needs or desires, our responsibilities to government or corporation or employer, even to the laws of the state or the expectations of society and culture—must be subservient to our relationship and responsibility to God. Whatever tends to come between ourselves and God sabotages our claim upon His grace and His primary claim upon us and makes us ineffective as His ministers and servants.

Our initial commitment to Him is well-meant and our daily profession of faith is probably generous and passionate, but self-surrender to God as King and Lord of all we are and have is a day-by-day, lifelong exercise—and a joy-giving experience.

God is patient, but seeks ever to draw us into loving obedience, challenging us to take the risk and discover the joy of taking up our cross to follow Jesus. It is a discipleship and a discipline for which we were created and into which we have been redeemed and out of which will come the fulfillment of our most intense longings.

Monday   *1 Corinthians 2:6–13 (A)*

Unworldly Wisdom

It is not surprising that our non-Christian friends and associates are unable to comprehend our apparently unreasonable faith in and loyalty to an unseen God. They have some understanding of what fuels automobiles or energizes machinery. They cannot be expected to apprehend that which fuels the Christian and gives him or her the hope and joy that keeps that person steady even in the midst of the uncertainty and instability of life in this disjointed world.

The faith of a Christian is secured by an unworldy wisdom, a wisdom that is beyond that of the great intellects and talented people who inhabit this planet. It is the "secret and hidden wisdom of God" imparted to His children by way of His Spirit. It means that even the uneducated Christian possesses a wisdom that may be superior to that of the most profound scholars. The Christian may know little about science or history or economics or medicine but, being in touch with the Creator, is in touch with the eternal and the infinite, and while he or she may not be able to communicate with more educated people, the Christian possesses a far more profound and important experience and knowledge than anything the earthbound creatures of this world can assimilate.

We will probably not impress our more intellectual and talented peers with our comprehension of worldly activities and events. We may, however, by our attitudes and actions reflect something of God's divine love and power to people in need.

Tuesday   *Mark 1:40–45 (B)*

A Very Special Challenge

Like a symphony that gently introduces us to a theme of music and gradually builds it up through the first and second movements only to burst forth in glorious, breathtaking beauty and power—with every instrument, melody, and countermelody revealing the full sweep and the culmination of the theme in the final movement—so Christ, the son of a carpenter, a man among men and women, yet God-Incarnate and God-Revealed, began gradually to bring the divine touch of the almighty and loving God to people in His path. He first spoke and taught with authority; he exorcised a man possessed by a demon; He healed a woman of her sickness. Now He met a very special challenge by curing and cleansing a leper. Thus the symphony of God's grace moves on—still in its first movement.

Mark, in his brief and pertinent Gospel, singled out only those divine acts that had a particular significance for his writing project. The healing of a leper was, no doubt, a very special challenge in that it could not possibly be credited to magic or witchcraft or trickery. Lepers were always accounted as incurable—as the walking dead—and their only hope, if indeed there ever was hope, lay in the special intervention of God. Jesus, God's Son, met that challenge; He was that Intervention.

69

The great God, who has forgiven us our sins and reconciled us to Himself, abides with us and within us today. He is also the Great Enabler, who can empower us to face up to whatever challenge comes our way as we travel and labor in His course for our lives. We, the very sons and daughters of God, are now His interveners and enablers in the broken lives that cross our paths.

Wednesday   *1 Corinthians 9:24–27 (B)*

Lest I Be Disqualified

I am a son of God. I am justified by faith. It is still necessary, however, that I keep the faith. The failures of my life are and will be forgiven, but the failure to rise from defeat and persist in my walk with God may disqualify me for the final reward.

It means that I give priority to the business of being a Christian, that I make whatever sacrifices are necessary to keep this first and foremost in my life.

There is a reward for those who keep the faith. It is not some sentimental, harp-playing, cloud-hopping, pearly-gate nonsense. It is eternal reality—and the answer and fulfillment of one's deepest needs and longings. It is the guaranteed result, not of continual success but of staying close to the Lord and being faithful and persistent in the Christian conflict.

We don't need to be disqualified. We live in an era of divine grace. If we submit ourselves to God's love and to obedient servanthood, we will run the race successfully and are assured of the ultimate prize.

Thursday   *Luke 6:17–26 (C)*

Words That Disconcert

Some of the words that are attributed to Jesus are downright disconcerting. He speaks the consoling words of blessing and promise to the poor and the hungry and to those who weep in sorrow amid their unfortunate circumstances. To those who have everything they want, who enjoy full stomachs and love the life they lead and have won the respect and admiration of their fellow beings, Jesus appears at times

70

to speak the disturbing words of doom. Most of us, comparatively speaking, are rich in the things of this life, reasonably content, and generally respected. We are among the 10 or 15 percent of this world's population that travel first class on this spaceship called earth while the masses of this world travel in steerage. If we take the words of Jesus literally, it appears that we may be among the damned.

Our loving, forgiving God accepts us as we are—even if we are not poor or hungry or persecuted. Nevertheless, the four "woes" of Jesus' sermon that day are destined to keep us restless and deeply disturbed about the inequities of our society and world, and to lead us to a determination to invest whatever we can to help alleviate the tragic differences between the "haves" and the "have-nots" on this planet. They commit us, as well, to corporate repentance and social renewal, along with our primary mission of proclaiming God's saving love through Jesus Christ.

Friday   *1 Corinthians 15:12, 16–20 (C)*

Life Beyond Death

The high point, the constantly recurring theme, and the grand climax in the great symphony of the Gospel is the resurrection of our Lord Jesus Christ. He died for our sins, and He arose from the dead victorious over sin and death. If we subtract this from our message of love and hope, we really have nothing to say. We must be sure of this— Christ's resurrection—and we can be. It was witnessed by many before us. It has or can be experienced within us.

Maybe other people can discover motivation for good works apart from the commands and promises of the Christian faith, but it is the fact that death in this world is followed by everlasting life in the next that gives me the courage to go on—even to the point of risking my life and possessions on behalf of others.

We shall indeed be raised from the dead. Our God has not given to us an explanation as to just how this shall be done. Our three-dimensional insights would not be capable of comprehending it even if He had. But this we know: The perishable shall become imperishable and the mortal will become immortal on that great day. And this is all we need to know. It provides all the motivation we need to labor committedly and sacrificially in the purposes of our Lord.

71

At a Time of Decision

The words of this Old Testament lesson are the words of Moses to the people of Israel. Forty years earlier the parents of these Israelites had come to a similar place, the edge of the Promised Land, and were commanded to cross over into the new country. They refused—and lived and died in the wilderness. Now their children faced the same choice. Moses, the leader, rendered a sort of baccalaureate or graduation address on this momentous occasion. "Choose life," he said, "that you and your descendants may live, loving the Lord your God, obeying His voice, and cleaving to Him. . . ."

We have already chosen life when we have embraced Jesus Christ as our Savior and Lord. We have crossed the river and entered the new land. As with the Israelites, however, so with us—the new land and the new life are fraught with pitfalls and precipices, with temptations and trials of every sort. Whereas His grace has led us to the ultimate choice and decision, there are rivers to navigate and paths to tread and enemies to confront. Almost every day of our lives involves decisions. We don't have to be afraid, because God goes with us. But we do have to be wise, cautious, and finely attuned to God and His will and purposes for us if we are to remain in harmony with Him.

"Love the Lord your God, obey His voice, and cleave to Him," said Moses. This remains the key to right decisions and effective living and serving as His sons and daughters.

Seventh Sunday
After the Epiphany
Matthew 5:38–48 (A)

Outrageous Exhortations

If there are texts or portions of the New Testament one might wish to extirpate from the Scriptures, this would be one of them. Jesus says many difficult things, but these are outrageous, inconceivable, incredible. We often get through them with some mushy, sentimental interpretations—or ignore them altogether—but they continue to stand as Christ's declaration of what authentic Christianity is all about.

Because we can't rid ourselves of these outrageous injunctions from our Lord, we must accept the humiliation they lay on us and determine to do something about them. They are obviously not normal or natural to the human spirit; they are utterly impossible. It is only by means of the Spirit of God that these Sermon-on-the-Mount challenges can be applied to our lives. Whereas they reveal our poverty, they reveal, as well, Christ's expectations of His disciples. They are not a vision of what we will be in some heaven or other; they are what God chooses us to be and would have us to become right here on this planet.

We have a long way to go—to "be perfect as [our] heavenly Father is perfect"—but the journey begins with our baptism into Christ and continues as His indwelling Spirit increasingly and determinedly accomplishes His purposes in and through us.

It is, of course, impossible to believe that we will ever reach all of these incredible standards Christ set up for us; it is equally unthinkable that we should ever cease to focus on and struggle toward them. And God will forgive us when we fail.

Monday   *1 Corinthians 3:10–11, 16–23 (A)*

Foundations and Roots

By the time the foundation of a prospective house is laid and settled, the construction company has its sign posted announcing to all who pass by who is about to build on that particular foundation. The foundation of true faith is Jesus Christ and His redeeming love for humankind. If our faith is attached to anything or anyone else, the product will be disastrous.

The fact of the matter is that scores of God-seeking people are building on faulty foundations—on human wisdom, reason, visions, or emotions, or on gifted personalities who egotistically replace true foundations with cheap facsimiles in the effort to acquire followers and fans for themselves.

This is the reason the world is full of cults and sects that lead people down dark paths to spiritual oblivion. We are to be God's temple indwelt with His Spirit. This means that our lives or roots must be lodged deeply in that foundation which is Jesus Christ. Any self-appointed leader who builds upon or proclaims anything else is a false shepherd and should be avoided like the plague.

"So let no one boast of men," for men are capable of leading people astray. For "you are Christ's, and Christ is God's."

Tuesday   *Mark 2:1–12 (B)*

The Incomparable Experience

Mark continues to relate those selected incidents in Christ's ministry that increasingly reveal Him to be God-incarnate. Jesus was noted as one who spoke with authority, who cast out demons, who healed the mother-in-law of one of His followers, who cleansed and healed a leper. Thus far, however, these acts could be ascribed, at least by the religious leaders of His day, to some strange magic or witchcraft. After all, healings and exorcisings were not entirely unknown at that time.

There was, however, something different about this event, the healing of the paralytic who was brought to Jesus. In this act Jesus went one step further in the gradual revelation of Himself as the Messiah, the Son of God as well as the son of Mary, God-incarnate in their midst. His first words to this victim of paralysis who was brought before Him was, "My son, your sins are forgiven." This really got a rise out of the scribes who witnessed this happening: "Why does the fellow talk like that? This is blasphemy! Who but God alone can forgive sins?" (NEB). Then Jesus proceeded to heal the cripple, saying, "Rise, take up your pallet and go home."

The scribes were right in stating that only God could forgive sins, but they refused to believe that this Jesus was anything more than some sort of magician. The paralytic, however, who was brought to Christ for healing, received far more than he dared to anticipate—the need for which he may not even have recognized. He came face to face with the incomparable experience of his life. By means of the divine touch of God he was delivered not only from the paralysis that bound his body, but from the paralysis that bound his soul. He was reunited, redeemed, restored to his loving God. "My son," said Jesus, "your sins are forgiven."

It is this miracle that our Lord performs on our behalf—today and every day of our lives. It is the incomparable experience—the forgiveness of our sins. And we can begin this day and every day with this blessed assurance.

Wednesday   *2 Corinthians 1:18–22 (B)*

Positive Thinking

"All things are possible to him who believes," said Jesus (Mark 9:23). "I can do all things in Him who strengthens me," wrote Paul to the Philippians (4:13). As realistic as Paul was in his confrontation with human nature—in himself and in others—he was resolutely positive in his apprehension and proclamation of God's amazing grace and power on behalf of His children. "All the promises of God find their Yes in Him," he said. Whereas an overemphasis on the "power of positive thinking" as it is interpreted by some religionists in this day may lead one astray, the lethargic faith that fails to fully embrace God's Word and promises and to live by them leaves one impoverished and ineffective as God's child and servant.

It is possible for a Christian to slander God. It can be done by incessant fretting when things are difficult or worrying when one's plans fall through. The child of God, of all people, is the one who should live and serve positively and confidently. "It is God who establishes us . . . in Christ, and has commissioned us; He has put His seal upon us and given us His Spirit," says Paul. Our confidence is not to be foremost in ourselves; it is—it must be—in God and His indwelling Spirit, for with Him "all things are possible."

Thursday   *Luke 6:27–38 (C)*

Turning the World Around

We live in an upside-down world. It is not at all what God planned and created it to be. Human creatures established their independence of God and as a consequence determined to run this planet according to their self-centered ambitions, becoming, thereby, consumers of God's good gifts rather than loving images and reflections destined to receive and channel these gifts to fellow creatures.

God in His mercy sought out His fallen creatures through Jesus Christ, God-incarnate, to restore His image and purposes in their lives. It was His plan to bring order back into the chaos wrought by men and women, to turn the world right side up again.

The Gospel lesson relates, in the words of Christ, the change that would take place should God have His way in the hearts and lives of His redeemed creatures. We would change from consumers into givers and sharers, from enemies into lovers. Jesus' injunctions are unrealistic, impractical, and far beyond the reach or comprehension of any man or woman. It is unreasonable to suppose that such attitudes would ever be accepted in a society where competition has become virtuous and winning heroic and where people's identity or value is measured in terms of the money or property they possess.

Yet these are the words of our Lord and the mark of the new kingdom He came to establish. They are, as well, some measure of just how much we have matured as the citizens of that kingdom. Because they are Christ's injunctions, we had better not ignore them, but rather rely on His Spirit to make them ever more real and applicable to our lives. May He help us to that end.

Friday   *1 Corinthians 15:35–38a, 42–50 (C)*

Questions, Questions

Paul implies that such questions are foolish. They obviously reveal the thinking of the natural man, who has no grasp of spiritual matters. Paul does not suggest any reasonable answers, perhaps because we could not comprehend them even if they could be put into the language of this dispensation, and probably because he could not comprehend much more than we can about the eternal mysteries of resurrection and life after death.

He knows only that our death is an essential part of the whole process of God's ongoing creation. And he has the faith to believe that, as with a bare kernel buried in the earth, new life will come forth.

The rest of the matter is none of our business; it is in the hands of God. This much, however, we can believe with Paul: There will be some kind of body, and for each resurrected being his or her own unique body or entity.

Whether such a body will be anything like the one we live within in this world is pure conjecture and won't make a particle of difference in that great day of our resurrection. The only answer we need be concerned about is firmly stated by Paul: "What is sown is perishable; what is raised is imperishable. . . . It is sown a physical body, it is raised a spiritual body."

Saturday   *Isaiah 43:18–25 (B)*

The Reality of Forgiveness

It was indeed a "new thing" that God was revealing through the words of Isaiah. It had nothing to do with offerings and sacrifices, but with the people's heavy burden of sin and iniquity. This "new thing" was forgiveness based not on the human creatures' offerings or good works, but upon the graciousness of a loving God. It was not a "new thing" in respect to God's plan for His creatures; He was and is eternally gracious. It was new to His fallible, stumbling creatures who endeavored to subdue the wrath of a holy God by their faltering adherence to laws and regulations and, failing that, by sacrifices and religious ceremonies.

Forgiveness—it is old but always new. It is the gift of God to His penitent children. It is applicable to everyone who embraces God's grace. It is complete, total, and blots out forever a person's guilt and, as far as God is concerned, even the memory of that guilt.

We will remember all too well—at least the more pronounced failures and sins of our past. Perhaps it is good that we do, lest we continue to repeat them. But forgiving is synonymous with forgetting in the mind or heart of God. Today is a new day in our relationship with Him, and we need not be weighed down or hindered by the sins and errors of yesterday. We are forgiven!

Eighth Sunday
After the Epiphany
Matthew 6:24–34 (A)

Security in an Insecure World

If we are to find security in a very insecure world, we will obviously have to seek it on a far different level than do most people today. We will have to return to the Christ, whom we have so often ignored or bypassed while clutching our ephemeral material securities, and embrace once more His person and teachings as they are presented in our Gospel lesson.

Jesus begins with a word of *warning:* "No one can serve two masters. . . ." If we are to experience peace within revolution, security within instability, we must be set free by God to serve God. There must be total and irrevocable committal to Him and His purposes.

Jesus follows His warning with a *promise.* "Your primary concern in life," He is saying in contemporary terms, "must not be with those things that keep you alive—job, income, pension, food, clothes, reputation, status. Your citizenship is in the kingdom of God. You can well afford to lose your possessions, even your very lives, as far as this temporal world is concerned, for you are sons and daughters of God, and God your Father will never fail or forsake you."

The final word of Christ in this lesson is one of *exhortation,* to "seek first His kingdom and His righteousness," to give first place to His kingdom and to do what He requires and let the chips fall where they may. And this injunction is followed by the guarantee that the things we really need in the course of committing ourselves to this kind of relationship and carrying out the terms of this kind of loyalty will be provided.

Monday   *1 Corinthians 4:1–13 (A)*

As the World Regards Us

As "the wisdom of this world is folly with God" (1 Corinthians 3:19), so it is with what this world considers to be true values. Earthly riches, honor, respect, or reputation—none of this is promised to the servants of Christ. Even life itself, as important as that is to us, is not the Christian's greatest value. The people of the world are not likely to regard highly the disciples and servants of Jesus Christ.

If we seriously embrace the commission of Christ, we cannot begin to imagine to what heights—or depths—our discipleship will take us. There will be moments on the mount. There will be hours down in the valley—down where there is no honor or recognition, only loneliness and persecution, even suffering and imprisonment, as we seek to identify with the victims of war and poverty and oppression and injustice and to communicate the love and healing of Christ to those who are ready and willing to receive it.

Whatever the rewards for faithful service in some future realm, we are the sons and daughters, disciples and servants of God. Our appointment as such is reward enough. God grant that we may be loving and faithful and obedient.

Tuesday   *Mark 2:18–22 (B)*

Bottle-Bursting Christianity

As Jesus demonstrated before the religious leaders of His day, so He would to us, that the Gospel and life He brings cannot be confined to our concoctions and formulas; but like new wine bursting old wineskins, His life and power—true Christianity—will blow sky-high the self-made forms and notions we sometimes parade as Christianity.

What are some of these homemade formulae which might be construed as bottled-up religion today?

One has to do with a *God-in-a-box* concept adopted by many religious people. They bring God down into something or someone who can be comprehended, packaged, boxed-in in such a way as to no longer be a threat to their way of life—someone they can take or tolerate as it suits them.

Another formula is the *big-thumb-in-the-sky* concept. When the pressure is severe, the pains intense, many people are quick to find some god to latch on to. When the clouds clear away, the blue skies resolve into broken promises and the true God is left high and dry. There are so-called Christians who are unwittingly attempting to pack Christ's potent truth into the old bags or bottles of their bigoted and self-made notions, or who regard Christianity only as a haven in a time of storm instead of meaning and motivation for day-by-day living.

It is rather risky to allow Jesus to have His way in us. It will result in some bottle-breaking as He embraces, cleanses, redeems, and claims

79

us fully for Himself and His purposes. But when it happens, beauty will be restored where once there was ugliness, forgiveness where once there was sin and guilt, potency where once there was weakness, and our Christianity will become real and joyfully vital.

Wednesday   *2 Corinthians 3:1b–6 (B)*

Confident in Christ

Paul didn't say much, if anything, about self-confidence—as important as this is to us at times—but he repeatedly focused his confidence on Christ and properly credited Him for whatever was accomplished through his life.

While some people seem naturally to possess the courage and confidence to face anything that comes their way, many of us tip-toe through life's corridors—especially when it comes to carrying out our Christian witness among our peers.

I need to be reminded that fear is often a symptom of faithlessness. If I rely on my own knowledge or skill in my day-to-day relationships, I may have good reason to be afraid. If I, however, rely upon the Spirit and power of God, I *am* qualified to be a minister of the "new covenant" and the Spirit will bear witness through my words and deeds related in love to my fellow beings.

We are not assigned to demonstrate a new law or discipline. Nor are we expected to pass out formulas for proper living. We are here to proclaim and manifest Jesus Christ. We cannot do this by peddling the good news as newsboys peddle papers. We are called upon to offer our lives, to give of ourselves to our fellow persons' needs, and let God take care of the consequences.

And this we will do—if our confidence is in Him.

Thursday   *Luke 6:39–45 (C)*

Togetherness

We are aware of the necessity of recognizing God's love and of loving Him in return. In this Gospel portion Jesus is, in essence, introducing to His disciples the need and necessity of loving their fellow beings—

implying that love of God will inevitably result in "togetherness."

God is Love. The only way one can resemble God is in loving. Our neighbor is, in a remarkable way, God's representative in this distorted world, who is appointed by God to receive the sacrifices of love and service which we are to offer God through our neighbor. All is from God and for God, but His gifts of love showered upon us are to be returned to Him by way of the human priesthood—the priesthood of all believers to one another. A Christian has little of his or her own to give; a Christian is an instrument through which God's redeeming love reaches humankind. A Christian is called to be Christ to his or her neighbor.

Christian ethics—in terms of interpersonal relationships—is to *judge never, criticize seldom, forgive always, love intensely, live sacrificially.* This is the recipe or formula for "togetherness." "Beloved, let us love one another," wrote John, "for love is of God, and he who loves is born of God and knows God. He who does not love does not know God; for God is Love" (1 John 4:7–8).

Friday   *1 Corinthians 15:51–58 (C)*

It's a Mystery!

We shall not all sleep, but we shall all be changed—in a moment, in the twinkling of an eye—at the last trumpet? And at the sound of the trumpet the dead will be raised imperishable? It's incredible! To most people utterly unbelievable! This was, however, Paul's conviction—and continues to be a conviction that energizes and motivates Christ's disciples today.

Of course it's a mystery, and very foolish to worry about when and just how all this is to transpire. Paul was content and thankful to know that the victory through Jesus Christ is assured.

So let us be awake and aware—always. Even as we rest in what God has done on our behalf, let us be on the tiptoe of expectancy. Let us be working, giving, loving, keeping the faith, and demonstrating that faith to the world of men and women about us. The time will come soon enough when we shall experience together the eternal wonders of the next dimension. As for now, we need to hold on to one another in our love, serve God and our neighbor in our daily vocation, and dedicate ourselves in loving service to God and humanity.

Justice Be with You

It may be that the "peace" greeting is intended to include justice, but we often use it haphazardly without realizing that if there is to be peace or love in our hearts and in our relationships to our fellow beings, there must be justice.

Perhaps the Israelites were unable to fully comprehend God's ancient command to love their neighbors—or at least to understand all that this entails. They had no excuse for not understanding and carrying out God's command to "execute justice one with another." Only "then I will let you dwell in this place, in the land that I gave of old to your fathers forever."

What God may be saying to us today is that we can remain in the center of His will, where He through grace has brought us, only as long as we continue to walk with Him in loving obedience. We are commanded to love our fellow beings, and we on this side of Easter ought to know what that means. Loving one another—even our enemies—is possible only by way of His Spirit within us and involves a continual process of spiritual growth. To "execute justice," however, in respect to all peoples throughout our world, is something we are mandated to do *now*, and God will accept no excuses for our reneging on that issue.

We begin with justice in relation to God's creatures on this world; we proceed, by His enablement and inspiration, toward love.

Last Sunday
After the Epiphany
(Transfiguration)   *Matthew 17:1–9(A)*

Valley to Vision—and Back Again

Twelve men had left their jobs, homes, and families to follow Jesus Christ. Maybe they assumed that their sacrifices would resolve in eventual positions of wealth and glory, deluding themselves into believing that Jesus was Israel's future king and they his right-hand men. It wasn't working out that way and, after several months of following Him, He was no closer to earthly power and glory than when He was baptized in the Jordan River. They were in need of a vision, and in view of the trials-by-fire they would experience in future months and years, three of the disciples were permitted such a vision.

We, too, become bored with valley-living and occasionally need mountaintop experiences, something that might put a glow into the daily struggle, cast a halo about our perpetual conflicts, renew the meaning and purpose of this continual battle with life. And there are occasions when we get just that—oases along our desert paths that refresh and revitalize our weary spirits. They might come in the form of a Bach chorale or a Beethoven symphony, or during a walk in the woods, a conversation with a dear friend, a Bible class or worship service, or a meeting with a stranger who is an angel unawares.

Then it is back to the valley again, the hours of pain and frustration, our own defeats, our friends' suffering. But through it all there is joy—deep, profound, inexplicable—the joy of knowing that we are God's sons and daughters, His servants and ministers, that all that is His is ours, that we are His forever. From valley to vision and back again—and the living Christ is with us all the way.

Monday   *2 Peter 1:16–19 (A)*

A Valid Faith

We cannot say with Peter that "we were eyewitnesses of (Christ's) majesty," or that "we heard this voice borne from heaven." Peter was beset by human fallibilities as much as any of us, but he would not be

83

conned into following the "cleverly devised myths" that attract many religious people today. He knew his faith in Jesus Christ was valid; he had *seen* and *heard* the grandeur and glory of God.

But how can we possibly swallow this irrational God-stuff in a world of computers and satellites—and suffering, striving, dying people?

We know that Christ is real, that God is alive and well and lovingly concerned about each of us, because we have seen Him through the eyes of faith, have witnessed His miracles in our lives or the lives of others around us, and have experienced His forgiving and life-giving love in our own hearts. We know Him; He is real to us, and He is the source of our joy.

It is this grand experience we are dedicated to sharing with others, the experience of loving fellowship with God. It is this ever-growing and enriching experience that confirms our personal worth as God's redeemed children and draws us into a warm and loving relationship with one another.

Tuesday   *Mark 9:2–9 (B)*

A Necessary Experience

We can only guess why just three of the disciples accompanied Jesus up the mountain on this significant day. Perhaps it was because these three would be especially responsible for continuing the minstry of Christ after He left them. *James* would need the recollection of this experience to cool his intolerant spirit, temper his ambition, comfort him in Gethesemane, and nerve his faith as he laid his head on Herod's block. It was probably, in part, this mountaintop vision that kept *John* from fleeing in haste at Jesus' betrayal and crucifixion and enabled him to endure his exile to Patmos. *Peter* would often need the memory of that vision to strengthen his wavering courage and enable him to stand against persecution, comfort other believers amidst their trials, and testify to millions throughout history that he was an eyewitness of Christ's majesty and heard with his own ears the voice borne from heaven, "This is My beloved Son; listen to Him."

It is not surprising that these men, particularly Peter, wanted to settle down with Jesus on that mountaintop for the rest of their lives. It was not meant to be. It was back to the valley for them—to those places between a rock and a hard place where they were to continue, enriched and renewed by what they had just witnessed, to lovingly and faithfully serve in the difficult arenas of this world. The Transfiguration was a necessary experience for them, but it was not the grand finale. It was designed to equip them for service in the new kingdom, to better enable them to face and overcome the hardships and sufferings involved in witnessing concerning that kingdom on this planet.

Sometimes We Wear Masks

Moses wore a veil or a mask to shield his people from the glory of God that shone through his countenance. They were not ready for that kind of closeness to the Almighty, All-righteous God. The religious leaders of Christ's day could not perceive Christ as God's Son and His teachings as God's truth because of a different kind of veil that covered their hearts and minds. We also tend to cower behind veils or masks even today which obscure God's truth and prevent others from perceiving it in and through us.

God's truth has been unmasked. His love for His creatures is revealed through Christ-incarnate, His judgment upon sin satisfied through Christ's sacrifice on the cross. And His revealed truth has unmasked us—confronting us with our fallen condition and with His forgiving mercy that reconciles us to Himself.

There is no longer any need for masks. Our relationship to God is marked by self-surrender, and our relationship to our fellow beings by self-disclosure. We have nothing to hide from God, and we are to be open and aboveboard with one another. Only then can the Spirit of God be reflected and channeled through our interpersonal relationships.

Mountains and Valleys

When they "went up on the mountain to pray," the three disciples along with Jesus, they received far more than they had bargained for. It was a majestic vision, something clear out of this world. Peter was so flabbergasted that he immediately wanted to set up shelters for three figures within this mountaintop vision. "Master, it is well that we are here," he exclaimed.

There is point and purpose to the Transfiguration event. It provided a prophetic picture of the glory in which Christ and His followers will ultimately appear—a brief glimpse into the dimension of the spiritual and eternal. Though the disciples may not have realized this at the moment, it was designed to alert them to the fact that they were destined for something far better than this earthly sojourn, that Christ's kingdom was not to be centered upon this globe nor in this space-time concept we call life, and that eternity and spiritual reality is something that can never be comprehended by the finite faculties of the human creature.

What ought this vision mean to us? Among other things, it means that there is a victorious conclusion to this valley experience that we are a part of, this conflict in which we are engaged. It means that we need not put so much emphasis on temporal values; that poverty or lack of success here, though uncomfortable, is not tragic; and that affliction in this life, though painful, does not have to be bitter and incapacitating.

It was a great and grand event, this mountaintop experience. Now it is back to the valley again—and the transfigured and resurrected Christ is with us to transform us and transmit through us His resurrection power.

Friday   *2 Corinthians 4:3-6 (C)*

Some People We Deal With

While we intend to shed our masks and veils in the disclosure of ourselves to others, some of the people we deal with are not about to allow us through the veils they hide under. They are not capable of trusting us or accepting the message we would bring to them. Blinded by the things of this world, they cannot comprehend the beauties and delights of another dimension, and that renders them deaf to the blessed Word of God.

In other words, there are instances when our preaching appears to bear no fruit and, in our interpersonal relationships, the witness of our lives may be the only message some people can see or hear. Thus it is necessary to let the Light shine "who has shown in our hearts to give the knowledge of the glory of God in the face of Christ."

Verbal witness or proclamation is ultimately necessary. Some people, however, are not ready for it, and the Holy Spirit may prepare them for the verbal witness by means of the silent yet effective witness of joy and love that is expressed in and through us as we relate to them in work and play relationships.

Moses on the Mountain

When Moses went up the mountain, his colleagues could only accompany him part way. His actual meeting with God was between him and God alone. While Moses was very special—chosen by God to carry out a momentous task with the children of God—the incident serves to point up something about your and my meeting with God.

We celebrate and worship together as God's sons and daughters. We need each other in our relationship within the kingdom of God, and He speaks to and through each of us as we fellowship together. Yet there are very important occasions when God deals with each of us as individuals, when we retire to our secret meeting place and allow God to work with us as He wills.

We must not approach Him in fear, for He is our loving Father; but we must come to Him as we are, holding nothing back, and willing to accept His message and do His bidding whatever that may entail.

Because God deals with us as individuals, these periods of solitude are very important to our growth as Christians—and they are very precious. Let us not ignore them or pass them by.

First Sunday in Lent
Matthew 4:1–11 (A)

The Conflict Before Us

The glories of the Epiphany season are now behind us. It was an exciting time. We were witnesses to a series of manifestations of Jesus' majesty—in His baptism, His miracles, His revelation of Himself as the Son of God at the Transfiguration on the Mount. These were some pretty heady experiences.

Now we have come back to earth—to our three-dimensional world and the sufferings and conflicts that plague us here. This is the first Sunday in the church season called Lent. While it is designed to prepare us for the high festival of Easter, we do have to consider some things of a very serious nature if we are properly to understand the meaning of Christ's resurrection—things like sin, death, temptation, repentance, crucifixion.

We are introduced to our Lord's conflict with the spiritual forces of evil—the same forces we confront daily in our sojourn and service as the children and servants of God. The temptations Jesus confronted are, in many ways, comparable to those we face. They were, in essence, Satan's attempt to cross out the cross in the ministry of our Lord. Had the devil succeeded in doing so, salvation would not have been offered to us, sin would not have been atoned for, we would never have known the experience of redemption, God's human creatures would die eternally in their sin, and the spiritual forces of evil would be forever victorious.

Whereas Satan failed in his temptations of the Christ, he has and is too often succeeding with many of us, primarily in the temptation to cross out the cross in our relationship with God. As we focus on the cross of Christ during this and every season of the church year, may we embrace and faithfully obey our Lord's injunction to take up our cross and follow Him.

From Sin to Grace

We are aware that all God's human creatures are sinners—that disease and death, physical and spiritual, have permeated the whole human race. We know, as well, that the laws of God, and the precepts of men and women who tried to find and follow God, were initiated to bring order and harmony into humanity's chaos. It was these ancient laws that revealed to man and woman their inner sickness and estrangement from their Creator.

God's love, however, is far greater than the evil that brings death and destruction. His grace is more powerful than human wickedness. It was this that was revealed through Jesus Christ, and it is this that grants us eternal life.

What we cannot comprehend we can still celebrate. For it was through the sacrifice of our Lord Jesus Christ, God's act of grace and love, that we have been made the very sons and daughters of God.

Temptation

Temptation—it often takes the shape of bread that promises to satiate my hunger or water to slake my thirst. It promises fulfillment and happiness—poking into my dark hours with beckoning fingers of hope, interrupting my drudge-laden routine with moments of tantalizing excitement, relieving my pain with experiences of pleasure and delight.

It never lets up. I have sometimes envied my Lord who had angels to succor Him after His 40-day ordeal in the wilderness. I wonder if it's fair that I, composed of such human stuff, should be so constantly exposed to that which cannot be humanly resisted.

But I am exposed—and I discover very realistically that I cannot win them all. It is said that temptation is necessary to Christian maturity. It can be used by God to develop my dependence on Him. It ought to result in keeping me close to Him. I am supposed to grow stronger in the heat of conflict and even to discover that my weaknesses can become channels of divine power and sustenance.

God doesn't send temptation, but He obviously allows it. And with every temptation He promises the grace to resist it. I must learn how to tie on to that grace.

We Are Secure

Nothing, nothing at all, can come between us and our loving God. Our feelings of guilt and depression will rise up to haunt us, but they will in no way alter God's redeeming and accepting love. The tragedies and conflicts of this life will frighten and discourage us, but they cannot change God's attitudes or stifle His love for us. Failures and defeats may trip us up, but they do not affect our relationship to God.

Our boat will rock; the earth will tremble. Revolutions will shake up governments and institutions. Our traditions may be nullified, our convictions threatened. Every temporal security may crumble. God's love and reconciling grace are forever, and He will never let us go. If our allegiance is to God and our faith is fixed on Him, the very atrocities that threaten to destroy us become the means by which He carries out His will in us and through us.

Nothing, absolutely nothing can separate us from the love of God as revealed and proclaimed and demonstrated through Jesus Christ. We are the sons and daughters of God, His servants and disciples forever.

Crossing Out the Cross

It is probably a gross oversimplification to state that Satan's whole purpose in Christ's temptations was to cross out the cross in the life and experience of our Lord. As far as Jesus was concerned, it was a vain attempt, for Jesus had set His face toward Jerusalem, placing the cross at the very apex of His plan for the salvation of the human race, and nothing would deter Him from that course.

The spiritual conflict before us does, however, reveal the pattern of temptation as it pertains to all of God's children. Although the devil failed in his temptation of Jesus, he succeeds all too often in the temptations that come our way. There is the temptation to use God to meet our human needs and wants rather than allowing Him to use us in the accomplishment of His purposes. There is the incessant quest on the part of some churchgoers for entertaining, consoling, head-patting, peace-giving, get-ready-for-heaven, Christ-is-coming-soon sermons, the desperate search for ecstatic experiences, the common concept of God as a sort of dispenser of good things for good people. There is the temptation to be crowd-gatherers, convert-counters, recognition-seekers, to promote our own image under the guise of Christian servant-hood. There is always the temptation to compromise—with the state in promoting destructive wars, with the status quo in perpetuating injustice against the powerless, with the middle class in maintaining high living standards at the cost of oppressing the poor.

Even while we cling to the cross Jesus bore on our behalf, and are fairly successful in fighting off less profound temptations such as pilfering and philandering, we all too easily yield to the temptation to avoid the cross our Lord has commanded us to bear on behalf of our fellow beings.

Friday *Romans 10:8b–13 (C)*

Authentic Faith

"For man believes with his heart and so is justified. . . ." Let us understand, however, what it means to "believe" and to proclaim and promote such belief through our confessions of faith. We ought to know that it is not accomplished totally through well-formed phrases or impressive liturgies. This could be as phony as a sales pitch. Our pious exercises may be a ridiculous facade that obscures the real condition of our hearts. To "believe" is more than "calling upon the name of the Lord." We tend to do that every time we are plunged into some dire crisis.

To "believe" is to trust in the redemption wrought by Christ, with the result that we surrender and submit all we are and have to God's loving control. This means that God and His purposes become the consuming passion of our lives, and His purposes point directly to a relationship of loving concern for—and action on behalf of—our fellow persons about us.

If we truly "believe" in Him—in what God has done for us as revealed through Jesus Christ—then we *are* saved, and this is true irrespective of our race, color, ancestry, social status, or church denomination.

Saturday *Genesis 22:1–18 (B)*

The Supreme Test

This incident in the life of Abraham is certainly one of the more troublesome stories from the Bible. The God of Abraham, in this instance, does not appear to be the same God who is revealed to us through Jesus Christ. Is it possible that Abraham assumed that his commitment to God and His purposes would be tested in this manner?

Assumption or whatever, the end result is a grand revelation of Abraham's devotion to his God. More important to Abraham than his very son, who was the focal point of God's promises and the seed that would become Israel and culminate in the coming of the Messiah, was Abraham's personal relationship to God. Abraham proved to himself and to us that he was truly a man of God and could therefore be trusted to carry out God's purposes. Abraham was not devoted to mere human convictions, and certainly not to the tradition of child-sacrifice that may have been prevalent among the religions of his day; he was devoted to God. Another sacrifice was provided to express that devotion, and the purposes of God were carried out through Abraham and his seed.

Jesus also said some very difficult things to His disciples—things like hating one's own father and mother and wife and children or cutting off one's hand or plucking out one's eye if these come between a person and God. While we are not about to take this literally, we get the message—from Abraham and from Jesus—that our response to God's love must be total, unconditional, and more important than anything else in this life.

Second Sunday in Lent
John 4:5–26 (A)

From Futility to Fulfillment

Back of the glitter and painted scenery out front in our lives there is naked reality—and often disorder, confusion, and excruciating futility. There is the futility of contradiction, conflict, unsatisfied desire, meaninglessness, and purposelessness. We feel something of the strain and stress of Cosette in Victor Hugo's *Les Miserables*, tugging away at her heavy bucket, wishing deeply that she could "fly, to fly with all her might, across woods, across fields, to houses, to windows, to lighted candles."

The message of this Gospel lesson is that futility can give way to fulfillment, that our great God has taken upon Himself the heavy load we are so frantically struggling with, that there can be meaning and value, point and purpose in our daily conflict.

Jesus began His ministry to the Samaritan woman by making her conscious of the futility in her heart and life. He then reached out to offer His fulfillment. She had left home for the purpose of drawing water—expecting, of course, to continue on in the purposeless, vicious futility she had always struggled with. What she found at the well was water of a different sort—a new heart, a new life. She met Jesus and became a new creature.

"My soul thirsts for the living God," said David. Indeed it does. This is the basis of our futility—the thirst in our lives for the living water which Christ offers so freely. We must cease culling our comfort and consolation from an abstract, unknown god and consecrate ourselves to God-revealed, the living Christ—to receive from Him, delight in Him, love and serve Him. Then our futility will give way to fulfillment.

Monday   Romans 4:1–5, 13–17 (A)

Our Salvation—God's Gift

From the very beginning of God's dealings with His chosen people, even from the time of Abraham, our great God made it quite clear that His acceptance is not the result of good works on the part of His creatures, but His own incomprehensible, incomparable love. And yet, though it may be very subtle, most of us are still afflicted in some measure with an insidious work-righteousness concept in respect to our relationship to God. Even in our generous proclamations concerning God's grace, we still come down heavy on the side of the Law as well as the assumed "dos" and "don'ts" of the Christian life.

It is so natural to tie our faith to certain acts that we do, to rituals and ceremonies and little sacrifices that we engage in. While these things may be of value, they in no way reconcile us to God.

God's saving love, His eternal righteousness, is a gift, not a reward for good works. We are to embrace that gift, that righteousness as revealed through Jesus Christ, to recognize our obvious inability to measure up to the demands of the Law, to claim our freedom from sin's condemnation with its eternal consequences, and to live and serve as the true sons and daughters of God.

Tuesday   *Mark 8:31–38 (B)*

From Salvation to Discipleship

It had been a sort of kindergarten experience up to now for these 12 men who had followed Christ. The time had come when they must be prepared for commitment and service. "And He began to teach them that the Son of man must suffer many things. . . ."

They were shocked, flabbergasted, bowled over. This was something they could not comprehend—this lovely, gracious, all-powerful Christ who was well on His way to becoming Israel's king was now predicting His own execution.

This is possibly what happens, in some degree, to each of us. As long as our preachers talk about dear old God who comforts and coddles us while allowing us to live pretty much as we please, indulging in our material gifts, using them for our personal aggrandizement while continuing to acquiesce to our sin-ridden desires and instincts, nobody is provoked and church and religion are accepted as an integral part of our lives. But when religious leaders break through the periphery of Christian teaching and talk about cross-bearing and dying to sin, when they go beyond the "take the love He brought" presentations with which we can readily agree and begin challenging us to "lead the life He taught," then many of us either cop out or crawl more deeply into our kindergarten apprehensions concerning religion and never discover what Christianity is all about.

"Let him deny himself and take up his cross . . .," said Jesus. This is as much a part of Christianity as the cross Jesus bore on our behalf.

To "take the love He brought and lead the life He taught"—it is only in Christ, our Savior and Master, that we find the grace and the strength to do both.

Wednesday   *Romans 5:1–11 (B)*

We Are Accepted

The truth of the matter is—and this in spite of our foolish efforts to placate God by means of rules and laws and traditions and customs—that we *have been* accepted by God through Jesus Christ. This is where we now stand; this is what we ought to be celebrating. This is no vain hope; it is the Gospel truth. God's love and Spirit *do* abide within us.

It is when we accept and cling to this that God has done for us through Christ, irrespective of our human feelings and frailties, that the very conflicts which beset us, and may even threaten to destroy us, become God's tools to grind and polish and temper our spirits and prepare us for loving and obedient service.

Let this day be filled with praises! We *are* reconciled to God; we are His forever! Now we can lend ourselves to good works on God's behalf and begin to reflect and transmit to others something of our joy as God's children and of God's saving love extended to them.

Thursday   *Luke 13:31–35 (C)*

The Darkness Around Us

Some of us have wondered, as we follow Christ through His hours of suffering that led to His ultimate sacrifice at Jerusalem, why our paths should be so smooth and our way so easy. Refusing to yield to Satan's temptations to take the easy road to worldly acclaim and power, Jesus chose the painful path of sacrificial service to make possible our salvation. While we claim to follow Him, most of us have found little in our course through life that resembles suffering or sacrifice for the sake of others.

One of the reasons for Jesus' suffering was the hostile reactions of the national and religious leaders to His ministry of redeeming love. In the tradition of the ancient prophets, He courageously spoke out against the oppressive policies of Herod and repeatedly exposed the hypocrisy of Israel's professors and teachers of religion. And it was the "church" of His day that set in motion the machinery that eventually executed Him.

Our Christianity is of little effect unless we begin to live by our Lord's precepts, and this will take us beyond profession into practice, beyond pie-eyed contemplations around spiritual ecstasies into the hard, painful realities of daily living and loving. Along with our brothers and sisters in Christ we have the obligation not only to proclaim God's love but to bring something of that love into our world and to work toward making our society just and equitable. Among other things, this must include the courage to stand up and be counted in respect to our abhorrence of injustices perpetrated by the rich over against the poor or by majorities over against minorities, and the risk of reaching out to correct such inequities wherever they may appear.

Tragedy and violence, poverty and oppression, fear and darkness are as rampant today as they ever were. Maybe we are a part of the problem. May our gracious Lord help us to see it if we are!

Friday   *Philippians 3:17–4:1 (C)*

Keep the Faith!

"Stand firm thus in the Lord," exhorts the apostle Paul to his friends and co-ministers at Philippi. He even dared to enjoin them to imitate him—"and mark those who so live as you have an example in us." Paul was writing this injunction while in one of the several prisons in which he and his colleagues were often incarcerated. From that time until this, jail sentences have often been the lot of those who have sincerely, if not always wisely, sought to follow in the steps and the teachings of Jesus.

Paul was not, of course, suggesting that a jail sentence was inevitable if one is to "obey God rather than men" (Acts 5:29). Man-made laws are supposedly for the benefit of all—pagans and believers alike. Conflicts, adversities, sufferings of one sort or another are inevitable. They are sometimes the consequence of keeping the faith; they are always associated with living in this disjointed world and are as much a part of life as our very environment.

Over and above this life and this world in which we live, however, is the inevitability of life everlasting, the sure hope and assurance that "our commonwealth is in heaven," the guarantee that "the Lord Jesus Christ . . . will change our lowly body to be like His glorious body."

Thus we are enjoined to keep the faith. It will be worth it despite all of the difficult and painful things that happen here. As Paul writes in another of his letters, ". . . the sufferings of this present time are not worth comparing with the glory that is to be revealed to us" (Romans 8:18).

Trust and Obey

"So Abram went, as the Lord had told him. . . ." "By faith Abraham obeyed when he was called to go out to a place . . . and he went out, not knowing where he was to go" (Hebrews 11:8).

Whatever may have been the medium by which God communicated with Abraham—dreams, visions, spoken word, inner conviction—this man was certain that God had spoken and had made His will known. It must have been an exciting, even traumatic experience in the life of Abraham that resulted in his severing all ties with homeland and friends and secure surroundings to launch out into a strange and unknown world. The consequences of his obedience, not totally revealed to Abraham, are known and celebrated by God's children to this very day.

"You are My friends if you do what I command you," said Jesus to His disciples (John 15:14). Our great God continues to reveal Himself and His will through His Son, our Lord. He does not, anymore than He did with Abraham, reveal the immediate consequences or results of doing His will. God commands; our response to His love, His grace, and His commands must be obedience. This is what authentic faith is all about. There are many things about which we presently do not know the will of God. There are other matters in which we do know His will, and all our quibbling and procrastinating only forestalls and inhibits its accomplishment and endangers our relationship to Him.

Let us go, "as the Lord has told *us,*" as did Abraham of ancient times, in scorn of cost or unknown consequences. In no other way can God accomplish His purposes in and through our lives.

Third Sunday in Lent
John 9:1–41 (A)

The Problem of Pain

The most common malady of humankind is that of suffering. It is so commonplace that it becomes almost routine, and we tend to become hardened and calloused to it—at least in regards to the suffering of others. Every newspaper screams it out in black headlines. The electronic media give form and voice to it in every news broadcast. But until it personally touches us or our loved ones, it is just so much water over the dam and we continue to nurse our little aches and pains even while we ignore the millions of suffering and pain-ridden souls in the world about us.

Jesus healed the man born blind, but He made no effort to adequately define or explain the sufferings that plagued His world and ours. He accepted them as part of this distorted, sin-permeated planet, confronted them, and brought the power and grace of His loving Father to bear upon its victims. He was revealing the God who is greater than His creatures' sufferings and can cure them of their maladies—or use them in the accomplishment of His loving will and plan for this world's inhabitants.

We will not discover in Jesus Christ any logical answer or explanation for the sufferings of our world or the pain and problems that may come our way. His takeover of our lives, however, will always produce miracles. It may be the miracle of immediate healing or the eradication of the pain—or the supernatural grace of God that enables us to handle our sufferings and even to use them in the accomplishment of God's purposes in and through us.

Monday   *Ephesians 5:8–14 (A)*

Walking in the Light

Our immediate goal in respect to the week before us is not to be people-pleasing. It is to be God-pleasing. This is God's will for us this week, as it is every week. "Try to learn what is pleasing to the Lord," Paul enjoins the Christians at Ephesus. There is no guarantee that we will thereby please the people about us, but it is the only way we can truly serve God and properly communicate to the human family the grace and the power of our loving God. And it is the only way we can bring the divine and eternal light of God into the darkness that confuses and threatens the inhabitants of this planet.

The light that broke into the darkness of our world through Jesus Christ is now to be transmitted through us. This necessitates our walking in the light. Our self-surrender to God is to be reflected in our self-disclosure to His created children about us. We are to walk as Jesus walked, in honesty and openness, and in loving, self-denying concern for others.

It will not always be popular or make us popular—our walking "as children of light." It means that we cannot participate in some of the everybody-does-it, shady, shadowy activities that people consider natural and necessary in their day-by-day existence. It may mean that we will have to make some controversial decisions and support some unpopular causes. It may, on the other hand, compel or encourage others about us to leave the dark paths of fruitless striving to discover Jesus as the Light of the world.

Tuesday   *John 2:13–22 (B)*

A Time for Anger?

It is difficult to conceive of Jesus Christ as ever being angry. Perhaps this is because we foolishly assume that there is no room for anger in love or in loving relationships. We can more easily accept anger in a person such as Paul, who told his constituents at Ephesus to "be angry but do not sin" (Ephesians 4:26); and yet the degree of anger demonstrated by Jesus within the circumstance of our Gospel lesson may disturb us at times.

Both the humanity and the divinity of the loving Christ may well have been indicated in the temple incident. We may sincerely question what might be the reaction of Jesus to some of the "temples" we have erected to the glory of God—the Jesus whose concern for the poorest of the poor is far above any multimillion dollar sanctuary that His more affluent children may raise up and support in His name.

99

There is a time for anger. We ought to be angry about anything that comes between a person and God, about people's misguided focus upon places in which to worship rather than persons to serve, about questionable activities in God's house, about sexual immorality, about drug abuse, about poverty and injustice and war, about the self-centeredness of most of us who put our personal comfort and welfare above the dire needs of millions of God's human creatures that inhabit our planet.

There are times when it may be sinful *not* to be angry in our kind of world. We need to be aware, however, that God-pleasing anger results in the kind of actions that heal those who hurt, succor those who suffer, and bring God's love to bear upon those who are estranged from Him.

Wednesday   *1 Corinthians 1:22–25 (B)*

What Foolishness!

What foolishness!
—to buy into the nonsense that the crucifixion of a carpenter-turned-preacher could somehow be interpreted as God taking upon Himself the sins of the world. Yet this is what we as Christians hold to, that in which we hope, in which we invest our whole lives—past, present, and future.

What foolishness!
—to believe that a God of love reigns over this fractured, violence-ridden world of ours, that He really cares about the starving millions, the imprisoned, the deprived, the victims of disease and torture, terrorism and warfare, and the natural calamities that almost daily befall the inhabitants of this planet. Yet this is what we claim; this is the proclamation we joyously fling into the teeth of pagans and unbelievers about us. "Cast all your anxieties on Him, for He cares about you" (1 Peter 5:7).

What foolishness!
—to insist that God is in our midst, that He abides within us, that He loves us and cares about us as His own beloved children, that He is personally concerned about each one of us and has a plan for our lives on this world and guarantees life everlasting in the kingdom to come.

Yet this is indeed what we believe; it is this that keeps us pushing on through sunshine or rain, highs or lows, whatever the conflicts and calamities that stand in our way.

"For the foolishness of God is wiser than men. . . ."

The Gospel of Another Chance

It is true in respect to most churches; it may be true about our lives as well. There is a good deal of foliage. There may be some colorful blooming now and then. But the real test of faith and obedience is in the fruit that is borne as a consequence of our lives and living. It may be impossible for us to make any judgment in this matter, but the Master of the vineyard has a right to expect fruit-bearing and productive living. We must wonder at times whether or not we measure up.

We don't believe that evidences of fruit-bearing or productivity have to be statistical—or always visible to the naked eye. Fruit-bearing is not necessarily synonymous with good works or service for God. Fruit is what we are; service is what we do. We are required to bear fruit—wherever God has placed us: the shop or the school, the home or the office, Main Street or marketplace. We are to "live" Christ—not the narrow, severe, critical, unloving Christ as interpreted and reflected by some people, but the Christ of the Gospels, the joyful, loving, patient, kind, gentle, selfless Christ of Christmas and Good Friday, Easter and Pentecost. It means that we are to be kind among people who are cruel, tolerant among those who are irritable and complaining, self-controlled among those who live by their appetites, joyful among the unhappy and ungrateful, generous among the poor and needy, and loving and concerned in all situations—even when we have to take a prophetic stand against injustice and prejudice and greed.

And this is where all of us have failed—again and again. Let us be grateful for the Gospel of another chance. It is as if Jesus were interceding on our behalf: "Give them another chance, Father. I will stir them, prune them, and allow some hard times to refine and renew them and teach them how to rely on divine grace, but give them another chance. . . ." Our great God is merciful and patient, and He will make us into fruit-bearing Christians.

101

Overconfident?

"With most of them God was not pleased," wrote Paul about his ancestors who followed Moses out of Egypt. We become the unworthy recipients of God's saving grace in our baptism. Paul is alerting us to the fact that a fall from grace is indeed possible, that among the multitudes who call upon His name and faithfully fulfill the requisities and forms of Christian worship and expression are those with whom He is not pleased. "Therefore let anyone who thinks that he stands take heed lest he fall," he warns the Corinthian Christians.

We may disagree with Paul, or misinterpret him, when he says that God "will not let you be tempted beyond your strength. . . ." Many of us have indeed been tempted beyond our strength and have fallen on our faces in shame and despair. We celebrate with Paul, however, the conviction that "God is faithful and . . . with the temptation will also provide the way of escape. . . ."

There may have been a temptation that we were not "able to endure" and we grieved the Spirit of God and hurt someone we love. We did not fall from grace; God loves us, and He is still faithful, always faithful. There must be confession and repentance, a renewal of our commitment to the grace of God, His forgiveness, and the strength He promises to enable us to resist the temptations that confront us today. Let us be aware that our confidence is to be in the grace of God—not in self-engendered feelings about Him or in some of our work-righteous attempts to please Him.

Unforsaken

"I will turn the darkness before them into light, the rough places into level ground . . . and I will not forsake them." The word of the prophet was proclaimed on behalf of the Israelites and dealt particularly with God's concern for them. It is equally applicable, as revealed through Jesus Christ, to every one of God's human creatures who follow the Christ. We are the people of God, and His word as spoken to the ancient Israelites is His word to us today.

What a precious word and promise it is as we grope fretfully and fearfully through the clouds of darkness that often close in about us! There will be dark clouds and rough paths in the journey before us, but we have in Jesus Christ a Shepherd to guide us, a Light to beckon us, a Presence to accompany us whatever this day or the coming week may hold for us.

There are, nonetheless, those hours in which we will feel the chill and loneliness of encompassing darkness, and may stumble painfully on unseen obstacles that litter the trail before us. We need not fret nor fear these circumstances or episodes. Darkness will give way to light; rough roads will level off—it's a promise from God Himself. And whatever the obstacles in our path or the blindness that often hampers us, there is the grand assurance in respect to every one of God's children that He "will not forsake them."

Fourth Sunday in Lent

Matthew 20:17–28 (A)

Leadership and Servanthood

"Whoever would be great among you must be your servant," said Jesus. In the eyes of the world, leadership is usually associated with power and prominence—and is often sought by very egocentric people. This was possibly the feeling of the mother who naturally and proudly wished for it on behalf of her sons. She didn't understand, nor do many of us, that the kingdom of God is to be served and promulgated by those who serve others and that its leaders are those who become the servants of all.

It is certainly true in respect to those who are chosen and gifted to assume positions of leadership in the family of God: their greatness or effectiveness is determined by the quality of their servanthood. As Jesus has been our servant—even to the high point of dying on our behalf—so we are made to be His servants, and we carry out that servanthood by serving our brothers and sisters in the human family.

Jesus is not calling us to positions of leadership. He is sending us forth to be servants and to regard such servanthood as more important than our very lives, to carry out that service without concern for consequences and even less concern for accolades or accommodations. It is those who lovingly serve in this manner who, even without official appointment or recognition, become the real leaders in the kingdom of God.

Monday   *Romans 8:1–10 (A)*

The Matter of Mind-Set

It's the truth; it's a fact! We need only to claim it and celebrate it! We are not to be judged under the Law, nor are we to be condemned in our Law-breaking. When we accept what God has done for us through Christ, we are delivered completely and forever from the guilt of sin. This is what Christ did for us some two thousand years ago. In the moment that we lay claim to God's great gift of forgiving love, it is applicable to us—here and now.

There is still, however, the matter of mind-set. While we celebrate what God has done for us through Christ, we need daily to set our minds and focus our energies on living "according to the Spirit" rather than "according to the flesh." While we cannot blot out forever the natural, fleshly thoughts and feelings that haunt us daily—lust, greed, envy, pride, self-centeredness, apathy—we are responsible for crowding out these pernicious thoughts and feelings with a mind-set that embraces the fruits of the Spirit—love, joy, kindness, concern for others, thanksgiving to God. It won't be easy and we will often meet with failure, but it is a blessed struggle that leads to ultimate victory.

"To set the mind on the Spirit is life and peace."

Tuesday   *John 3:14–21 (B)*

The High Cost of Loving

We are aware of the high cost of living. We are not so nearly aware of the high cost of loving. "God so loved the world that He gave His only Son. . . ." This is the story of the Incarnation—from the manger-birth to the cross on Calvary's hill. This is the ultimate example of love, and it is the pattern and model of the kind of love that we are enjoined to manifest in response to God's love for us.

There are not any of us who can fathom the price of true love as it is demonstrated by Christ's crucifixion and all that it means to us in respect to our relationship to God. "But we see Jesus," said the writer of the Letter to the Hebrews, "who for a little while was made lower than the angels, crowned with glory and honor because of the suffering of death, so that by the grace of God He might taste death for everyone" (Hebrews 2:9). And we see in Jesus the kind of love we are to extend to the human family about us. "This is My commandment," said Jesus, "that you love one another as I have loved you" (John 15:12).

It is going to cost something to love—the addicted and the perverted, the selfish and the corrupted, those of classes and races other than our own, even our neighbors down the block or some of the people we worship with in our own churches. Our great God who gave us His love will now extend that love to others—through us.

Teach us and enable us to love, O God, regardless of the cost or consequences.

105

Made to Be Good

"For by grace you have been saved through faith . . . it is the gift of God. . . . For we are His workmanship, created in Christ Jesus for good works."

Whereas God's saving love is a gift which cannot be merited by human efforts to aspire to divine standards, God's deliverance from sin and self-service sets us free to give our lives to good works, to love God and communicate love to humanity about us. We were not saved for our welfare alone. We were indeed saved to serve, and in serving God by serving His human creatures we thus fulfill the destiny for which we were created.

It is not meant to be a laborious duty—our serving others—but a glorious response to God's love for us. Whatever our life's vocation—farming, teaching, clerking, mothering, building, nursing, writing—our gifts and efforts are generally expended in the process of service to humankind. The Christian is privileged to do this, and to go far beyond this, in the process of serving people out of God-engendered love. It is this that turns drudgery into joy and gives meaning and purpose to our lives, for today and every day.

Thursday   *Luke 15:1–3, 11–32 (C)*

Only Sinners Are Eligible

A Roman philosopher is recorded as saying: "It is impossible for a man of himself to escape. It must be that someone stretch forth a hand to draw him out." It was said about Jesus—and this by His enemies: "This man receives sinners. . . ." We discover in these worth-quoting statements both the dilemma and the deliverance, the latter being personified in the man, God's Son, Jesus Christ.

God knows how we have sought for ways of escape. There were times when some of us have become so filled up and fed up with life's bellyaches that we wanted to go over the hill and "hang one on." Usually we took the route of frenzied activity or, like the Prodigal Son, the road of sensual indulgence. We only discovered how impossible it was to run away from life's conflicts and problems. We discovered, as well, that the basis for such conflicts lies deep within us, that we were born out of orbit with God—at odds with His plan and purpose for our lives—and that our past failures, present conflicts, even our fear of the future are part and parcel of this nature of ours. And then we discovered, and it continues to be a perpetual, ever-new discovery in our lives, that our honest acknowledgment of our condition is not the end but really the beginning of life. It makes us eligible for divine deliverance, for new life, health and happiness. "This man receives sinners," was the self-righteous murmur of the Pharisees, and they never realized how right they were. It means, praise God, that Jesus receives us, accepts us, loves us, forgives us, reclaims us, and reinstates us as His own, and that we then live out His purposes for our lives.

"He was lost, and is found," said the father of the son who finally "came to himself" and returned to the ranch to be reclaimed and reunited with his family. Isn't this what the Gospel—the good news of salvation—is all about?

Friday   *1 Corinthians 1:18–31 (C)*

To God Be the Glory

"He is the source of your life in Christ Jesus. . . ."

It is often affirmed that one can't argue with success. When it does happen to us—success, that is—it is right that we feel good about it, celebrate it, rejoice in it. When some popular faith-healer, however, insists that the power is God's and he or she is only the instrument, or some preacher responds to a compliment with a "give God the credit" cliché, it sometimes sounds a bit superpious or something of a put-on.

We are indeed to rejoice in the occasional successes that come our way, but let us be aware lest we revel in them. We are to be encouraged by them without being overwhelmed. They do not make us any more important than anybody else, nor do they increase our worthwhileness in the eyes of God.

May our rejoicing resolve in gratitude, in praise to God rather than praise of self, for "He is the source of your life [and of all your successes] in Christ Jesus. . . ."

"Let him who boasts, boast of the Lord."

What a Day!

The ancient prophet envisioned an exciting, fantastic event that would come upon the children of God. What a day that would be—the Day of the Lord! On that day the hearts of God's people will be filled with thanksgiving. They will sing songs of joy to the God of their salvation. Their lives will be filled with love, and they will embrace each other as brothers and sisters in the great family of God. Those who claimed their freedom from sin and its guilt through their loving Redeemer will then know that freedom totally, and they will be set free from the evil that tempts, the suffering that inhibits, the fears and doubts that once obscured their God. The encompassing darkness of this world will forever be dispelled, and they shall sing and shout for joy as the beloved children of God.

There is light at the end of the tunnel. Whatever today may bring forth, there is that Day to anticipate. While we cannot evade the trials and burdens of today, we ought to find them lighter and less threatening as we look forward to the Day of the Lord.

Fifth Sunday in Lent
John 11:1–53 (A)

We Shall Live Forever

It is absolutely true: The sons and daughters of God shall live forever. What Christ has promised has already been granted. It is the abolition of death and the gift of eternal life. The atrocious event of death that threatens and appears to destroy what God has created becomes His very servant that swings open the gates to life everlasting. Jesus has overcome death's evil intent and power by rising from the dead.

We are already citizens of the new kingdom—and this status does not change when we leave behind the known and the familiar of our earthly existence. Thus we need not fear that ultimate event. It only guarantees that we shall hereafter know and experience fully the splendor and beauty of the new kingdom where we can live and serve in supreme joy without the limitations and temptations of mortal life upon this planet.

It is true: Because we accept the life Jesus has come to bring, we shall live forever.

Monday   *Romans 8:11–19 (A)*

We Are Identified

"For all who are led by the Spirit of God are sons [and daughters] of God," writes Paul to the Church at Rome.

We are identified! We are the very sons and daughters of God. It is this, actualized by the Spirit within us, that enables us to turn from self-service and its resultant estrangement from God to godly service and love of those about us. It is this that makes life significant and gives point and purpose to our living. It is this that puts us back into God's orbit for our lives and welds us to Him in a union that nothing can dissolve.

"O God, now I know who I am. You gave me my identity in the moment I was brought to the font. You touched me with Your cleansing power and filled my heart with Your Spirit. I am Your child, fallible and often very foolish. When I stumble in my childish attempts to follow You, You pick me up and dry my tears and heal my wounds and draw me back into Your loving embrace. I am Your servant. I am here to serve my fellow beings, to retain and further comprehend my identity in losing my life on behalf of others. I am Your minister destined to represent Your purposes, to demonstrate Your love, to communicate Your healing touch to the fractured, sin-bound creatures in my path. Thank You, dear God, for snatching me out of the pit of self-centeredness and restoring my identity as a member of Your eternal Family."

Tuesday   *John 12:20–33 (B)*

"We Wish to See Jesus"

I was rather startled, I remember, when I stepped into the pulpit of a church in Shanghai, China. Carved on the inside of that pulpit in such a way that it could be seen only by the preacher were these words: "Sir, we wish to see Jesus." I never forgot them. I honestly tried during that service—and have ever since—to proclaim the Gospel in such a way that Jesus could be seen or sensed by those who listened to what I had to say.

There are times when Jesus is obscured by inadequate presentations. There are also those times when Jesus is not seen nor His message understood because people are not really seeking Christ and His Word or they are looking for the kind of Christ that might fit their preconceived notions and fill their assumed needs.

If we want to see the loving, miracle-working Jesus, the tender, caring, concerned Christ, the consoling, protecting Shepherd of our souls and the answer to our needs and longings, we must also see Him as the One who died and arose again on our behalf, who accepts us as His brothers and sisters, and who empowers and appoints us to be His disciples. If we truly embrace this kind of Christ and yield ourselves to His will and purposes, we will see Him—again and again—in His Word to us, in the words and deeds of our colleagues, in the dire needs of those who suffer around us.

God help us to accept His Son, Jesus Christ, as He really is—not as we may selfishly desire Him to be.

For Those Who Suffer

"Although He was a Son, He learned obedience through what He suffered. . . ." Our loving God does not initiate suffering; it is the consequence of living in this world into which He put us—and often the consequence of our own foolish mistakes. If Jesus suffered—and it was on our behalf and because of our sins even though it was perpetrated by the people who pinned Him on the cross—can we as God's children through Christ's redemption expect anything else?

We may not be able to understand how Jesus learned obedience through suffering, but He was obedient even to His final words while on the cross: "Father, into Thy hands I commit My spirit." He didn't reject His suffering; nor did He rebel against it. He faced it, accepted it, and it became the means of redeeming human, sin-ridden creatures for God.

This, then, must be our answer to the problem of suffering: Face it, accept it—and *use* it. Allow it to teach us obedience, to make out of us vessels fit for the Master's use and vehicles of healing and blessing to those who suffer about us.

The Risk of Loving

The parable that Jesus related reveals something of the risk of loving. The owner of the vineyard sent one, two, then a third servant to his tenants. They were beat up and cast out. Then he sent his son—and they killed him. And God's human creatures have thus responded to such love from that time until this.

The God of love refuses to let go or give up; He continues the risk of loving. He keeps loving even those who reject His overtures—even until they break and destroy themselves by their own resistance. He loves men and women at their worst; ". . . while we were yet sinners Christ died for us," wrote Paul (Romans 5:8). "I will send my beloved son," said the owner of the vineyard, "it may be they will respect him."

The God who took such a risk on our behalf has every right to expect that we begin to take some risks on behalf of our fellow beings. We have a position of trust and responsibility in the vineyard of the Master; it is to love our brothers and sisters in the human family. This is our primary vocation in life, regardless of our various avocations. There is a risk in this kind of loving. There are times when those we love are not able to understand, receive, or assimilate such love. Then we are hurt and frustrated; we pull back and become cautious about extending our love to others.

Loving others does involve pain and suffering, discomfort and inconvenience. At the same time, the very effort to love serves to stretch our souls and enlarge our capacity for enrichment. "He who does not love abides in death," wrote John in his First Letter (1 John 3:14b). At least we are truly alive when we reach out in love—whether that love is responded to or not.

Friday   *Philippians 3:8–14 (C)*

And So We Press On

Jesus Christ is sufficient—and so is the righteousness He imparts to us. We don't earn or merit it by following certain rules or rituals; we receive it as the gift of God's love. We possess this righteousness even now by faith in Jesus Christ. We have no need for any other.

This by no means indicates that we have arrived, that we have reached the ultimate in respect to our natural state or being. And so we "press on," in painful yet joyful struggle, to surrender our total beings to God—to let Him have His way with us. This does not come easily. It involves the crucible of conflict—even failure and defeat. But even when we fall, we fall only to rise again, to "press on," acknowledging but never nursing our failures, knowing that our loving God understands and perpetually reaches out to draw us to Himself.

Thus we press on that we "may know Him and the power of His resurrection. . . ." We "press on to make it [our] own, because Christ has made [us] His own."

"Let those of us who are mature be thus minded" (v. 15).

Saturday   *Isaiah 43:16–21 (C)*

The Past Is Past

"Remember not the former days, nor consider the things of old. Behold, I am doing a new thing."

When the days darken and the times in which we live become unstable, at times even unbearable, we are tempted to look back to those years or episodes in our lives when, we assume, we were happy or more content. Or, on the other hand, we may still be burdened by some failure or sin in the past that continues to rattle its bones or inhibit us in respect to our daily activities or our outlook on the future.

The prophet was singing a song of hope and comfort to his people out of his inspired glimpse of God's plan for the future. This vision of what God was about to do would surpass or overcome the joys or the tragedies of the past. Nevertheless, his message may well be God's word to us at the end of a difficult week. "Remember not . . . nor consider the things of old. Behold, I am doing a new thing." We are not really enjoined to forget the negative things of the past, lest we repeat them. And it is often past gifts and blessings that encourage us to boldly face our uncertain future. Hope means that God still reigns and that He loves us and is working out His plan for our lives in this world, that we need not be forever crippled or hampered by past errors or events. A new week and new opportunities lie ahead of us, and God will, if our hope is in Him, continue to do "a new thing" in and through us.

Sunday of the Passion (Palm Sunday)

Matthew 27:11–54 (A)

What Shall We Do with Jesus?

It was initially Pilate's question, and he answered it for himself by symbolically washing his hands of this whole sordid affair that was laid on him by the Jewish religious leaders. Judas betrayed Jesus. Peter, who once said he would risk his life to protect his Master, recoiled in fear and denied any relationship with the Christ when Jesus was indicted. The mob called for Jesus' crucifixion, and most of the disciples looked for someplace to hide.

Perhaps all of us have wondered at times just what would have been our reaction had we been on hand to witness what was happening to the Lord Jesus Christ.

While most of us do respond to the Christ as revealed through His Word by *doing* something with Him—using Him, ignoring Him, running from Him, even trying to run with Him—the question is no longer "What shall [we] do with Jesus?" it is "What has He done and what does He seek to do with us?"

Actually, there is nothing we can *do* to or with Jesus. He is Lord and King, Savior and Master. "I am the way, and the truth, and the life," He said; "no one comes to the Father, but by Me" (John 14:6). God's refusal to violate our personhood allows us to shun Him, to refuse to honor Him, to worship self-concocted gods and idols rather than our Creator and Redeemer, but we have no power to do anything with Him. What we, empowered by His Spirit, are enabled to do is to open our hearts and lives to Him, return to Him, relate to Him as He reveals Himself to us, and embrace Him in faith and obedience.

Monday   Mark 15:1–39 (B)

"My God . . . Why?"

"My God, my God, why hast Thou forsaken me?" It is the question that each of us, at one time or another, has screamed into cold and gray

114

skies—in the face of the little crosses that have come our way or the heavy crosses laid upon those we love. "Why God, why?"

Some people get no further than this agonizing query and live most of their lives under the shadow of that twisted question mark. They make for themselves a veritable hell on earth.

Our Lord also asked "Why?" but before He breathed His last breath on the cross, He turned the apparent tragedy of His crucifixion into a basis for universal blessing with the song of victory: "Father, into Thy hands I commit My Spirit" (Luke 23:46). It is in this act that we discover the key to a proper and beneficial response to our sufferings. It is true that Christ's sufferings were on our behalf, but they also came as a consequence of living in this distorted world.

Our great God does not afflict us with suffering. He does, nonetheless, enable us to bear it and even to discover meaning and often some purpose for our conflicts and afflictions. What is the Christian's answer to suffering? Again it is this: Face it, accept it—and *use* it. Allow it to make out of us vessels fit for the Master's use and vehicles of blessing to those about us who suffer. And this becomes possible only by the grace of God.

Tuesday   *Luke 23:1–49 (C)*

Why Did You Let Us Do It?

I always had a problem with the Passion Story in my childhood readings of the gospels. In those days of heroes and happy-ending stories this kind of termination to Christ's life and ministry seemed tragically out of character in respect to the hero I had made Him out to be. Every time I arrived at this final episode in Jesus' ministry I was secretly hoping that my Hero would suddenly turn on His persecuters, those stupid, blind religious and political leaders, and demolish them with a bolt out of the blue. But it never happened that way. He who had set His face toward Jerusalem had now arrived—and His miracle-working ministry of love was to be cruelly terminated in His execution.

My comprehension of those Holy Week happenings enlarged a bit as I grew up. It eventually implicated me in those excruciating hours of my Lord. I gradually began to realize that if I had been living in those days I probably would have been one of that jeering crowd that egged on Jesus' tormentors. Or, at least, I would have been like those disciples who took to the woods in fright when the authorities viciously plotted and carried out their objective to destroy the beloved Master. Now, having inherited the same human frailties and blindness that afflicted

Jesus' contemporaries, I can only phrase the question that has plagued the minds and hearts of most Christians from time to time: "Why, O God, did you let us kill Him?"

If I, like writers before me, presumed to answer that question on behalf of the almighty, all-loving God, it might go something like this: "How else could I get through to you? How else could I convince you of My love for you? I could not just ignore sin. There was simply no other way to deal with the enormity of your sin and selfishness. I didn't want My Son to suffer and die. In His suffering I suffered; in His dying I died. This is the measure of My love. I created humankind with the freedom to believe or to doubt, to obey or disobey, to love or hate, to build or tear down, to give life or to destroy it. You had to have this freedom in order to know the meaning of love. But the first man and woman—and every other person since then has chosen to disabuse My love, to ignore My will, to walk a self-chosen course in life. And you do these things even now. If I sent My Son to visibly inhabit your world today, you would probably crucify Him again."

O God, be merciful to me, a sinner!

Wednesday   *Philippians 2:5–11 (A, B, C)*

The Mind of Christ

Jesus "emptied Himself, taking the form of a servant. . . . He humbled Himself and became obedient unto death. . . ." And this is the "mind" that Paul enjoined his constituents to demonstrate "among yourselves."

It is rather far-fetched, to say the least, and bears little resemblance to the "me" philosophy that has pervaded our generation. It is obvious that we need to recognize and joyfully accept our own identities. We would hardly have anything to give if we failed to discover who we are—our individual validity as a son or daughter of God. That validity, however, tends to diminish if it turns in upon itself. Jesus knew who He was, the very Son of God, and this enabled Him to commit Himself to His Father's will and purposes, to take "the form of a servant" among God's human creatures—even to the extent of dying on their behalf.

The old "saved to serve" cliché, though simplistic, is still true. Our value as individuals, though inherent by way of our creation and redemption, is truly enhanced and fulfilled in our dedication to servant-

116

hood. As Jesus came to serve us, and thereby to serve His Father, so we are upon this planet—within the kingdom of this world—for the express purpose of serving our fellow beings. "Have this mind among yourselves, which is yours in Christ Jesus. . . ."

Maundy Thursday   *Luke 22:7-20 (C)*

You Are My Body!

"This is My body," said Jesus as He broke bread and distributed it among His disciples. We have categorized Jesus' statement as an incomprehensible mystery or translated it into the assurance of His real presence among those who commune together, that as we receive the bread and wine of the Eucharist we receive in a very special way the Lord Jesus Christ.

While we are not about to discredit that concept, there may be an additional meaning to Jesus' pronouncement that would enhance the validity and importance of Holy Communion for our lives and the life of the church. Jesus knew that His body was about to be offered upon the cross. He knew that, after His resurrection, He would no longer carry on a visible ministry in this world. It is possible that He was also saying, in effect, "You are, from now on, to be My visible body in your world. Partaking of Me and empowered by My Spirit, you are to communicate and demonstrate My Father's love and purposes in the world about you. I will make the supreme sacrifice, but you will now become My visible body and assume My role in representing and channeling God's saving love to the masses upon your planet."

Such a concept has serious implications for us. It means that we are members of Christ's body. It assures us of His loving acceptance and gracious appointment and of His strength to accomplish His purposes —to do what He would do had He remained in our world. It places upon us a tremendous and unique and joyful—yet frightening—responsibility to carry on our assigned tasks. It warns us of the terrible dangers of eating and drinking with other members of His body if there is malice toward them in our hearts. It makes us aware that, as we come to receive from Christ, we must come to give of ourselves to Christ and His purposes in our world.

So we continue to come, with our brothers and sisters in Christ, the many members of Christ's body, to eat and drink of the bread and wine, the body and blood of Jesus, to be touched by God's forgiving love and assured of His Spirit-giving presence, and with our fellow-participants to be united and empowered for continued service in the kingdom of our Lord.

Good Friday   *John 19:17–30 (A, B, C)*

"It Is Finished!"

"He said, 'It is finished'; and He bowed His head and gave up His spirit."

The agony was over. He no longer felt the terrible pangs of crucifixion nor heard the taunts and insults of a blood-thirsty mob. The fiendish minds of men had done their worst. Their fury had been spent—and so, too, the fury of a righteous God upon sin and disobedience. No longer were felt the thorns upon His brow, the stripes upon His back, the nails through His flesh. No longer was felt the soul torture and bitterness of separation from His heavenly Father. His heart had now ceased to beat. "It is finished."

But there were, in that stifling silence following Jesus' death, other sounds: the sounds of bursting fetters, breaking chains, crumbling prison walls, the rending of veils, the overthrowing of barriers, the opening of gates. Christ's last words were not the words of defeat, but the cry of victory, the shout of triumph, the sound of a trumpet. "It is finished"—finished was the work of redemption, the last payment for the guilt of sinful man and woman. "Finished" was the terrible ban of judgment upon the ages, the power of darkness and desolation, the curse of sin upon humanity.

What Christ finished, however, has scarcely begun for us. He accomplished what we could not. He closed the unbridgeable gulf between God and humankind, the Creator and the creature. Now the work of His visible presence was done and the work of His invisible presence was to continue through the followers He left behind. It is sometimes very difficult to believe, but we, forgiven by Christ and empowered by the Spirit of God, are by His grace qualified and commissioned to be members of that great body of Christ that is elected to carry on and continue that which He made possible when He said, "It is finished."

Nothing but a Promise

The lights had gone out. It appeared in those hours following the burial of Jesus that Christianity died with the Christ and was laid with Him in the sepulcher. There was not a single human being who believed it would be possible ever to see Him again. What remained for the disciples but to return to their homes and their fishing nets as tragically disappointed, disillusioned men and try their best to forget the whole amazing experience? There never were men more utterly depressed and dispirited than were the disciples of Christ in those hours immediately following His crucifixion.

There was nothing left but a promise—a promise that went as far back as Moses, that was reiterated by the prophets, that was clearly ennunciated by Jesus Himself before this tragic event. But the disciples appeared to pay little attention to that promise. For them the lights had gone out.

We live in a day of promise-fulfillment—a fact we shall happily celebrate in the next seven weeks. Yet we too are people of a promise—the promise of God's total revelation and our complete enjoyment of Him and His kingdom on the day of our resurrection. There will be those hours of pain and darkness in our daily walk through life, but encompassing us through it all is the promise of God's love and our eternal salvation. And this, on the basis of Christ's crucifixion and resurrection, is enough to enable us joyfully to press on, knowing full well that God's Word can be embraced and trusted and "there is none that can deliver [us] out of [His] hand."

The Resurrection of Our Lord

Matthew 28:1–10 (A)

Christ Alive—and for Real

Christ has arisen; He is alive and for real. Do we want proof of this amazing event? Then let us consider the consequences of Easter and Pentecost in the lives of His first followers. Their faith, which died when Jesus died, was suddenly revived. They report that Jesus arose and that they saw Him. They tell us about their visits to the empty tomb, and how He appeared to Mary Magdalene, to the other women, to Peter, to the two on the way to Emmaus, to ten of them at once, to eleven of them at once, to James, and to the five hundred.

These were more than the verbal reports of excited, exuberant men. The amazing thing is that along with these reports of the resurrection of Christ was the indisputable resurrection of Christianity. After Easter and Pentecost the once defeated and disillusioned disciples became men set on world conquest. They who sought for thrones were now fearlessly expecting persecution and death. These few men—ordinary, fallible, blundering men—were changed from inferior failures into flaming messengers, ready to go boldly into the very city that had crucified their leader and to proclaim Him as the world's Savior. Their faith was no longer a consoling convenience, but a consuming passion. They were electrified with a new power; they proclaimed a new message; they sang a new song. Christ is alive! Christ is for real!

When God's Spirit moves us to faith in the resurrection of Christ, giving us God's love and power to live and act on the basis that it is so—that it really happened—then we will discover, as millions have before us, that Christ is alive—in us, through us, and forever.

Monday   Colossians 3:1–4 (A)

Is It Really True?

The resurrection of Christ—is it really true?
"No, it cannot be," say some people. "It simply does not fit my idea

120

of God and the world. I didn't see any resurrection. I can't feel it. It doesn't do anything for me. I can see the flowers and the trees. I can celebrate the newness of life as evidenced in the beauty of spring that follows the deadness of winter. But I can see nothing of a living Christ in this distorted, violent, hate-ridden world of today."

Perhaps most of us have, at one time or another, been under the dark cloud of unbelief in respect to the resurrection of our Lord. Equally serious is the possibility that we, in our lives and attitudes, may have contributed to the unbelief of our brothers and sisters in the human family—even while sincerely confessing and joyously celebrating the resurrection event. The unbelieving masses about us are not likely to put much stock in some historical event if the followers of the living Christ continue to live primarily for the things of this world or have little concern for the hungry, oppressed, and suffering creatures about them.

When we speak to others about Christ being alive and for real, many will believe this only if it is dramatized here and now—through the lives of His followers through whom He is able to communicate His love and healing power in this very hour.

We will continue to celebrate Christ's resurrection. It is even more important that we "set [our] minds on things that are above, not on things that are on earth." Only then will we be lovingly compelled and enabled to concentrate and act upon our responsibilities as Christ's followers within our world.

"For you have died, and your life is hid with Christ in God."

Tuesday   *Mark 16:1–8 (B)*

We Can Prove It for Ourselves

The central core and factor of Christianity is the bodily resurrection of Jesus Christ from the dead. We believe that it really happened—among other reasons, because of the millions before us who believed, and because of the fantastic transformation that took place in the lives of men and women who met the resurrected Christ or who have believed in the risen Christ from that day until this.

Even more pertinent to us today is the witness of men and women in this hour who truly believe in the resurrection of Jesus Christ. Most of us know that something indefinable and incomprehensible happens to people who really entrust themselves to the risen Christ. There are pathetic contradictions and inconsistencies—the scores who verbally claim to believe and yet remain but self-centered blobs on the fringe of genuine Christianity—but there are changes that take place in the lives of those who truly commit themselves to the risen Christ that confound the skeptic and help to assure us that Jesus really did arise from the dead and that it is the risen Christ and the eternally living and loving God whom we worship today.

The grand truth is that we can prove the resurrection of Christ for ourselves. We cannot do this with historical evidence or contemporary analysis—and we may not be able to do it for anybody else—but we can prove it for ourselves. We can enter into this truth-revealing experience (which continues daily to affirm the Easter event) by living and acting on the basis that it is true irrespective of whether or not our feelings and emotions immediately attest to it. It is belief in spite of scientific evidences or lack of such, but it is also life and living in scorn of consequences. It is the only way to discover for oneself the authenticity of Christ's resurrection and personally to experience His life and power.

Wednesday   *1 Corinthians 15:19–28 (B)*

It's a Fact

"But in fact Christ has been raised from the dead. . . ."

Paul never hedged in his proclamation of the living Christ. It was a fact; it was his unfaltering conviction. His Damascus experience—the light from heaven driving him to the ground, the voice identifying Jesus: "I am Jesus, whom you are persecuting," the divine command instructing the blinded Paul to submit to God's will for his life—was enough to convince him that "Christ [had] been raised from the dead." It was an experience Paul never forgot. It became the thesis and basis of his preaching from that time to the hour of his martyrdom.

Through Paul, through the apostles who saw the risen Christ, through the multitudes who have followed this Christ and witnessed to Him, who have preached and written about Him throughout the centuries, God has spoken to us.

The fact of Christ's resurrection resolves into another astounding fact: We shall, indeed, be raised from the dead. "The last enemy to be destroyed is death," wrote Paul. It is not logical or comprehensible to our three-dimensional insights; it is a fact, nonetheless, and a glorious hope that gives us the courage to joyfully march on—and even to risk our lives on behalf of others.

It I Really Believed

"These words seemed to them an idle tale, and they did not believe them," it was said about the disciples when the women brought the news of their shocking experience at the empty tomb.

I say that I believe that Christ has risen. I confess my faith in the living Lord every time I attend my church or pray in His name. But do I really believe? What would happen in my life or as a consequence of my living if I really believed?

If I really believed that Christ arose from the dead, I would fling aside my garments of self-righteousness, the camouflage, the window-dressing of my life, and fall on my face before the living Christ in repentance of sin.

If I really believed in the living Christ, He would be the most important factor in my life. He would take over first place among all loyalties and allegiances in my life.

If I really believed that Jesus lives, my life would be filled with joy unspeakable, peace incomprehensible. I would not be commiserating over guilt feelings out of the past or be overanxious about the future.

If I really believed in the resurrected Christ, no problem or difficulty, weakness or sin, no insufficiency or inadequacy could destroy me. I would discover that the power which raised Christ from the grave cannot be baffled by my thwarting frailties—that the God who performed this amazing feat of might and glory could certainly handle my small pains and problems.

If I really believed in the risen Christ, I would realize anew my identity and validity as God's child and servant, take up the cross assigned to me, and dedicate my gifts and energies to the splendid task of proclaiming and demonstrating that Christ is alive and that His saving grace and abundant life are available to every human creature.

If I really believed . . .

Lord, help my unbelief!

Keep On Believing

The high point, the constantly recurring theme, and the grand climax in the great symphony of the Gospel is the resurrection of our Lord

Jesus Christ. He died for our sins, and He arose from the dead victorious over sin and death. If we subtract this from our message of love and hope, we have nothing to say. We must be sure of this—His resurrection—and we can be. It was witnessed by many before us; it has or can be experienced within us.

These are the "terms" in which Paul preached to the church at Corinth: "the Gospel, which you received, in which you stand, by which you are saved, *if you hold it fast.*" I have meditated on what would happen if I really believed in the living Christ. Equally important to our salvation is the necessity of holding fast, of keeping the faith, the determination, in spite of the pluses and minuses in our lives, to keep on believing and rejoicing in the Easter event. This does not eradicate the probability of nagging doubts from time to time. It necessitates our returning, again and again, to the resurrection event, to the renewal of our convictions—repeatedly exposing ourselves to and grappling with the consequences of the resurrection of Christ in the lives of His followers throughout the centuries and embracing the power and grace of that glorious event for our own lives.

We need often to prostrate ourselves at the foot of the cross in confession of our sins. We need, as well, to look into the empty tomb in order to be reassured that Christ lives and is ever present to enable us to hold fast the faith amidst the doubts that plague us from time to time.

And this we will do—by the grace of God.

Saturday   *Isaiah 25:6–9 (B)*

It Is Done

It is done! What Isaiah, inspired by the Holy Spirit, prophesied has been accomplished! "The covering that is cast over all peoples, the veil that is spread over all nations" has been removed. Death has been swallowed up, and the Lord God has wiped away all tears.

This is what we have been celebrating this week—and will celebrate throughout the Easter season. "Lo, this is our God; we have waited for Him, that He might save us. This is the Lord . . . let us be glad and rejoice in His salvation."

We are no longer waiting for our salvation; it is ours in this very moment—as is the gift of eternal life. As Christ was raised from the dead, so we are guaranteed such a resurrection. These mortal coils and entanglements can no longer bind us. We have been set free to be perfectly reunited to our loving God and Creator forever.

Even while we shuffle along the corridors of this disjointed, broken world, we do so in victory and joy. Even while we cling to our lives and possessions—and taste the afflictions and sorrows of this earthly journey—we do so with the conviction that we have nothing to lose, "that the sufferings of this present time are not worth comparing with the glory that is to be revealed to us" (Romans 8:18).

"Let us be glad and rejoice in His salvation."

Second Sunday of Easter
John 20:19–31 (A, B, C)

When Believing Is Seeing

Some of us envy Peter and Paul and those other apostles of the first-century church who saw the risen Christ, talked to Him, and were challenged by Him. Had we been in their sandals, we too might have been faithful and courageous—even to the point of martyrdom. But we live in a fractured world. We see so many unsaintly and unsanctified things within us and about us that bear no resemblance whatsoever to the resurrected Christ. There are problems we cannot solve, tragedies we cannot explain, conflicts we cannot handle, and we become "tremulous Thomases" who pine for more tangible evidence of divine power— that power which was supposed to have been made available through the resurrection of Jesus and the indwelling Spirit of Christ.

As with Thomas, our cry is often, "If I could see, I would believe." The answer of Christ is always, "If you would believe, you would soon see. Blessed are those who have not seen and yet believe."

Along with the New Testament proclamations of God's loving and saving grace is offered the faith to embrace that grace. It begins when we really believe—when we stop talking *about* God and walk right into His invisible presence to talk *to* Him, throwing our full weight upon Him, plunging into the ocean of His forgiving and sustaining grace and love. We may not feel anything very significant, or see miracles take place before our eyes, but there will eventually come, in response to our believing and obeying, a sense of added strength, new insights, increased courage, and the dawning realization that we are in touch with divine power, the same power that raised Jesus from the dead, the kind that will make a real difference in our lives.

Monday   *1 Peter 1:3–9 (A)*

Response to Easter

"Without having seen Him you love Him; though you do not now see Him you believe in Him and rejoice with unutterable and exalted joy." This is the Christian response to the Easter event, the resurrection of Christ. It is "as the outcome of [our] faith [that we] obtain the salvation of [our] souls." Jesus died for the sins of the whole human family; He arose from the dead as victor over sin and the death that follows as a consequence of sin. Faith, believing without seeing, "the assurance of things hoped for, the conviction of things not seen" (Hebrews 11:1), is that God-imparted faculty or grace which receives and appropriates God's gift of forgiveness and eternal life.

It is genuine faith, imparted by God, tested in the crucible of suffering, demonstrated in believing without seeing, expressed in rejoicing "with unutterable and exalted joy," that formulates the proper response to Easter. God grant that our faith, tempered by the hot fires of adversity, be enlarged and increased. May our love for God and our brothers and sisters about us be made more honest and generous. And may it result in our do-or-die determination to please God and serve our fellow persons regardless of the cost or consequences to our lives.

Tuesday   *1 John 5:1–6 (B)*

Everyone Who Believes

"Everyone who believes that Jesus is the Christ is a child of God. . . ." The word "believe" is often shallow and misappropriated in contemporary use. We who have committed our lives to God as He is revealed through Jesus Christ *are* the children of God. And then John says, in essence, that as children of the same Father we are brothers and sisters, and in loving our divine Parent we also love one another.

It is both a command and the response of genuine belief or commitment—love of God equals love of our fellow persons. John is not reluctant about calling it a commandment. We realize, as well, that such love is a consequence of God's love for us. When we allow something to come between ourselves and each other, that something obscures and may cloud our relationship to God. We demonstrate our love of God—and respond to His love—by loving one another and thereby living in obedience to His commandment. Because we obey as a response to God's love for us, the commandment to love one another is "not burdensome"; we obey joyfully even when our obedience leads into suffering and sacrifice on behalf of others.

John assures us that it is this kind of response and obedience, loving one another even as we love God as revealed through the resurrected Christ, that will grant us the ultimate victory over the rebellious, anti-God forces of the world and society in which we live.

On to Victory

"I am John, your brother, and as a follower of Jesus I am your partner in patiently enduring the suffering that comes to those who belong to His Kingdom" (v. 9a TEV).

John speaks with authority, and the recounting of his revelation is a message of encouragement and hope to his peers as well as to each of us in our tumultuous times. "Hang in there! Keep the faith!" he is saying to us. "These are difficult times for Christians, but the final victory is God's—and ours!"

This is not the time for despair; it is the time for celebration. Jesus has come; He is present with us amid the trials of this tempestuous world. "Fear not, I am the first and the last, and the living one; I died, and behold I am alive for evermore." He is about ready to come again and gather His faithful followers into the fully revealed and eternally reigning kingdom of God. At that time the suffering martyrs, the struggling saints, the priests and prophets, servants and disciples of all the ages shall be united together to sing the praises of the resurrected Christ, their eternal Savior and King.

Let us begin the celebration even now!

We Are Witnesses

"This Jesus God raised up, and of that we all are witnesses."

This was Peter's first and grandest sermon. At least it had a great effect on a large number of people. He was in the right place at the right time. He was indwelt and empowered by the Spirit of God. He had a good text (Psalm 16:8–11). His bottom line in this lesson is the clincher: "This Jesus God raised up, and of that we all are witnesses." This glorious fact gave Peter's sermon the impact it needed on this unforgetful day.

It isn't likely that any of us can be very effective in our proclamation of the Gospel unless we are witnesses and participants in that Good Friday-Easter event in the life of Christ. "We were buried therefore with Him by baptism into death," wrote Paul, "so that as Christ was raised from the dead by the glory of the Father, we too might walk in newness of life" (Romans 6:4).

In a very wonderful sense the children and servants of God *are* witnesses. The death and resurrection of Jesus Christ became real to us as we embraced Him by faith and dedicated our lives to His service. Very few of us will witness the kind of results Peter did when thousands were converted to Christ as the consequence of his preaching, but when we proclaim and demonstrate the Gospel as witnesses of and participants in the power of God as manifested in the living Christ, there are and will be results, for "we all are witnesses."

Friday   *Acts 3:13–15, 17–26 (B)*

The Continuing Witness

This is Peter's second sermon—following an act of healing that turned a group of bystanders into a body of witnesses as to the power of the resurrected Christ. What an act to follow! Now Peter could really speak with authority and to an audience that would hang on to his every word. He was quick to take advantage of this remarkable event to credit God publicly for the miracle they had seen and to make it clear to his listeners that the crippled beggar was healed in the name of the risen Christ. The once undependable, half-comprehending, sometimes compromising Peter was becoming the courageous, responsible apostle that Jesus had chosen and destined him to be. And John and Peter were the first disciples of Jesus to be arrested—partly as a result of Peter's second sermon.

Peter's message on this occasion turns out to be a bold and vigorous proclamation of the Gospel. Building on the recorded words of Moses and the prophets, Peter portrays the resurrected Jesus as that long-promised Servant of God who has come, and will indeed come again, to save and bless His people. Like John the Baptist before him, Peter calls on his listeners to repent and turn to the God of their fathers that their sins may be blotted out.

Peter and John were arrested by the religious leaders, the consequence of their courageous and joyful witness, but hundreds more were added to the fold because of their faithful ministry.

The Compulsion to Obey God

The continuing witness of the apostles rapidly built up the Christian fellowship. It also brought down the wrath of the leaders of Israel, who saw their own prestige and authority wearing thin in the light of the glowing success that followed these preachers and healers. Astounding things were happening among the ever-enlarging crowds that gathered around these men. When the chief priests slapped them into jail in an attempt to stifle their dangerous declarations, even the jail could not hold them, and they were back in the streets again "obey(ing) God rather than men."

The apostles were not living dangerously in order to please or satisfy their heavenly Father or to win some crown or other in some other dimension. They were joyously compelled to risk their lives, to bear beatings and imprisonments, in order that the message of the living Christ might be heard by the people. They were filled with faith and trust in God, and the consequence was the abandonment of all that most mortals hold dear in order to commit their minds and bodies to God and His purposes as well as to their fellow creatures and their needs.

We obviously don't impress God by suddenly becoming interested and concerned about His purposes in our world. We must first recognize and appropriate His eternal love for us—no matter how wretched or miserable we are—and then allow His gracious Spirit to fill, enervate, and propel us toward obedience and toward a committal of all we are and have to Him and His purposes.

Third Sunday of Easter
Luke 24:13–35 (A)

The Road to Emmaus

Their quiet country walk to Emmaus was immersed in despair for a couple of Christ's disciples as they reviewed the horrible happening in the city they left behind.

The darkness and depression that enveloped these two men are often reflected in our lives today. Whatever may be the distant goal of our travels, our Emmaus, we abide in a time of despair. We are economically strapped; there is little security in the things we have pinned our hopes upon. Jobs are scarce, and we are confronted with the fact that the ladder of success we have been climbing doesn't go any higher. Our nation is no longer the affluent leader of the world. The traditions we have so avidly clung to are not as relevant as they once appeared to be. The church institutions we assumed were perpetually secure are shifting precariously with the winds of our tempestuous times. We reach back for yesterday because we are uncertain of today and afraid of tomorrow.

A stranger joined the two men on their way to Emmaus. Eventually revealing Himself as the resurrected Christ, He transformed their day of despair into the most glorious experience of their lives. It is this same Christ who accompanies us on our daily walk to our Emmaus. It is He who seeks to transform our darkness and despair into brightness and joy. The ugly and painful things that happen to us are not the end of life. We may have lost a loved one, but we need not lose our faith. We may have little worldly security, but our salvation is still intact. We may know the agony of pain even while we abide in eternal peace. We may be terribly lonely, but we are never alone. The death of Jesus resolved in life eternal; the dying that is a part of our daily walk will give way to resurrection.

Christ has arisen; we shall live forever!

131

We Are Ransomed

Peter was older and wiser at the time he wrote his letters than he was in those exhilarating, exciting days following the resurrection of Christ and the coming of the Holy Spirit to indwell the lives of God's children and servants. He had, sometimes through trial and error, at other times because of persecution and imprisonment, developed into a mature, sensitive leader of the early church. He had learned—what some Christians apparently never learn—how to balance the theology of suffering with the theology of glory, the cross with the resurrection. He was no longer expecting Christ's imminent reappearance as most of the apostles initially did, but was solemnly alerting his constituents to the probability of much suffering and the possibility of violent death if they persisted in following the teachings of the living Christ.

Peter's proclamations, at least as evidenced by his writings, were not a promise of perpetual ecstasy but a theology of hope. "You were ransomed . . . with the precious blood of Christ," he wrote. "Through Him you have confidence in God, who raised Him from the dead and gave Him glory, so that your faith and hope are in God."

We may never face the kind of conflicts and sufferings the early Christians had to deal with—and that thousands of contemporary saints are struggling with today—but each of us who follow Christ have conflicts of our own. There are times when the pain evoked by the cross we carry obscures the joy of the resurrection. But hope, though severely tested, need never die. Foolish, weak, sinful, unworthy, we are "ransomed . . . with the precious blood of Christ." Nothing can change that; it is our eternal condition.

"Handle Me and See"

The wonder and splendor of our loving God will never cease to astound us—unless, that is, we become insensitive, stupefied zombies. Above all, the great resurrection event is beyond all human comprehension. Through Christ-incarnate, God came to us as a baby. He died on the cross at the hands of His own creatures. Now, following His resurrection, He marches right into our dull, sinful, earthbound natures and says, "Handle Me and see." It is utterly impossible to even imagine what more a loving God could do for His created children than what He has already done and is doing to heal them, redeem them, and restore them to His divine family. "Handle Me and see." If God has to come as man and submit to the curious, groping, ever-doubting hands of the very beings He created in order to assure them of His eternal love, even that will be done and was done that humanity might return to Him. "Handle Me and see."

The disciples were ultimately convinced that their Lord and Master had risen from the dead. Jesus, the resurrected Christ and as yet, for most part, the still unrecognized Christ in our world today, still bids us, challenges us to recognize and embrace Him as the living Christ. He has conquered death; He has set us free from sin and its eternal consequences. And we are assured that the same power that raised Him from the dead is available still, not only for our salvation but also for our daily sustenance and the accomplishing of His purposes in and through us. He can meet all our needs. He can satisfy the hunger of our barren souls. He can give us, even in the midst of this bewildering and chaotic age, an eternal peace, a vibrant joy like that experienced by those first followers when they finally recognized the risen Christ.

"Handle Me and see."

Wednesday   *1 John 1:1–2:2 (B)*

The Resurrection Made Applicable

Easter, as properly understood and accepted, means happy endings and new beginnings. It means that there can be a happy ending to the control and' reign of sin in our lives, to the loneliness, the doubts, anxieties, and fears that plague us, even to the fear of death. It means, as well, that there can be new beginnings in our lives in terms of joy and effectiveness and love and service.

John tells us how we can respond to the Easter event in such a way as to make all this happen. He writes as a witness and participant in the great Easter happening and is sharing this experience in order that "our joy may be complete," the out-of-this-world joy of being reconciled to God, of being reunited to His kingdom, His orbit and purpose for our lives. John's message is a glorious outpouring of hope—that we can have fellowship with God, that in the midst of our darkness and despair there is divine light, and that we can live and serve within that light amid the darkness and violence and contradictions of our world that press in upon us. "If we confess our sins," he writes, "He is faithful and just, and will forgive our sins and cleanse us from all unrighteousness."

If this happens—and even this can happen only by the enabling power of God—there is the blessed guarantee of God's forgiveness and of our restoration to His redeeming and reconciling love. This will truly make "our joy . . . complete."

Thursday   *John 21:1–14 (C)*

Business as Usual?

Easter Sunday had passed. It was a great happening—a grand climax to all of the tragic and glorious events that had befallen the disciples. Now that the excitement had subsided and there was nothing better to do, Peter turned to the men he had traveled with for the better part of three years and said bluntly, "I am going fishing." "We will go with you," said the other disciples, and off they went, boats, nets, and men, to business as usual—a business they had at one time assumed they had left behind forever.

It is a glaring portrayal of so many of our post-Easter activities. Like the disciples, we have experienced something of the excitement and joy of Easter. We believe with all our heart that Jesus arose from the dead. But on Monday it is business as usual—the same commonplace routine, the same problems, anxieties, defeats, bondages as the week before. Easter has impressed us, as it does year after year, but it somehow fails to empower us with a bit of the divine energy that brought Christ from the grave.

The disciples "caught nothing" in their post-Easter fishing expedition—until they recast their nets in response to the order of a stranger on the beach. Then they caught their fish and came up with a post-Easter recognition of their beloved Master, the Lord Jesus Christ.

If we take the great event of Easter seriously, it will no longer be "business as usual" in the days and weeks and years following Easter. It will be a new life lived in the grace and power of the risen Christ. Then we will discover the real meaning of Christianity and how we may become effective channels and communicators of love and healing to lonely, unhappy, defeated people in the Monday-through-Saturday world about us.

The Act of Worship

Worship is, in the words of J. B. Phillips, "a declaration of God's worth." This lesson from John's Revelation is his vision of a gigantic worship service, millions of God's creatures, from elders to angels, saying or singing in a loud voice: "Worthy is the Lamb who was slain, to receive power and wealth and wisdom and might and honor and glory and blessing!" They were declaring God's worth, or more explicitly, the worth of His Son, the One who was slain and who lives again.

The dominant note of John's vision is *celebration*—and what a celebration! It is proper, and in some cases long overdue, that this become the dominant note of our worship services. Jesus died for our sins; He arose from the dead as Victor over sin and death. Let's celebrate, not only through the Easter season, but throughout the church year.

Worship must take into account other things—such as *relationships*, the need to recognize and celebrate our unity with and our need for one another as God's children. Worship includes *action*—as Paul indicated when he stated that worship is the presentation of our "bodies as a living sacrifice, holy and acceptable to God" (Romans 12:1). If our celebration is genuine, as was that of the creatures in John's vision, it will lead to loving relationships and dedicated activities in respect to God's will and purposes for humankind.

God is indeed worthy of our worship. Let us declare His worth. May our lives be perpetual acts of worship as we seek today and always to do His will.

Under No Other Name

One can imagine the consternation, even the anger, that would prevail in any of our congregations should the pastor suddenly announce one Sunday morning that he was informed through some vision or voice from another dimension that the Gospel he had been preaching, and which has been embraced by Christendom for the last twenty centuries, was no longer adequate or relevant.

If we can imagine that, we may be able to understand something of the feelings and reactions of the priests and elders, rulers and scribes, that Peter accosted in his explanation concerning this cripple who was healed as a consequence of their ministry. While Peter was not demeaning the ancient traditions and the sacred Scriptures that these learned leaders lived by and which were the basis for the very existence of Israel, he was proclaiming the name and deeds of One who was far superior and who was the very culmination of everything the prophets had declared. Peter was brazenly and bluntly announcing to these officials that the salvation of Israel could only be realized under the name of Jesus Christ, whom they had crucified. Is it any wonder that Peter and most of the apostles were immediately blacklisted by the leaders of Israel?

We are probably more prudent than Peter—and not nearly so courageous—but this is the message of the New Testament that we profess to hold to: "There is no other name . . . there is salvation in no one else . . . [than] by the name of Jesus Christ. . . ." We may not impress or convince our peers from non-Christian religions or sects by blasting it out as did Peter, but we are expected to live and serve on the basis that we *do* believe that "there is salvation in no one else." It is clearly the proclamation of the New Testament; it ought to be the issue of our daily lives.

Fourth Sunday of Easter
John 10:1–10 (A)

That They May Have Life

If we were to speak of the primary subject of the New Testament, the ultimate purpose of religious organizations and movements about us, the aim of all sermons preached and services conducted, the object of God made incarnate and dwelling among us, the significance of the suffering, death, and resurrection of Jesus Christ, it would add up to one word: LIFE. "I came," said Jesus, "that they may have life, and have it abundantly."

It is this Christ, God-incarnate, who is the authentic Door to life in respect to the *physical being* of His creatures. The New Testament teaches that God is not simply Lord of a particular aspect of human nature, such as the spiritual or the moral, but is the ultimate ground of all being; He is Lord of all. "Your body is a temple of the Holy Spirit within you," said Paul (1 Corinthians 6:19).

Jesus Christ is the Door to life in respect to a person's *intellectual faculties.* "Brethren, do not be children in your thinking . . . in thinking be mature" (1 Corinthians 14:20).

Jesus Christ is the Door to a person's *moral life and nature.* "The body is not meant for immorality, but for the Lord" (1 Corinthians 6:13b).

Jesus Christ is the Door in respect to a person's *spiritual nature.* ". . . it is the Spirit Himself bearing witness with our spirit that we are children of God" (Romans 8:16).

Truly, the resurrected Christ is the Door to abundant living, to fulfillment and enrichment, meaning and purpose. "I came that they may have life, and have it abundantly."

Monday   *1 Peter 2:19–25 (A)*

To This You Have Been Called

"Christ also suffered for you, leaving you an example, that you should follow in His steps." Perhaps Peter remembered Jesus' words to His disciples just months before His crucifixion. After He had informed them of His impending death and subsequent resurrection, He said that those who follow Him must deny themselves and carry crosses of their own. Now, several years later, Peter understood the meaning of Jesus' words.

It is doubtful that Peter would go along with much of the positive-thinking, ecstasy-seeking jargon that attracts and hooks multitudes of "born again" Christ-followers today. Suffering was an integral part of Christian discipleship in Peter's day. He prepared his converts to Christ for it and sought to support them within it. This is no less true today. Most of us will escape the kind of violence that befell so many of those first-century Christians, but few if any of us will escape suffering.

"By His wounds you have been healed." And—of course in a far lesser sense—by our wounds others about us may discover healing and wholeness. While we are not about to seek or cause suffering if it is within our power to evade it, we need to be aware that our suffering, the crosses we bear or share on behalf of our fellow persons, is to be expected, willingly embraced, and may even be necessary for our life and growth as disciples of Jesus Christ.

"For to this you have been called. . . ."

Tuesday   *John 10:11–18 (B)*

Christ Is Our Shepherd

"I am the Good Shepherd," said Jesus. Either this Christ is a silly fraud, even a dangerous one, as are scores of self-appointed "Christs" enticing the masses today, or He is truly the Son of God, for this is what He claims to be. Moreover, His claims are stronger and more persuasive than when He first made them, for He now presents Himself as the resurrected, living Christ.

Jesus gives His reasons for declaring Himself the Good Shepherd. He is the *Owner* of the flock. "I know My own and My own know Me." He is not hired to care for them; He is their Owner—they are His possession. He came to possess His possessions, to redeem His sheep, to complete and secure His fold.

He is *Caretaker* of His flock. "Behold, He who keeps Israel will neither slumber nor sleep," said the psalmist. He is never off-duty, but with watchful eye and cocked ear is ever attentive to the needs of His lambs.

He is *Provider* for the flock. "He makes me lie down in green pastures; He leads me beside still waters," sang the psalmist. "Seek first His kingdom . . . and all these things shall be yours as well," Jesus promised His disciples (Matthew 6:33). Truly, "The Lord is my Shepherd; I shall not want."

He is *Defender* of the flock. "They shall never perish, and no one shall snatch them out of My hand," promised Jesus (v. 28).

The Lord is our Shepherd—and we are His. This day and every day our lives and all that we are and have belong absolutely and unconditionally to Him, for the Lord is our Shepherd and we are His forever.

Wednesday   *1 John 3:1–2 (B)*

We Know Who We Are

The fact is: We are God's children now! This status and relationship is not something we work for or wait for; it is ours here and now. It is the gift and consequence of God's eternal love. We are His children by way of His creation. We are His children by way of His redemption and our adoption into His kingdom. We are His children by way of His indwelling Spirit. We are His forever.

"We are called God's children—and so in fact, we are," writes John. "My dear friends, we are now God's children" (1 John 3:2 TEV). "Those who are led by God's Spirit are God's sons [and daughters]. . . . The Spirit makes you God's children, and by the Spirit's power we cry out to God, 'Father! my Father!' " (Romans 8:14–15 TEV).

We have discovered our identity and significance. We do not have to be fearful of this world's condemnations nor be dependent upon its acceptance. Our response to its enmity is self-sacrificing love. It means that we can abandon ourselves to God's purposes and follow His design and destiny for our lives, an exciting, risk-filled style of living that guarantees freedom and joy in the midst of this world's oppression and pain.

We know who we are and to whom we belong and where ultimately, if not presently, we are going. For we are God's children now.

Thursday   *John 10:22–30 (C)*

Profile of a Christian

What ought to be some of the characteristics or marks of our lives if we truly believe in Jesus Christ?

For one thing, we must be *belongers.* "You do not believe, because

139

you do not belong . . . ," said Jesus. He is stating emphatically that believing is belonging when it comes to a person's relationship with God. If we do belong, we shouldn't have to prove it. There ought to be stamped upon our attitudes, manners, and personalities the brand of God's ownership. We are God's property, God's possession, and we should speak and act as such.

We are *listeners.* "My sheep hear My voice," said Jesus. While the devotees of this materialistic existence cock their ears to the sensuous sounds about them or are taken in by the bright promises of socialism or communism or capitalism, we should be listening for the voice of God. He may speak in a "still, small voice," but He can also be heard in the whirlwind, the lightning and thunder, the chaos and catastrophes of these times in which we live. We must be listeners, for how else will we be able to steer our frail crafts through the storm except we be in communication with our God?

We are *followers.* "My sheep hear My voice . . . and they follow Me," said Jesus. Following means serving Him; serving Him means serving our fellow beings on His behalf. We do this, first of all, in our family and in our daily calling. But Jesus also leads us out into fields of battle—the world, the community, even the political and economic and civil-rights struggles of our society. Here, too, Christ is—where the suffering, shepherdless children of darkness grope for meaning and purpose. Here is where, as recipients of God's love and grace, we should desire to be—as belongers, listeners, and followers of Jesus Christ.

Friday   *Revelation 7:9–17 (C)*

A Time to Celebrate

This is not a time for despair; it is a time for celebration! The resurrected Christ is with us. He is present with us amid the trials and tribulations of this tempestuous world. He is about ready to reappear and to gather together His faithful followers into the fully revealed and eternally reigning kingdom of God.

This great, long-awaited event is about to take place, and the suffering, celebrating children of God of all nations and generations are invited. Christ will once and for all time reveal Himself as the living, conquering, victorious Lord of heaven and earth. Evil will be eradicated; all stumbling blocks will be removed; those who oppose God and His people will be overcome; the spiritual forces of evil will be bound and destroyed.

Sorrow will turn to joy, night into day. Tears will give way to laughter; ugliness will yield to beauty. "Every knee [will] bow . . . and every tongue confess that Jesus Christ is Lord" (Philippians 2:10–11). On this great day the suffering martyrs, the struggling saints, the priests and prophets, the servants and disciples of all ages will be united together to sing their praises to their eternal Savior and King.

Words cannot describe it—this incredible event about to take place, but Jesus is coming soon to take His church to Himself. Let us begin the celebration even now!

Saturday   *Acts 6:1–9, 7:2a, 51–60 (A)*

The Cost of Discipleship

The apostles paid for their courageous and enthusiastic proclamations with numerous arrests and beatings. It was one of their converts, selected and ordained by the apostles to relieve them of their "lesser" duties so as to enable them to give their full attention to the all-important responsibility of preaching, who became the first Christian to pay the ultimate price of discipleship, the first to be martyred as a consequence of his faithful witness.

His name was Stephen. The same Spirit who indwelt and spoke through the apostles seemed to speak with even more courage and wisdom through this newly converted "deacon" than He did through the men who witnessed the crucifixion and resurrection of Jesus. While most of the converts in the first-century church were avid witnesses to their faith in the risen Christ, Stephen's activity as a proclaimer of Christian truth was outstanding. He went farther than most of the apostles in his proclamations by radically insisting that Christianity was destined to supersede Judaism—and this is probably what bought down upon his head the wrath of the Sanhedrin. Stephen, after turning his defense into an opportunity to undermine the errors and hypocrisy of the religious leaders and lift up the risen Christ as the way of salvation for all, was cast out of the city and stoned to death.

Stephen's martyrdom introduced a heroic period of persecution in the early church, and the cost of discipleship has been extremely high in every century since the resurrection of Jesus. It is not always evidenced in martyrdom, but strong opposition is or will be the experience of most genuine followers of Christ, whatever the form it takes.

Fifth Sunday of Easter
John 14:1-12 (A)

Cure for Heart Trouble

The disciples of Jesus were on the brink of the greatest catastrophe of their lives. The One whom they had left all to follow and to serve was soon to be taken away from them and executed on a cross. They were becoming apprehensive as the enemies of Jesus were rapidly closing in on Him, and Jesus (who knew what His course would be) was preparing them for this tragic event. He prescribed a cure for anxious, troubled hearts. It was to "believe in God, believe also in Me."

It is significant to note that Jesus was not passing out some every-cloud-has-a-silver-lining platitude. Such an admonition, even if it included some vague reference to an unknown, invisible God, would do little to brighten troubled spirits. A false optimism is worse than extreme pessimism because it knows not life nor its meaning and refuses to face life as it is, to probe the basis of its tragedy and despair. Referring the troubled in heart to some distant God is like pointing to some opaque blur. Jesus, however, was authorized and able to say, "Believe also in Me." The human creature cannot come to God; God in His love found a way whereby He could come to His creatures. Jesus presents Himself as God come to earth, God made visible and available, as "the Way, and the Truth, and the Life," and this is not rosy optimism or sentimental good cheer that He dispenses; it is divine truth.

The cure for heart trouble is heart trust. We are not to trust in some vague concept of divinity, but in Jesus Christ, who is God with us and within us. He plumbed the depths of sorrow and suffering. He conquered over death and darkness. He arose from the grave. He lives—and because He lives, we shall live forever. We need not allow the anxieties of this life to trouble us overmuch. We need to listen and to accept in faith the words of Jesus: "Let not your hearts be troubled; believe in God, believe also in Me."

142

We Are the People of God

"You are a chosen race, a royal priesthood, a holy nation, God's own people. . . ."

We who have sampled God's grace and know that He accepts us as His children and remembers our sins no more are just beginning to realize the magnitude and immensity of that grace. Now it is time to grow in that grace, to put aside our childishness and become mature, dependable Christians. Like blocks that firm up and reinforce a building, we ought to be the kind of men and women that build up God's kingdom on earth. Our great God has accepted us as His sons and daughters and appointed us to be His ministers. We, with Christ as our Savior and King, *are* the kingdom of God.

There are, however, many other blocks, still unprepared, that need to be shaped and formed to fit into this great temple of God. Our Lord has made us the blocks that hold together other blocks—and the artisans that assist in hewing and shaping others to find their places in this structure that God is building. We are to do this by declaring the love of God for all His human creatures and demonstrating that love in our daily contacts and in our sacrificial deeds of kindness on behalf of God and for the benefit of humanity. It is this profound responsibility that shapes our lives and guides our activities in our remaining years on this planet. We can well afford to lose our material possessions, worldly acclaim, even our physical lives in this splendid task—and yet lose nothing at all because we are the people of God and belong to Him forever.

This is the way of love, our response to the gift of divine grace that drew us into the family of God. Let us walk in it.

How to Be Truly Happy

We may not have the right to be happy. If such happiness is designed to satiate our egos or pacify our self-centered natures, we can hardly, as Christians, claim that right. We do have the right to joy—not because we merit it but because God offers it. Nowhere and at no time does God promise sensual happiness, but His Word is full of promises of joy.

It is only as joyous Christians that we can bear fruit. This Gospel lesson underlines the *necessity of fruitfulness* in our lives. "By this My Father is glorified," said Jesus, "that you bear much fruit, and so prove to be My disciples." Jesus is informing us that we have been cut away from the forest of sin, redeemed from its ugly consequences, and engrafted into the Vine, into Christ, not only to bask in His glow, wonder at His miracles, and anticipate eternal rewards, but in order that we may bear fruit toward the accomplishment of God's purposes.

Jesus reveals, as well, the *key to a happy, joy-filled, fruit-bearing life.* "I am the Vine, you are the branches. He who abides in Me, and I in him, he it is that bears much fruit." We don't have to clutch at Christ like a drowning man to floating debris, we need only to "abide," to remain, to rest in Christ the way a baby rests in the mother's arms. This "abiding" is a state of faith; it is perpetuated by faith. As we entrust ourselves to Him by faith, so we "abide" in Him and will remain with Him forever.

It is when we truly abide in Christ—and we invite and allow Him to abide in us, permitting His Spirit to have His way in and through us—that our lives will be full of joy and will bear the fruit of that joy.

Wednesday   *1 John 3:18-24 (B)*

From Doubt to Assurance to Obedience

Our confession of faith that we participate in every Sunday morning does not eradicate forever all doubts about our relationship to God. There are the blue-Monday doubts and the gray, beclouded skies that often obscure the bright sunshine of God's forgiving, accepting love. They do not stifle or smother His love for us, these doubts that plague and harass us, nor do they change our status as God's beloved children. But they do send us scurrying back to God's blessed Word that assures us of His love and mercy. Even when "our hearts condemn us . . . God is greater than our hearts," and so therefore is His mercy and grace.

It is not enough, however, to make confessions or proclamations concerning our faith. We are indeed saved by faith in God's ever-abundant grace—not by works. Yet a genuine faith in God is marked by obedience. We live in obedience to God when, while believing in Him, we lovingly and actively reach out to meet the needs of our fellow beings.

Apart from this level of obedience, according to John, our faith may be in question—and so our relationship to God.

Oh, continue to assure us of Your eternal love, dear Lord!

Something Old, Something New

"A new commandment I give you, that you love one another . . .," said Jesus to His disciples. It was actually not a new commandment, but the old one made new by the life and teachings of Jesus Christ. It was more a declaration of the truth than a command, a fact of life (the Christian life) rather than a directive. "When you love your neighbor," said Kierkegaard, "then you resemble God." What is new about this commandment is that if we are to follow Christ, to be His disciples, we must by the grace made available to us through His resurrection love our brothers and sisters within the human family. Our faith apart from or without this inevitable expression would be little more than blasphemous posturing, a ridiculous facade. Our neighbor, in a very real sense, represents the invisible Christ, and Jesus declares that what we do for our neighbor—even unto the least of our brothers and sisters—we do for Christ.

The standard or quality of love is also made new by the life and teachings, the death and resurrection of Jesus Christ. ". . . Even as I have loved you, that you also love one another," He said. The springs of love are in God, not in us. He must give to us through His Spirit the will and the ability to love. We must somehow see Christ in our neighbor, or we must see him as one whom Christ loves and seeks, as one for whom He died and arose from the dead.

"By this all men will know that you are My disciples, if you have love for one another," said our Lord. It would appear that the sole, sufficing evidence of our Christianity is our love, a genuine, sacrificial, Christ-inculcated love for our fellow beings. It doesn't come naturally, nor all at once, but it is something we must be empowered to do and learn to do. And we had better begin now—right where we are.

God Is with Us

John's vision illuminates the great event that will ultimately take place. God's faithful children—clothed in His righteousness—can believe it and hope for it and ready themselves for it, because it will happen. When it does happen, all the pain and suffering that encompassed them in this world will be forgotten in that glorious revelation of Christ as King and God ever-present with His people in the world to come. For "He will dwell with them, and they shall be His people, and God Himself will be with them." What a harbinger of hope and comfort John's Revelation must have been to the suffering, persecuted Christians of his day! It continues to offer comfort and hope to God's children and servants in our day.

There is even greater hope and comfort spelled out by John and the other apostles in the assurance that God is already with us amid the conflicts and trials we encounter today. He is not visibly present in this hour, but through His indwelling Spirit walks and works and worships with us, whatever our course through life. Our conviction about this ever-present God is demonstrated in our faith, which accepts the fact of His presence despite the pains and problems of this life. There are ample evidences of that presence—in the words of those who witnessed Christ's resurrection and the coming of His Spirit to indwell them; in the lives of thousands of His children who testify as to His wonder-working power in their experiences; in those times when we have felt His loving interventions in our own lives; in the Eucharist, where He touches us in a very special way through the bread and the wine we receive.

"Behold, the dwelling of God is with [us]."

Saturday   *Acts 13:44–52 (C)*

Joy and the Holy Spirit

"And the disciples were filled with joy and with the Holy Spirit." Though we know that the apostles were filled with the Holy Spirit, it doesn't always appear that they had a great deal to be joyful about. They were constantly on the run—proclaiming the blessed Gospel and then leaving behind them an angry mob that drove them out of their city. It happened here; it would happen again in Iconium, the next city where they would minister.

But their joy superseded any fear for their own welfare. They were proclaiming the Gospel of God's saving love as revealed through the risen Christ and, wherever they went, they sowed seeds that would take root and bear fruit unto the great, eternal kingdom of God. Furthermore, such fruit-bearing was not to be limited to the people of Israel but would continue among the Gentiles—unto all the nations of the world. They understood now what the ancient prophet meant when he said that the salvation of God was destined for the Gentiles as well as the Jews, "to the uttermost parts of the earth."

What a ministry they had! And what a commission we have! There may be a price to pay along the way—as there was for the apostles—but we also have a part to play in enlarging God's kingdom. We may not always see much fruit as a consequence of our seed-sowing, but our witness in life and word will bring results. We can indeed be "filled with joy," knowing that the Spirit of God works and speaks through us. Let us be faithful to our ministry, as were those first-century disciples.

Sixth Sunday of Easter
John 14:15–21 (A)

We Are Not Alone

"I will not leave you desolate," said Jesus. "He dwells with you and will be in you," He said concerning the Holy Spirit. The church of Jesus Christ is privileged to proclaim the profound truth that we are not alone. It is this message that we are responsible not only to proclaim but essentially to demonstrate to God's creatures who inhabit our community and world. We are to do this not through ecstatic manifestations or supernatural gifts that attract and amaze people about us, but through sacrificial acts of love.

Our Lord's words announced the Spirit's indwelling, which was to be the fruit and crown of His redeeming work. It was for this that man and woman had been created. If it were not for Pentecost, the Father's purpose and Christ's own work would never have been accomplished. Christ knew that His disciples would not understand at this point; but He discloses the divine secret that, when He left them, their loss would be compensated for by a greater blessing than that of His bodily presence. Another would come in His place, to abide with them, to dwell in them forever.

Of course we are not alone. It is time that we stop cheating ourselves out of that divine power so needed and so available, and cheating our fellow beings out of the divine touch that can redeem their empty, meaningless lives, and yield ourselves totally, abandon ourselves completely, to the control of the Holy Spirit and allow Pentecost to happen to us. It has happened to us—even from the time of our baptism into Christ. Now let it happen to others through us, and it will become increasingly apparent that we are not desolate.

Monday   *1 Peter 3:15–22 (A)*

Suffering That Is Honorable

The Christian witness to a rebellious world will involve pain as well as blessing. There will be negative reaction as well as positive response. Whereas there is no call for a martyr complex and we cannot assume, as do some cultists, that the abuse received as a result of witnessing on this planet guarantees special consideration in some future heaven, suffering can be honorable and may result in some maturation in our lives as well as progress in the advancement of God's kingdom. It is far better to bear patiently the hurts that others may inflict upon us than to be the cause of their pain—or to be guilty of not making any effort to alleviate their suffering.

It is not so tragic or unfortunate that we suffer. It is probable that such suffering will enrich our lives and enlarge our faith. Jesus Christ Himself, God's Son, suffered much in the course of His brief life upon this strife-ridden world. How dare we expect any less?

While we will not seek suffering, conflicts and trials come to all of us at one time or another. They cannot be avoided or ignored. They are real—and they hurt. But we need never be ashamed of suffering for Jesus' sake. May God grant to us the kind of love and courage we need to enter into suffering, if such is necessary, in order to declare in witness and good works God's love and salvation for disoriented people in a disjointed world.

Tuesday   *John 15:9–17 (B)*

The Responsible Christian

We continue to affirm that salvation is by faith—the acceptance of God's loving, forgiving, redeeming grace as revealed to us through the crucified and risen Lord Jesus Christ. Salvation—the forgiveness of our sin, eternal life, our adoption into the very family of God—all this is a gift of God. It is not deserved; it cannot be merited or earned; it must be acknowledged and embraced through repentance and faith.

Yet there is more to the Christian life. There are responsibilities to consider, commands to obey, directives to carry out. "If you keep My commandments, you will abide in My love. . . . This is my commandment, that you love one another. . . . You did not choose Me, but I chose you and appointed you that you should go and bear fruit. . . ."

While it is correctly understood that a total commitment to the saving love of God will resolve in sacrificial discipleship and obedient servanthood, in fruit-bearing, in being a responsible Christian, we realistically insist that the journey from salvation to servanthood is often a long and painful (as well as joyful) experience. Christian growth comes by the grace of God—as does forgiveness and love—but only if we responsibly walk in that grace and in obedience to the commands of our Lord.

What are the commands of Jesus? "Love one another." "Go and bear fruit." Every one of us is called to full-time service for Jesus Christ, to be His servant and minister in the parish or arena of life and activity in which we find ourselves today. God help us to be responsible Christians, not only to accept Him and live by faith within His saving grace, but to obey Him and by His grace to commit ourselves to the desperate needs of the human family about us.

Wednesday   *1 John 4:1–11 (B)*

The Acid Test

"Do not believe every spirit," writes John. In his day, and in ours, there were and there are other "spiritual" forces seeking the loyalty and allegiance of men and women. It is not always easy to spot them— and many who initially came to faith by way of God's true Word have been led astray by self-styled religious con artists who concoct a gospel of their own and for their own self-centered purposes. One test that will separate the shepherds from the goatherds, the false prophets from the genuine article, is whether or not they confess and proclaim Jesus Christ as God's Son—God in the flesh, God-incarnate, who has come to redeem us from our sins. If they do not proclaim the Christ in this manner, they must be avoided like the plague.

After all, the proof of our adoption into the family of God is love. That adoption begins with our being drawn into God's gracious love as revealed and granted through God-incarnate, Jesus Christ. We cannot come to God by way of our good works; we come only by way of His grace and by way of Jesus Christ, who communicates that grace to us. In response to that grace we are lovingly compelled to love one another —willingly and joyfully to love our fellow creatures with the love that God's grace sows and brings to fruition in our hearts and lives.

The Ascension of Our Lord

Thursday   Luke 24:44–53 (A, B, C)

Left Holding the Bag

He lives! He reigns!

He left His beloved disciples "holding the bag."

It is a rather colloquial expression, but the fact remains that what Jesus began the disciples were left behind to continue. At least this appears to be the case until we begin to understand that our Lord didn't really leave His disciples at all. He "parted from them" or disappeared. He became invisible; He returned to that dimension which is near us and about us but not visible to our eyes that are designed for three-dimensional landscapes.

Before He parted from His faithful followers, He left them with a commission and a promise: a commission to witness of the things they had seen and experienced, to proclaim the Gospel they had heard, and a promise that they would be fully equipped to do the job they were commanded to do. It was not in God's eternal plan that the visible Christ should try to cover all the bases by Himself. So He "parted from them" only to invisibly, through His Spirit, indwell, empower, and carry out the purposes of His Father through the bodies and brains of men and women who would embrace His salvation and commit themselves to His service.

The disciples of Christ, after receiving the Holy Spirit, proceded to do this very thing—most of them being martyrized in the process. Thousands followed in their wake. The Gospel of God's saving grace was proclaimed throughout the world, and millions were redeemed and are being redeemed by His forgiving, life-giving love.

Now we are the disciples of Christ, authorized and commissioned to continue the ministry of the suffering, resurrected, and reigning Lord Jesus Christ in our world today. And we are, enabled by His Spirit, equipped to do the job. Our God and Christ, working through our fallible, failure-fraught bodies and spirits, will continue to carry on His purposes in our community and world today.

From Dust to Deity

The Genesis story of creation tells how "God formed man of dust from the ground, and breathed into his nostrils the breath of life; and man became a living being." In a strange and wonderful way the living Lord is still involved in creating—taking the dust of this world's darkness and oppression, the wrecks that humans make of their lives, and breathing into them His deity. The very heartaches and agonies, the inscrutable difficulties, the insurmountable problems of peoples' lives are as important in this process of creation and transformation as are the joys, the hours of achievement and accomplishment, that are the portion of God's human creatures.

There is a secure basis for attacking and overcoming, or for learning how to live with, the sufferings and conflicts and dark hours that come our way. For one thing, there is the *love of the Father.* "If a man loves Me, he will keep My word, and My Father will love him. . . ."

There is the *indwelling of the Holy Spirit.* ". . . The Holy Spirit, whom the Father will send in My name, He will teach you all things. . . ." The dust of this existence can be inhabited with deity. The Spirit of the living Christ clothes Himself with the very bodies of problematic, sinful fishermen and tax-collectors, men and women of all races, temperaments, and walks of life.

There is the *peace of Jesus Christ.* "Peace I leave with you; My peace I give to you," said Jesus. "Let not your hearts be troubled, neither let them be afraid." It is not the kind of peace found in some distant world of make-believe, nor is it life separated from the turbulence of this frustrating existence, but the kind of peace that can be ours right here in the very midst of a world of trouble and trial. What a formula for joyful, effective, secure living—and for meeting the adversities of life with confidence and courage!

The Big Event

What about that great day in which God's kingdom shall be revealed? Is there any way we can picture that glorious event?

Some have had visions; others have dreamed dreams. But it is not possible for our small minds to visualize the glory of God's eternal kingdom. Our images are earthbound. Our words are like the babbling of babies. Our imaginations are utterly incapable of grasping the majesty, beauty, and power of the glory that awaits the children of God in that great day. We see but minute glimpses of His eternal glory in the elements about us, yet even these are beyond the comprehension of our finite thinking. The pictures we compose are crooked lines or abstract blobs that barely represent ultimate truth.

This, however, we believe: With the dawn of that magnificent day Christ shall be revealed in all His glory and majesty. All the hosts of heaven will be gathered to sing His praises. And every human creature upon this earth, along with those who have gone before us, will know that this One who walked among us, who revealed God's eternal love and suffered in His own body the consequences of our faithlessness and disobedience, this One, the resurrected Christ, is Lord and King of this earth, the universe, of heaven itself, for all eternity.

Unfortunately, not all of God's creatures will greet the big event with joy. The faithless among His created children are not citizens of God's eternal kingdom; those who have not loved and worshiped Christ as King within this world will bow their knees and cover their faces in fear on that day. Only those of us who love and serve our God today can be assured of rejoicing in His manifestation tomorrow. We can regard that great coming event with joyful anticipation.

Seventh Sunday of Easter
John 17:1–11 (A)

Jesus' Concern for His Own

This great prayer of our Lord highlights His concern for the disciples He was about to leave behind. His earthly mission was about to be terminated in His betrayal and crucifixion. Whereas His visible ministry was almost completed, the work of God's kingdom as revealed through His Son had barely begun. The expansion of that kingdom, the accomplishment of God's objectives as initiated by Christ, was to be carried out through those Jesus left behind. It was for them, and for us who claim to be the 20th-century disciples of Christ, that Jesus prays and expresses His concern through His prayer.

We see this great concern of our Lord in the fact that *Christ prays for us.* "I am praying for them; I am not praying for the world but for those whom Thou hast given Me," said Jesus. The Good News concerning the past is that Christ has intervened in this realm of suffering and death, struggle and conflict, and made possible our deliverance from the eternal consequences of sin. The most consoling news concerning the present is that Christ intercedes on behalf of His disciples.

We witness Jesus' great concern for us in that *He regards us as His possession.* "They are Thine; all Mine are Thine, and Thine are Mine," He prays. We have unwittingly regarded God as some ethereal Being assigned to serve and please us. We have our wires crossed, for Jesus emphatically declares that we belong to God, that we are His possession, that we are expected to enlist our lives in His service. "You did not choose Me," said Jesus to His disciples, "but I chose you and appointed you . . ." (John 15:16). The surest guarantee that we are safe and secure, loved and accepted, and that we have nothing to fear amid the frightening circumstances that batter our world, is that we are God's possession, His property, His sons and daughters, His own forever.

Someone Does Care for Us

"No one cares for me," agonized the psalmist on one of the "blue Mondays" of his life (Psalm 142:4 TEV). The statement is attributed to David, spoken while he was hiding from King Saul in a dark cave.

There are caves along our sojourn through life, and we duck into them now and then to hide from something that frightens or threatens us, and there we moan out our loneliness and despair—telling ourselves lies about the Divine's indifference and our fellow persons' unconcern about our problems. We may have reason at times for doubting human concern. Our fellow beings are often too preoccupied with their own failures or successes to coddle us in our confoundment. It is true that God's love, usually transmitted by way of men and women who have encountered Him, is often made ambiguous by human insensitivity. Over and above the fallibilities of human beings is the perpetual and eternal truth of God's love and concern for us. "Cast all your anxieties on Him" wrote Peter, "for He cares about you."

It is time for us to emerge from our sorry little caves of morbidity and self-pity to face up to the "king Sauls" that intimidate us. We don't have to be afraid, for God really cares.

How Much He Loves Us!

This great prayer of our Lord was not offered, as was the "Lord's Prayer," in order to teach His disciples how to pray. This prayer is truly the Lord's Prayer, expressing, in view of His coming death on the cross, the deepest feelings of His heart at a very critical hour in His life. The real beauty and the consoling message of these precious words of our Lord are discovered in the rich expressions of love and concern for each of us.

Jesus prays that we may have *His joy fulfilled in us.* He is not referring to the effervescence and ecstasy that accompanies the religious experiences of some people, but to true joy, eternal joy, the joy that filled the life of Jesus even while He faced betrayal and execution

155

and that would abide in us even in the midst of this world's catastrophes and calamities.

Jesus prays that we may be *kept*. "Holy Father, keep them in Thy name, which Thou hast given Me. . . ." In an atrocious world with all of its pitfalls and temptations, we with all our weaknesses and fallibilities are the subject of God's promise and Christ's prayer that we will be kept by Him. We will often fail; we will at times become depressed and discouraged in our defeats and imperfections. In it all and through it all, we will be kept.

Jesus prays, not that we should be spared the conflicts and struggles of this cruel and contemptuous world, but that in the midst of it all we might *walk in the truth*. "Sanctify them in Thy truth; Thy Word is truth," prayed our Lord.

How much our great Lord loves us! It is when we really believe in this love, accept and abide in this divine, everlasting love, that we will become lovers and will be enabled to communicate this love to our fellow beings in our world about us.

Wednesday   *1 John 4:13–21 (B)*

By This We Know God's Love

"So we know and believe the love God has for us." It begins with our acceptance of God's love as it is revealed to us through Jesus Christ. It is further revealed and extended through our love for one another. This is what the God-life is all about. Apart from God there is no real love; apart from love God is not real in us and is not able to work through us. If we assume we can continue to bask in God's love even while we continue to harbor hateful, unloving thoughts about a brother or sister, we are deceiving ourselves.

We live in a fear-ridden world and foolishly allow these fears to permeate our lives and polarize our interpersonal relationships. If God's love truly dominates our lives, this will not happen, because it crowds out all fear and unites us to God and to each other.

God's love is perfect—and He loves us perfectly. Not only should this free us from the fears that plague our world; it should enable us to love our fellow persons without concern for consequences. This is our assignment in our world today: to be, as was Christ in His visible visitation, love-incarnate in our love-starved society.

Let us begin by genuinely loving one another.

Is Something Wrong with the Church?

In the great and beautiful "High Priestly Prayer" before His trial and crucifixion Jesus expressed His foremost concerns about those He was leaving behind to carry on the work He had begun. For one thing, He prayed that there would be *unity*, "that they may all be one; even as Thou, Father, art in Me, and I in Thee . . . that they may be one even as We are one."

Contrary to Jesus' earnest and devout prayer, unity is not generally known in the church today, and at times has hardly even been sought.

Fortunately, however, there now are many who believe that this unity for which Jesus prayed ought to be more visible to the broken world about them and regard it as their duty to yearn for and struggle toward a more visible and contributive unity within God's kingdom.

What is wrong with the church is clearly related to what is wrong in our own lives. Our lack of genuine love for Christ, for our brothers and sisters in Christ, for those for whom Christ died and rose again, even for the institutional church as it exists today, is certainly a part of the root cause for the failure of the church to dramatize and communicate God's saving love to our generation.

Teach us, O God, how to love even as You love us.

Hold On—He's Coming Soon!

This was the message John was sending to his persecuted, imprisoned, suffering brothers and sisters in the faith: Hold on—Jesus is coming soon! Whatever else his Revelation said to his readers—and there may have been much that they understood but which still remains a mystery to us—it was a message of hope and comfort to Christians trying to hold on to their faith and their lives in that violent world of their time.

Almost every generation, in times when things become unstable and the world appears about to go out of orbit, produces its prophets that herald something of the same message: Hang in there; Jesus is coming soon! The crowds they gather give some indication of how much the message is needed, of the fears and anxieties that harass people even today.

Some prophets, unfortunately, prophesy too much. They twist John's Revelation into saying or meaning something never intended by the writer—thereby confusing rather than clarifying the end-time message. The "Jesus is coming soon" message ought to be proclaimed to every generation, but it needs to be ungarnished, freed up from the tantalizing frills and thrills offered by popularity-seeking prophets and their overworked imaginations. Jesus *is* coming soon; that is all we know or need to know. There will be an end to violence, to all that is evil and ugly. There will be healing and joy, peace and rest, for those who "hold on" in faith—or allow God to hold on to them—and walk in obedience with the invisible Christ who directs their lives. The day is soon upon us when He will be fully revealed.

"I consider that the sufferings of this present time are not worth comparing with the glory that is to be revealed to us" (Romans 8:18).

Saturday   *Acts 1:8–14 (A)*

You Shall Receive Power

We are about to leave behind the Easter season even while we continue throughout the church year to rejoice in and meditate upon the Easter message. From now on, through the rest of the church year, we deal primarily with the consequences of the resurrection of Jesus Christ in our own lives. Like those first disciples we are thrust out into our world or our specific arenas of life and activity to communicate to the inhabitants of our world the Good News of God-incarnate, Jesus Christ, and His salvation made possible for all through His death and resurrection.

We are not left unarmed or unequipped. Jesus spend forty days following His resurrection talking to His disciples about the kingdom of God and their responsibility in building that kingdom. Just before His ascension He promised that the power they would need for this task would be granted by the indwelling of His Spirit within them. Then Jesus disappeared, vanished, ascended into heaven. God in the visible Christ had inaugurated His kingdom upon earth. From now on it was God and Christ working through the mortal, fallible, failure-fraught bodies and spirits of Their redeemed children who would carry on His plan to consummation, building the kingdom of God that would ultimately include His created children from all nations of the earth.

The disciples did not fully understand Christ's final words, but they held on to His promise. It was a promise or a prophecy that had been proclaimed years before by John the Baptist. It was now about to be fulfilled.

The Day of Pentecost
John 16:5–11 (A)

The Birthday of the Church

We are now on the threshold of the longest season of the church year—the Pentecost season. The event that took place on this day so many years ago is celebrated as the birthday of the Christian church. Pentecost proved that God became flesh not only by way of the womb of Mary and in the earthly sojourn of Christ but, in a sense, also by infilling, indwelling, and empowering the flesh of His human creatures. His indwelling, though different, is as real in us as it is in God-incarnate, Jesus Christ. It is Pentecost that inaugurated the perpetual presence of Christ in our world—through you and me and all of our brothers and sisters who follow Christ. As far as the here and now is concerned, Pentecost may be more important than Christmas. Pentecost makes Christmas a daily event in and through the lives of God's children. Whereas Christmas celebrates the event whereby God became man, Pentecost initiates the event when men and women became the vehicles and channels, the very temples of God Himself. It is Pentecost that makes us Christs-incarnate in the world today.

Luther called us "little Christs." The fact is, we are the only visible Christs that God has to advance His kingdom and carry out His purposes "concerning sin and righteousness and judgment" and concerning His great love for His creatures. We are in the midst of the twenty-centuries-long struggle to continue and carry on the work of God, so that He in His love for us and through our love for others may communicate divine love and healing to the lonely, unloved, frightened, and fractured people all about us.

And He has already equipped us for this task. Setting us free from sin's guilt and power and eternal consequences and reconciling us to His divine family, He has given us His Spirit. The power that brought the visible Christ into our world through the virgin Mary and raised Him from the dead on the day of Resurrection is the same power, the same divine energy, that abides within us. This is our equipment as the sons and daughters, servants and ministers of the living God, and it is more than adequate for the task our God has set before us.

159

Pentecost—It Has Happened to Us!

There is a new wave of interest in the Holy Spirit today. This is very good. A good many people who frequent our churches are quite comfortable with the manger scene and Calvary's cross—and especially with Easter and its grand tidings of victory over sin and death—but Pentecost is something totally incomprehensible to many religious people. There must be the Christmas, Good Friday, and Easter experiences in the life of every Christian, but this is to prepare the way for Pentecost. It is the culmination of everything that went before it.

The birth of Christ took place at night in the seclusion of a stable; Pentecost blazed forth in broad daylight with hundreds of people to witness this fantastic event. Unfortunately, the giving of the Holy Spirit is often still associated with particular signs—such as speaking in strange tongues or miracles of healing, and according to some people must be initiated by a second religious experience or second baptism. God may very well be the initiator and perpetrator of certain phenomena. But to insist that these mysterious, ecstatic experiences are necessary or synonymous with the Holy Spirit's infilling and control of Christ's followers is contrary to God's Word as declared through Jesus Christ. Wind, tongues of fire, and foreign tongues did indeed accompany the initial Pentecost event. God may occasionally use such phenomena today. It may take such happenings to move some people off dead-center and get them going for God.

Neither you nor I, however, have to sit around and wait for such strange, supernatural signs. Pentecost has happened to us; the Holy Spirit has been given. He entered our hearts at our baptism. He continues to abide within the lives of those who follow Jesus Christ. God is about us and within us this very moment. God help us to acknowledge that fact and set out in faith and obedience to walk in God's Word and will for us in order that the Holy Spirit may work out His divine purposes in and through us.

If Anyone Is Thirsty

The last day of the feast commemorated the amazing incident that happened during the Israelites' long trek through the wilderness when, while camping at Rephidim, Moses at God's command smote a rock to bring forth water to satiate his thirsty people. In celebration the priests poured out sparkling water with choral song.

While they stood with their empty vases, the temple's silence was pierced with a loud voice that proclaimed these words recorded in our Gospel lesson: "If anyone thirst, let him come to Me and drink." It was Jesus, the son of a carpenter and, unknown to the temple crowd, the Son of God, who spoke these words.

The scene and the ceremony change. Today there are thousands of rites and ceremonies—all geared toward the same goal, the quenching of thirst, the satisfying of humanity's desires, the fulfillment of the human creature's inner longings, the universal quest for meaning.

"If anyone thirst . . ." The basis of humankind's longing and desire is thirst for God. Jesus presents Himself as the answer and fulfillment of that thirst: "Let him come to Me." His first invitation and directive is to *approach Christ.* Our Lord stands before the human race as that One who knows its deep thirsts, takes account of the impotence of any created thing to satisfy humanity's inner needs, and assumes the divine prerogative by saying: "He who believes in Me shall never thirst" (John 6:35).

Jesus' second injunction is to *appropriate Christ.* "Let him come to Me and drink." It isn't enough to come to the Fountainhead; one must drink—embrace, enter into, commit oneself to, appropriate Christ and the life He offers to all.

Our Lord's injunctions are followed by a promise, one made by the prophet Isaiah centuries earlier. When one comes to Christ and receives Him, approaches and appropriates Christ, then "Out of his heart shall flow rivers of living water." The life-giving water is *applied* to parched lives about us.

It is the Holy Spirit working in and through us who makes all this possible in our lives.

Wednesday   *John 15:26–27; 16:4b–11 (C)*

And Now It's Pentecost

There must be Christmas, Good Friday, and Easter experiences in the life of every Christian; but they are meant to prepare the way for Pentecost. Pentecost is the culmination of everything that went before it. It is Pentecost that inaugurated the perpetual presence of Christ in our world—through us and our fellow-disciples in the Christian faith. Whereas Christmas celebrates the God-become-man happening, Pentecost initiates the event whereby man and woman become the vehicles and channels, the very temples of God Himself.

It appears that it was the ascension of Christ, His return to His Father, which made Pentecost possible. "It is to your advantage that I go away," said Jesus to His disciples. "If I do not go away, the Counselor [the Holy Spirit] will not come to you. . . ." The disciples understood nothing of this at the time. Now they learned through actual experience what Jesus was prophesying in these words of our Gospel lesson. While Jesus was with His disciples, the divine, supernatural power so necessary to the salvation of humankind was confined within the visible Christ. After He performed His mission on this planet and returned to His heavenly Father, the same divine, supernatural power responsible for Christ's resurrection and essential to the building of God's kingdom upon earth was to return to inhabit and empower His disciples.

And now it is Pentecost. It has happened. The same divine Spirit that ministered in the creation of the world, producing cosmos out of chaos, that had ministered through the visible Christ, has now returned to indwell and pour Himself out through the lives of all those who would in faith and obedience lend themselves to His infilling and outflowing.

We are the contemporary evidence of Pentecost, the recipients of that Spirit. God grant that He may work through us today.

Thursday   *Joel 2:28–29 (A)*

It Came to Pass

Much of what the Old Testament prophets had to say to their people appeared to be obscure. Many contemporary prophets and their imaginative interpretations of the ancient prophecies only further obscure the messages of these prophets of the past. Among the blessings and woes which the prophets pronounced upon the Israelites, however, were numerous gems of profound insight from the very heart of God. At least portions of God's plan for the distant future were and are revealed through their prophecies.

It is those prophecies of the Old Testament that are fulfilled in Jesus Christ and the times following His resurrection that are most significant to us. They underline the authority of the Bible, these Scripture lessons we meditate upon each day, and assure us that God indeed speaks to us through the written Word.

What Joel prophesied came to pass. On the day of Pentecost Peter immediately linked what was happening to him and the believers around him to the ancient prophecy of Joel. God's Spirit was being poured out upon human flesh, and accompanying that Spirit were supernatural gifts and powers such as healing and tongues and prophesying, making it obvious to all present that God was acting and His human creatures were being edified and equipped to carry on His purposes in the world about them.

It came to pass—for them and for us. The Spirit who was promised through Joel, and poured out upon the apostles and other believers on the day of Pentecost, is the very same Spirit who abides in each of us. As we truly believe this, it ought to make a real difference in the way we live and walk and act today.

Friday   *Ezekiel 37:1–14 (B)*

The Breath of God

One is tempted to out-prophesy the venerable prophet in his astounding vision, to mark this as God's promise that all of Israel, once cut off from God's grace and apparently without hope, will be raised from the dead to honor and serve the God of their fathers.

Such a temptation put aside, it is possible to find in this vision excitement and hope for the church at large, for the "spiritual Israel" which includes true believers out of all nations and tribes throughout the world. Is it possible that scores of people who frequent our churches and dutifully confess their faith are still comparable to "dead bones" because they have not allowed God to have His way in their lives?

The excitement and hope transmitted through Ezekiel's vision is that this does not have to be; this can be changed. Church institutions throughout our world are being brought back to life again as their members who once confessed only with their mouths begin confessing with their hearts the forgiving love of God. Many are returning to the covenant made between them and God at their baptism; and God is breathing upon them, restoring them to life and truth and joy and purposefulness by way of His Spirit, who is taking control of their whole beings.

This is the incomparable experience: restoration to the love and grace of God. It includes forgiveness, reconciliation, assurance of life eternal, peace and joy, purpose and meaning. It is like a resurrection from the dead, a new birth.

May God continue to breath upon us.

First Sunday After Pentecost

Response to a Suffering World

The world is in deep need. A thousand quivering moans herald each rising of the sun. If one is sensitive, one can almost hear the sighing of the oppressed, the whimpering of the starving, the pleading of the sick. Less evident but very real is the spiritual need in which so many millions find themselves. Idolatry, superstition, unforgiven sin, lack of purpose in life are everywhere.

What is to be our response to these manifold needs? It is not to hide behind the walls of our affluence and prosperity or even within the walls of our hallowed sanctuaries. It is to "Go . . . to all peoples everywhere and make them My disciples" (v. 19 TEV). Our Lord did not enjoin us to reach for the moon; He ordered us out into the world. He did not instruct us to stay close to our manmade sanctuaries and altars; He sends us into the world to relate to the oppressed and the affluent, of every color and race and creed, and to tell them about the salvation planned by the Father, wrought by Jesus Christ, and brought to us by the Holy Spirit. "Go therefore and make disciples of all nations."

Monday   *2 Corinthians 13:11–14 (A)*

Live in Peace

"Live in peace, and the God of love and peace will be with you."

We may not always nor need always to "agree with one another," nor have we yet all embraced Paul's injunction to "greet one another with a holy kiss," but it is possible and important that we "live in peace." We are the products of Pentecost. We are indwelt with the same Holy Spirit. We are confronted with the same overall command of Jesus to "Go . . . to all peoples everywhere and make them My disciples" (Matthew 28:19 TEV). With the love of God the Father, the grace of Jesus, and the fellowship of the Spirit empowering us, we can do great things in spreading God's kingdom.

We can be assured that "the God of love and peace will be with [us],"

164

and can confront each day of our lives with the determination to love one another and allow the Spirit of God to bring His eternal love and grace to those who cross our paths.

How to Start Over Again

It is one of life's most precious gifts: the opportunity and the privilege to begin anew, to start over again.

We were born into a discordant, disease-ridden humanity. We inherited a sinful, error-prone nature. Inculcated into our souls, however, was the longing for better things, the grasp for perfection, the urge for something that hovers tantalizingly beyond our reach.

We flail the air with desire but fail to obtain. We run but never arrive. We seek but do not find. We grovel or grapple with the things of this life only to lapse into depression and defeat, our souls empty and unfulfilled.

Our great God has shown us how to start over again. It begins with a new birth, a reentry into this finite dimension with the realization of divine acceptance and grace. It is the gift of the ever-loving Father. It is revealed through the redemption of His Son. It is received and appropriated by faith worked by the blessed Holy Spirit.

We may still be haunted by failure and plagued with defeat. The new birth does not promise the end to guilt feelings or to the sins and weaknesses that cause them. But even while clothed in the blemishes and flaws of mortal flesh, we are the adopted sons and daughters of God. Our failures do not damn or destroy us. They drive us back to the sufficiency of God. There we find forgiveness and acceptance. There we are granted' the opportunity to start over again.

His Spirit Within Us

"For the Spirit that God has given you does not make you slaves and cause you to be afraid; instead, the Spirit makes you God's children . . ." (v. 15 TEV).

Can you imagine people dying of malnutrition with hundred-dollar bills stuffed into their mattresses? And yet it happens from time to time. A similar malady is common among Christians. While God through His indwelling Spirit provides us with all that is needed to live effective, contributive, joy-filled lives, we are often afflicted with spiritual malnutrition.

It is indeed necessary that we are "born again." While this happened to us in the covenant God made with us in our baptism, we need daily to confront our finitude and failures and return to that covenant and embrace God's forgiving love anew. We need, as well, to be continually reminded and assured that Pentecost has happened, that God's Spirit dwells within us. It is this that establishes our credentials as God's children and equips us for the service we are called to render unto Him as His servants.

The faith that justifies us, that by God's grace enables us to tie into and respond to that grace, is the same faith that accepts our inheritance as God's children and the indwelling of His Spirit. "God's divine power has given us everything we need to live a truly religious life . . ." wrote Peter (2 Peter 1:3 TEV).

Thursday   *John 16:12–15 (C)*

Power to the People

We hear a great deal about power today. Our lives are enriched or frustrated, and may even be destroyed, by the various energies and powers that surround us. Whether we wake or sleep, we are sustained or threatened by the powers that press in upon us.

There is, however, another power, a far greater power, available to us: the Spirit-given power to love, to discover truth, to create and to heal, to bring light into darkness, beauty into ugliness, goodness into evil, sweetness into bitterness, joy into grief-stricken situations. Apart from it we could well become monsters that murder; with it we can become men and women who minister, sons and daughters of the living God destined to reflect and channel His love and grace to a broken, distorted world. The power of the Holy Spirit indwells us as God's special and divinely endowed representatives assigned to bring Christ's powerful salvation into the fractured lives of the ailing and lost all about us.

It is time that we cease being clods that clutter up the church of Christ and become what we are destined to be—vibrant, pulsating vehicles of spiritual power. That power is within us. We need only to submit to the Source, the invisible Christ, and yield ourselves totally to His control and use.

Accepted by God

The truth of the matter is—and this in spite of those fine religious people who attempt to placate God by means of laws and rules and traditions and customs—the truth of the matter is that we *have been* accepted by God through Jesus Christ. This is where "we stand." This is what we ought to celebrate.

We can well afford to celebrate this even amid the difficult circumstances that harass us. Whether it be physical pain or mental anguish, material loss or excruciating sorrow, this does not separate us from God or alter our relationship to Him.

When we accept and cling to what God has done for us through Christ, irrespective of our human feelings and frailties, then the very conflicts that beset us and may even threaten to destroy us become God's tools to grind and polish and temper our spirits and prepare us for loving and obedient service.

This is no vain hope; it's the Gospel truth. God's love and Spirit *do* abide within us. Let us move into this day before us under this conviction and by the power of God's Spirit, for we are the very children of God and no one can take that truth and experience away from us.

There Is No Other

"Know therefore this day . . . that the Lord is God in heaven above and on the earth beneath; there is no other."

Our Old Testament text is from one of a series of addresses made by Moses to his people prior to their crossing over the Jordan to occupy the new land to which God was leading them. The Book of Deuteronomy is a record of Moses' inspired pronouncements ranging from commandments and rules his people were to obey to prophecies of what would happen to them on the other side of the Jordan River and promises of God's care and guidance that would accompany them if they put their trust in Him. Throughout these lengthy discourses run Moses' constant reminders that their God is the only true God, a fact often proven throughout their long wilderness journey, and the guarantee of God's judgment upon all who create gods or graven images of their own to worship. "Lay it to your heart," said Moses, "that the Lord is God in heaven above and on the earth beneath; there is no other."

This injunction of Moses is as relevant to us as it was to the children of Israel. We need to be reminded from time to time that God, as revealed through God-incarnate, Jesus Christ, is the only true God. "There is no other." False shepherds are persistently hailing and propagating false gods, cults, sects—sometimes well-intentioned groups that use divine names and sacred Scripture and take on a "form of religion but deny the power of it" (2 Timothy 3:5). There are, as well, the more obvious "graven images" that tempt Christ's followers, such as wealth or position and various philosophies that promise self-fulfillment.

Lest we be seduced by those gods that seek our allegiance only to betray and possibly destroy us, let us begin this day's journey with a reminder from Moses and a renewed and revitalized conviction "that the Lord is God in heaven above and on the earth beneath; there is no other."

Second Sunday After Pentecost

Matthew 7:21-29 (A)

Salvation—Then What?

I have been a Christian since my baptism into Jesus Christ when I was an infant. Not until a decade or two later did the implications of God's free gift of salvation really begin to take hold of my life. A transformation began in my thinking and feeling that was as dramatic as is the initial conversion experience to scores of "born again" people in our society. I began to realize that I needed to take seriously some of the hard words of Jesus such as those recorded in our Gospel lesson for today. The purpose was not to assure me of my salvation or to pile up credits in some future life, but to respond to God's grace, to accept the implications of my sonship with God. As Jesus bore the cross on my behalf, so I have been chosen to bear a cross on behalf of others in my world.

The words of this lesson are indeed difficult, and sometimes disturbing, for Jesus may be speaking to us. We need to understand that our Lord's words are not suggesting that our salvation is dependent upon our good works. He clearly implies (v. 17) that these do not make us right with God. Our Lord insists, however, that those who abide in God's grace must respond to it in terms of hearing and doing the words and will of God.

"Conversion, in its original meaning," according to Jim Wallis, "meant that those who had been transformed by Jesus Christ experienced a change in all their relationships to the world, to their possessions, to the poor and dispossessed, to the violence in their society, to the idols of their culture, and to the false worship of the state."

Maybe some of us need a second conversion, one that embraces our Lord's will as well as His life and salvation.

Monday   *Romans 3:21-25a, 27-28 (A)*

Back to Square One

"They are justified by His grace as a gift," wrote Paul.

"The Gospel of the grace of God awakens an intense longing in human souls and an equally intense resentment . . .," said Oswald Chambers. "I will give my life to martyrdom, I will give myself to consecration, I will do anything, but do not humiliate me to the level of the most hell-damning sinner and tell me that all I have to do is to accept the gift of salvation through Jesus Christ."

We are reminded again that we cannot earn or win anything from God, that we must either receive it as a gift or do without it. Before we go back to the office, the marketplace, the school room, or the household chores, on this first working day of the week, it is well that we go back to square one, the fundamental of our faith, the grace of God—His unmerited, undeserved love for us, and this irrespective of our frailties and failures. We will deal much with good works, our response to grace, to God's love for us, and our resultant enlistment in His will and purposes for us as His children and servants. But we will be reminded again and again that our salvation, our justification, is "by His grace as a gift."

Let us celebrate that precious truth on this day—and always. If our celebration is genuine, it will result in the dedication of our lives to glorifying God through Jesus Christ and communicating His love to those around us.

Tuesday   *Mark 2:23–28 (B)*

Law Without Love

The Pharisees were guided by law, not love. Jesus introduced an entirely new element, one that superseded the laws and rules concocted by the religious leaders of Israel, who proceeded to make them absolutes that dictated the ethics and actions of the people. The Law was centered around the Ten Commandments and was intended to clarify and dramatize the ancient and essential commandment to "love the Lord your God with all your heart, and with all your soul, and with all your mind, and with all your strength" and "your neighbor as yourself" (Mark 12:30–31). Though the prophets at times indicated some understanding of what that kind of love was all about, it was Jesus who personified it, proclaimed it, and dramatized it.

This Law, and the hundreds of virtually impossible regulations added to it, was sacred to the Pharisees. It was what they strove to live by, what they proclaimed as the very absolute ordained by God. The apparent disregard of it by our Lord angered the religious leaders and was, in part, the reason for His crucifixion.

The Ten Commandments continue to be essential to our life and growth as Christians, but they are superseded by love—the kind of love taught and exemplified by Jesus and the kind He expects of His disciples. This kind of love becomes an absolute for us. It means that our standards must supersede the Law as stated and interpreted in the Old Testament. It is the kind of love that sets us free from the bondage of the Law in order to love as Jesus loved and thereby communicate God's love to people about us.

This does not come naturally. We will often fail to love one another as Jesus loved us. Having received God's eternal love and grace, and this by way of Christ and the cross, we who are the objects of His never-ceasing love are to dedicate our lives in love to the needs of our fellow beings and discover in God's great love for us the compulsion to love our neighbor.

Wednesday   *2 Corinthians 4:5–12 (B)*

Enjoying the Disagreeable

The selling point in much of the hustling that is going on in the name of Christian ministry today is joy, happiness, the highs and ecstatic feelings that are supposed to result from such a religious experience. This is not necessarily wrong. After all, Jesus certainly underlined joy as one of the prime fruits of "abiding in the Vine" (John 15:1–11), and John wrote his letter in order that "our joy may be complete" (1 John 1:4).

This is not the whole picture, however, and Paul tends to wet-blanket some of the excesses and extremes in this respect by pointing up a few of the disagreeable things that befell him and his colleagues as a consequence of their faithful witness: "afflicted in every way . . . perplexed . . . persecuted . . . struck down . . ." There doesn't appear to be a great deal of joy in these episodes that happened so often in their ministry. Yet these painful experiences did not smother out the joy of their relationship to God and their ministry for Him: "afflicted . . . but not crushed; perplexed, but not driven to despair; persecuted, but not forsaken; struck down, but not destroyed. . . ." Even these things inadvertently resulted in joy: "We are always being given up to death . . . that the life of Jesus may be manifested in our mortal flesh."

Is it really possible to enjoy the disagreeable? Only if our joy is divinely inspired and matured in the enthusiasm and delight of allowing "the life of Jesus" to be "manifested in our mortal flesh."

171

We are not about to seek out or choose the disagreeable, hurtful things that will happen to faithful disciples. If, however, they come as a consequence of obeying God and serving our fellow creatures, they will enhance and temper our joy as God's children and servants.

Thursday   *Luke 7:1–10 (C)*

The Gospel for Body and Soul

There are many instances when Jesus preached—particularly to His closest followers, that they might be purged and prepared for future service. To many people who came to Him, however, His ministry took the form of tangible acts of mercy in terms of problem-solving miracles: turning water into wine, giving sight to the blind, healing the lame and the ill, exorcising demons, and so on.

Some of us have been brought up under the illusion that the problems of people and their world would be solved or eliminated by simply preaching the Gospel, that our commission as Christians was only to talk about Jesus, to witness as to our faith in Christ, to get people ready for heaven. Whatever the source of such a misconception, it didn't come from God's Word. The early Hebrews recognized the difference between the sacred and the profane, but they did not divide the social from the spiritual. The social concern of the prophets is well known: "Seek justice, relieve the oppressed, judge the fatherless, plead for the widow," were their stern injunctions. Christ gave priority to the spiritual emphasis—salvation, God's forgiving grace, eternal life—but He never neglected the social emphasis.

The precious passages of the Gospel are those which exhort us to believe, receive, accept, and rely on Jesus Christ. We need to discover, however, that a relationship to Jesus Christ insists upon our acceptance of the passages that underline social action—our responsibility to His creatures about us.

It is not a comfortable Gospel that we accept and proclaim. It offers us redemption and life everlasting; it demands in return our total commitment to loving and living for God and for people. When we are committed to Jesus Christ as our Savior and Lord, both the spiritual and the social needs of our fellow beings become our foremost concern. We are truly evangelistic only when we begin to demonstrate that kind of concern in our relationships to God and to the human family about us.

172

Subverted Christians

It is astonishing and disconcerting when people are easily subverted from the Gospel as Jesus proclaimed it to chase after some subjective ecstasy, or go traipsing after a sign or miracle or vision, or fall prey to some half-truth that promises to make their lives more secure and exciting. One doesn't have to look far to discover false prophets twisting the Scriptures to say what they want them to say. They enclose our great God within their own shallow concepts and pass this sometimes poisonous concoction on to their avid followers. Paul had no kind thoughts about such individuals: "Let [them] be accursed," he said.

While we may not be inclined to judge so harshly such promoters of a religion, we need to avoid them like the plague and to make certain that the Gospel we submit to is the Gospel of Jesus Christ and not the pathetic mouthings of foolish and dangerous self-styled prophets.

In the meantime we need to recognize that we are all tempted, at times, to interpret the Gospel in ways that fit our assumed needs and seem most reasonable. This would result in some sort of compromise, and we are in danger of becoming content with something less than the whole Gospel of our Lord.

We need to be shaken up from time to time, to make sure that our reach for eternal truth far exceeds the grasp of our feeble understanding, and to continue resisting all attempts to bottle up our God in a closed system of select rules, regulations, or rituals that one can handle without too much discomfort or pain.

God, as revealed through Jesus Christ, is the true God whom we accept and serve; He is the One who loves and accepts and commissions us for service.

Blessing or Curse

Life or death, heaven or hell, good or bad, black or white. Maybe the issues were simpler in Moses' day. As we contemplate the last day of this week, decisions and issues appear to be far more complicated in our time. Our intentions were honorable—or so we surmised at the beginning of the week. Things didn't, of course, turn out quite the way we had hoped.

The same was true for the children of Israel. They carelessly or deliberately disobeyed God or attached their lives and fortunes to other gods along the way. The history of Israel is a history of human sinfulness and faithlessness and of God lovingly but sternly attempting to draw them back into a relationship with Himself. God did not have to zap them with frightful disasters; they aptly created their own by their refusal to listen to and obey the commands of their God.

We are the recipients of the Good News that the ultimate curse that is promised God's unbelieving, disobedient, sinful creatures has been borne by God Himself in His Son, Jesus Christ.

So, too, are the sins of our lives, the bad decisions, the failures and flops of the past week. We may still have to bear some of the consequences in one way or another, but God Himself forgives and forgets, and such unfortunate experiences do not stand between us and our loving God.

Tomorrow—and next week—afford us the opportunity to start over again. And all the while that we struggle to live according to His will and to reflect His attributes in our relationships with His creatures around us, He is with us to comfort, guide, enable, to work out His purposes through us, and to forgive us when we fail.

Third Sunday After Pentecost
Matthew 9:9–13 (A)

The Call of Christ

"As Jesus passed on from there, He saw a man called Matthew sitting at the tax office, and He said to him, 'Follow Me.'"

The most astounding, incredible fact of all history is the call of Christ to sinful men and women, the invitation to follow Him. It is extended to the meanest, greediest, most unpromising creatures on the face of the earth. No matter how fractured or distorted, failure-fraught or inadequate we may be, we are invited to follow Jesus Christ, to become the sons and daughters of God, servants and disciples of our Lord and Savior. It is, morever, not an invitation to casual acquaintance or weekly worship. It is not simply an offer of outside help when we are on the spot. It is the call to follow Him, to become exclusively attached to the Person of Christ, to love Him, serve Him, and crown Him Lord of every phase and facet, attitude and aspect of our lives.

Of course we *accept* Jesus Christ. This ought to flood our lives with the joy of sin forgiven and the assurance of life eternal. But if we are to be effective as Christians and obedient as God's children, we must *follow* Jesus Christ. Our Lord is not only inviting us to respect Him or honor Him or appreciate Him; He is calling us to follow Him, to join with Him, become one with Him, to die with Him and be resurrected with Him, and to reign with Him in that eternal kingdom He has come to establish and build.

It's incredible! It's true! As He called Matthew, that despised tax-collector, so He calls us—raising us out of our sin and despair to become, with Him, the very sons and daughters of God. "I came not to call the righteous, but sinners," said Jesus to the Pharisees. We are eligible; let us rise up to follow Him.

175

Hope Against Hope

"In hope he believed against hope. . . ." Abraham portrayed a very stubborn faith in God's promise "that he should become the father of many nations." This is the kind of faith we often need in our kind of world. The Holy Spirit, according to Jesus' promise, will accomplish the purposes of God in and through us. Abraham "did not weaken in faith when he considered his own body," but we often do. It is not particularly our age that concerns us, as it did Abraham, but our inadequacy. We still rely so very much on our human attributes and faculties and, by all appearances, they are incapable of carrying out God's objectives—especially in the role we are called on to play on this stage we call life. It is difficult enough to consistently believe that we are forgiven, accepted, loved by God, that we are through Christ righteous in His eyes. To believe that He is working out His will through us, that the seed we sow will bear fruit to the advancement of His kingdom, is well-nigh impossible.

It is, at times, a matter of "hope . . . against hope," of taking God at His Word and letting the chips fall where they may. Abraham's faith was "reckoned to him as righteousness." We are, through Jesus Christ, accounted as righteous; it is not at all a matter of how strong our faith is. And yet our faith is the means of embracing and believing that through Christ we are forgiven. It is also the means of overcoming our frailties and feelings of inadequacy, and it enables us to rejoice in the blessed truth that God will work out His purposes in and through us today.

The Family of God

"Whoever does the will of God is My brother, and sister. . . ."

We strongly affirm the emphasis on family life in these days when the forces of evil seem so intent upon and successful in their attempts to divide and destroy this all-important unit of society. Our Lord, early in His ministry, also referred to family life. It was, however, a far different family that concerned Him. He was speaking about something, thus far incomprehensible to His listeners, that was related to another dimension: the family of God. Human relationships were still important to Jesus, and He continued to reveal a human concern for His own family, noted especially in respect to the pain and sorrow His crucifixion was causing His mother (John 19:26–27). But even at that critical hour He was regarding the family relationship on a different level than we generally understand or experience.

We ought to cherish much our families and our relationships therein. We need, as well, to grow into an understanding of Jesus' pronouncements concerning the new family He had come to construct, the family of God. Jesus gave intimations about new, far superior relationships that would eternally bind together the people of God's kingdom. He said, in effect, that those who are related to God as their heavenly Father are brothers and sisters to one another—and are the very brothers and sisters of Jesus, the Son of God.

Whatever our race or heritage, class or status in society, our gifts or abilities, we are all the members of the family of God and are, with Jesus Himself, brothers and sisters in that family. It is an eternal relationship that is far more significant than the human family relationships we naturally cherish (or at least ought to). The Christians in our church, the members of Christian churches down the street, the hundreds of thousands of Christ's brothers and sisters all over the world— they are our brothers and sisters!

Wednesday   *2 Corinthians 4:13–18 (B)*

Do Not Lose Heart

We are "earthen vessels," clay pots, in the hands of God, Paul said in the verses preceding this lesson. And while every vessel has its flaws, God has chosen to deliver His eternal gifts to this world through such vessels. He may have to break and remake us from time to time, but use us He will—with our cooperation and obedience. He only requires that we gratefully submit our bodies and beings for His use and consecrate our efforts and energies to His purposes.

Of course we will have problems. There will be times when we are flattened by despair. There will probably be executioners about seeking to nail us to some cross. It is quite possible that we will lose status, popularity, friends, if we dare to let God have His way with us.

Whatever we lose we will regain a thousandfold in this life or in the next. This is the promise of our God. And he doesn't shortchange anyone.

The truth is, we don't have to be discouraged. We can be free even from fear of failure. Only then are we free to live—or to die—to joyfully spend and expend our lives for Jesus' sake.

So "do not lose heart." It's a great and wonder-filled life.

Thursday   *Luke 7:11–17 (C)*

Rise Up and Live

This Gospel lesson deals with Christ's confrontation with human grief and the event of death—and with His power to overcome both grief and death. It is designed to assure God's children of such power in respect to their lives and to eradicate once and for always their fear of this ultimate event. Death is a part of life, one single step from the front stoop of this three-dimensional world into the living room of everlasting union with God—one that Christians may well anticipate but certainly need not fear.

The fact is we are not likely to be of much use to God in this world until our eventual exodus from it, though at times fraught with apprehension, holds no real fear for us.

"Do not weep," Jesus compassionately exhorted the mother of the deceased man. "Stop crying," He is saying to doubting, griping, fearful, complaining Christians today. "Arise!" He said to the deceased man and is saying to all who claim His salvation and yet are sick unto death amidst the pains and pressures of our uncertain and insecure world.

Is it possible that some of us still haven't learned how to live, how to lay hold of the love and life made available through Jesus Christ and the death He died on the cross, a life that grants His supernatural peace and joy even in the midst of doubt and pain and insecurity?

It is only when we rise up and live in the joy and power of Christ, the resurrected Christ, that we can lovingly and helpfully respond to the doubts and fears, the burdens and sufferings, of dying people about us. It is when we do this that we are really living.

Friday   *Galatians 1:11–24 (C)*

The True Gospel

"For I would have you know . . . that the Gospel which was preached by me is not man's gospel." Nor is the Gospel we listen to in the churches we attend on Sunday. There may be some question about some of the popular media religious presentations that fill the airwaves at some time on almost any day, but most of us are secure in the knowledge that our pastor is preaching the Gospel of Jesus Christ.

It is true, nonetheless, that those of us who preach or witness have sometimes been guilty of less than spiritual motives in our presentations. While we often sense this to be true about some of the popular evangelists who charismatically draw viewers and listeners into their fold, we ought to be aware of the possibility that we may be doing the same thing in our little groups. God uses the message we proclaim because of us or in spite of us. We need to be sure, however, that we are mouthpieces, instruments, in the hands of God, and rid ourselves of any intent to seek our glory or the adoration of our fans or followers.

Responsible preachers of and witnesses to the faith pray sincerely that they may not come between people and God, but that they be channels of God's Word of comfort and challenge to people about them. Only then can they be assured that "the Gospel which was preached by [them] is not man's gospel."

We become God's servants by His grace alone. We preach and witness effectively only by His grace. The Gospel which we preach and to which we witness is the true Gospel.

Saturday   *Hosea 5:15–6:6 (A)*

God Is Faithful

God is faithful even when we are not. Like the foolish, unfaithful wife of Hosea, we turn from our loving God to pursue the foolish pleasures and temporal treasures, the creature comforts, within reach around us. We find ourselves, at times, in mind if not in body, whoring after the ephemeral delights of this world. Even then the love of our eternal God never ceases. He allows us to discover for ourselves, sometimes tragically, the emptiness of our lives and to taste the suffering we bring upon ourselves through our rebellion and unfaithfulness. God knows well that we may not find our way back to Him, so in His loving mercy He pursues us, suffering in Himself the judgment we incurred through our infidelities, seeking to draw us back into His forgiving heart and to restore us to a loving relationship with Himself.

God will not give up on us. Even while we insanely call down judgment upon ourselves, He is ready to forgive us. When we stumble into the pits that await us, He is waiting and ready to draw us back to His loving heart. God stands by to forgive the infidelities and heal the

179

faithlessness of His wandering children. If only we will confront our emptiness and loneliness, our great need for our true and eternal Lover, He will restore us to a loving relationship with Himself and within the family and kingdom of God.

Let us cease playing God with our own lives and return to the true God, our God who created and redeemed us. He will heal the wounds caused by our faithlessness. He will forgive and cast aside our iniquities. He will love and securely hold on to us forever.

Fourth Sunday
After Pentecost
Matthew 9:35–10:8 (A)

Christianity: Escapism or Involvement?

This Gospel lesson presents a concept of the Christian life that is sometimes lost among the soft, sentimental approaches that are often promulgated.

Jesus tells us that discipleship means involvement. He set the pace, and He expects His disciples to keep it. He identified with the agonies of humankind. He became involved in their crying needs. He even went so far as to bear the consequences of their sins. To be a disciple of Jesus means that we who accept Him as our Savior must also accept Him as our Lord and Master. We are expected not simply to criticize the distortions of humanity from the pews and pulpits of our churches, but to become involved in the blood and tears, the sorrows and sufferings, of God's creatures wherever they may be found.

Because we are involved in the sickness of our world, we must, as the disciples of Christ, become involved in its cure. Discipleship means involvement. As our Lord suffered on our behalf, we are expected to suffer on behalf of others, to lose our lives in service only to truly find life anew in the incomparable joy of being the children and servants of the living and eternal God.

"As the Father has sent Me, even so I send you" (John 20:21).

Monday   *Romans 5:6–11 (A)*

What God Has Done for Us

The preceding Gospel lesson underlines the necessity of involvement in the purposes of God by dedicating our lives to the good works of proclaiming and demonstrating God's love to the inhabitants of our world. This is followed by the Epistle lesson that draws us back to the center and core of our religion. Faith does not save us because it is a good work but because it is the hand that reaches out to take the salvation God has prepared for us. Daily repentance will not make or keep us Christian but is our realization of and response both to our

181

unworthiness and to what God has done for us in Jesus Christ. Nor does our obedience to God make us right with Him, but the suffering, death, and resurrection of Jesus Christ make us right with God. It is by the supernatural miracle of God's grace that we stand justified before Him, not by sorrow over sin or confession of faith or consecration to divine purposes.

This will always be a great mystery, something we can never quite comprehend, but it was Jesus Christ who reconciled us to God. What we cannot comprehend we can still celebrate. Through the sacrifice of our Lord, God's act of grace and gift of love, we have been made the very sons and daughters of God. We were once the enemies of God, totally estranged from Him, sick unto death with the disease that pervaded and permeated the whole human race. God's love for His creatures, however, is far greater than the evil that brings death and destruction. His grace is more powerful than human wickedness. This is the grace that was wrought and revealed by Jesus Christ, and it is this that grants us everlasting life.

Tuesday   *Mark 4:26–34 (B)*

God's Patience with Us

"He spoke the word to them, as they were able to hear it."

According to Mark, Christ's proclamations to the general public were almost always in the form of parables, "but privately to His own disciples He explained everything." From the ancient prophets of Old Testament times through the apostles in the first-century church, God patiently unfolded His eternal truth in the measure that they were able to hear it and thereby experience and proclaim it. In this very day, even concerning the truth as revealed through the Scriptures, it becomes our own in knowledge and experience as we increase in spiritual growth and maturity.

God has dedicated time and eternity to the project of making us what He intended us to be. He has redeemed us through Jesus Christ. By way of the Law and the Gospel, we have heard and made our own the truth of His eternal love for us. Yet God is not finished with us. As we are "able to hear it," He continues to let us find deeper insights about ourselves and about Himself and His purposes for us.

Thus we grow and mature as His sons and daughters, assuming that we are ever alert and obedient to His truth as He enables us to recognize and embrace it. Some of our brothers and sisters in the faith appear to grow more rapidly than others, and are enabled to hear and proclaim new dimensions of His eternal truth that may still be un-known or obscure to us. God won't give up on any of us. He loves each one of us and takes His time with each of us in order that all of us may be what He wants us to be. Some of this unfolding He does "privately," in our personal relationships with Him; much of it is done through our relationships with one another in the great family of God. Let us keep ourselves open to God and to one another in order that we may hear and recognize and respond to the truth as it becomes clearer to us.

Wednesday   *2 Corinthians 5:1–10 (B)*

The Walk of Faith

"We walk by faith, not by sight."

The few years we have on earth are precious to us. They are what we can consciously comprehend. But the same God who gave us this three-dimensional experience has promised us eternal dimensions far above and beyond anything we can imagine or comprehend. He asks only that we trust Him and demonstrate that trust in all-out commit-ment of all we are and have to Him and to our fellow persons for His sake.

This is what faith is all about. As a matter of fact, if we really knew what lay ahead of us in that eternal world that is to come, we would be too anxious to enter its portals and much too impatient about the few years and many tasks and hard problems of this temporal existence.

We can stop being cowards and begin taking risks for God. We are the inheritors of His great kingdom, heirs and joint-heirs with Jesus Christ Himself. Whatever we tenaciously hold on to in this life eventu-ally turns to ashes. Whatever we painfully, responsibly, and lovingly give away really enhances our lives here, and in the process of thereby serving others we serve our gracious God.

It is the risk we can well afford to take—one that we will begin taking when "we walk by faith, not by sight."

Thursday   *Luke 7:36–50 (C)*

Some People Can't Love

I have always assumed that the "unpardonable sin" referred to out-right blasphemy against the Holy Spirit. I now wonder if one's hatred

183

or even disregard or unconcern for a fellow human being nearly approaches this kind of blasphemy. Simon was a man who apparently could not love. Meticulous, well-disciplined, highly respected, extremely scrupulous, yet completely detached and noninvolved, he was like a cold fish. He demonstrated no affection whatsoever toward Jesus. He did not stoop to perform the host's function of providing water and washing a weary traveler's feet. There was no kiss of welcome, no oil for anointing. The only emotion he showed was an exclamation of horror or disgust over the entrance of a sinful woman and the manner in which she was acting toward the Christ.

There was, however, a woman who did love, a street-woman or call-girl, still carrying with her a tool of her trade, a flask of ointment. She heard that Jesus was near and sought Him out to express her love for Him. Ignoring the rules of tradition or ettiquette, she broke into that small assembly and in passionate devotion poured out her tears upon Jesus' feet and wiped them with her hair. Then, with utter disregard for the economics of the act or the restrictions of propriety or decorum, she poured the expensive contents of her flask of precious ointment upon Him and stooped to kiss His feet.

She is one of the two people ever recorded as having kissed Jesus. She kissed the feet of Jesus out of adoration and love. The other kiss was the kiss of betrayal bestowed upon the Christ by one of His own disciples—another man who was not able to love.

"Therefore I tell you, her sins, which are many, are forgiven, for she loved much," said Jesus about this woman, "but he who is forgiven little, loves little." It becomes obvious to me that I need God's forgiveness of my sins and His loving acceptance of me. Then, perhaps, I can learn how to love.

Signing Away Our Rights

"I have been crucified with Christ. . . ."

We vociferously and sometimes belligerently insist on our personal rights—to property ownership, free speech, the pursuit of happiness, or whatever else promises to please us. Not so, testifies Paul: "I have been crucified with Christ." This means many things, much of which we don't really understand, but it adds up to our signing the death warrant for the disposition of sin and self-rule in our lives, and the yielding over to Jesus Christ of every right that we claim for ourselves. We do not simply determine to imitate Christ or try to follow Him when it suits us; we have been identified with Him in His crucifixion. All that is accomplished for us on Christ's cross is also to be accomplished in us. We "die" to sin and our right to run our own lives and, by the grace of God, become His loyal and faithful disciples forever.

We remain human beings, each one unique and individual, but the mainspring is radically altered. Once estranged from God and His purposes, we are through Christ reunited to Him, made one with Him, restored to His orbit for our lives. We no longer insist on our own rights but carry out the rights and objectives of our Creator and Redeemer and discover that this is what we were meant to do from the very beginning.

"The life I now live in the flesh I live by faith in the Son of God . . . ," wrote Paul. This is really living! The limited satisfactions that are occasionally experienced by claiming our rights in this fractured world are small indeed when compared to the incomparable joy of allowing Christ to live out His life in and through us.

Saturday   *Exodus 19:2–8a (A)*

Remember Who You Are

"You shall be My own possession among all peoples. . . ."

Thus God speaks to Christians today as He did to the people of Israel in ancient times. The conditions as spelled out to Moses on the mountain were quite clear: "If you will obey My voice and keep My covenant. . . ." The people failed miserably and, except for a remnant, were dispossessed by God. Then through Jesus Christ, God not only spoke but acted to make His creatures His possession once more. God Himself fulfilled the necessary conditions. Humanity's rebelliousness and disobedience, the sins of every man and woman, were atoned for in the suffering and death of Jesus Christ. It is now possible for all of God's human creatures to be repossessed, to be drawn back into the circle of His love, to belong to Him forever.

It almost takes one's breath away, the fact that God would want to possess us, that He would give Himself over to suffering and death that such a thing might be possible. We just are not that much of a prize that God should go to such lengths to lovingly draw us to and keep us for Himself. His ownership was established at our creation. He permit-

185

ted us to break out of His circle of loving care and foolishly try to make it on our own. He seeks always to repossess us and make us His own for all eternity.

We who have been repossessed by and reconciled to God abide in the sweet comfort that we are His possession, and "no one is able to snatch [us] out of the Father's hand" (John 10:29). Let us remember that as we face the temptations that seek to trip us up today, or the adversities that cause us anxiety and pain.

Fifth Sunday
After Pentecost
Matthew 10:24–33 (A)

Christians on Trial

Many of us, as Christians, have coasted along with an anemic, bargain-basement kind of faith, worshiping a sort of mother-God who pacifies our hungers and secures our future. It has been respectable to be called Christian. It has been a warm, comforting, consoling, safe kind of faith that demands almost nothing in return. This may be the reason that we have difficulty understanding or identifying with the words and inferences of Jesus in our Gospel lesson, or with the words of a 20th-century martyr, Dietrich Bonhoeffer, who wrote: "If we refuse to take up our cross and submit to suffering and rejection at the hands of men, we forfeit our fellowship with Christ and have ceased to follow Him." When we return to the Scriptures and discover that authentic Christianity involves this kind of discipleship and this kind of suffering, it causes us some concern. We have basked in the serenity and security of modern religion, gratefully latching on to God's grace and Christ's promise of life eternal, but it may be a cheap grace that we have bargained for and, for most of us, involves very little sacrifice or suffering.

Thus far, at least, the words of Christ in this lesson may not mean very much to most of us. For those who seriously and sincerely obey Him, however, and who truly become His servants in our chaotic, hate-infested, sin-bound world, our Lord's words are words of *encouragement*. "It is quite possible that you will lose your lives if you follow Me, but don't be afraid," our Lord is saying: "You are of more value than many sparrows." He speaks words of *warning*. "There is an enemy that you must be concerned about," He may be saying to us today, "the apathy and neglect, the selfishness and self-centeredness, that can destroy your souls and rob you of eternal life."

We remain the children of God because He is loving, forgiving God. We pray that He will graciously and patiently lead us into a relationship with Himself that will honor and glorify Him by demonstrating His love and His life to the world about us.

Don't Blame Adam

While it is true that "sin came into the world through one man," the old "blame Adam" gimmick some of us have used to explain away some fault or failure in our makeup is sheer nonsense. According to one writer, sin is not explained as an accumulation of immoralities or wrongdoings in our lives, but is in reality our foolish and disastrous claim to our right to ourselves. It is, in essence, casting our God-Creator off the throne of our hearts and enthroning and enshrining self-will as god and master. It is this immoral and rebellious act that estranged us from God. Created to be His sons and daughters, we instead turned into tyrants and traitors, the very enemies of God.

We can't blame Adam. We are sinners with or without the contributions of our ancestors, for "all . . . are under the power of sin. . . . All have turned aside, together they have gone wrong . . ." (Romans 3:9, 12). We are responsible if we do not embrace the gift of forgiveness, the deliverance from the sin and guilt that holds us fast, the righeousness that Jesus came to grant us. "And this is the judgment," said Jesus, "that the light has come into the world, and men loved darkness rather than light, because their deeds were evil" (John 3:19).

How great is the grace of God! It is sufficient to cover all the sins of the human race—including yours and mine. The knowledge of this is that light which, through Jesus Christ, has come into our world. May that knowledge become our experience today and every day of our lives.

God's Grace Amid Life's Storms

World population is exploding. Our economy is on a rampage. Our environment is endangered through carelessness and waste. Our natural resources are being depleted. Our government is ineffective and often corrupt. Crime is increasing toward frightening proportions. Millions in our country are jobless. Hundreds of millions throughout our world are starving. Drought, earthquakes, natural and man-perpetrated calamities are wracking our world. I think we are beginning to feel something of what those disciples felt as the "storm of wind arose, and the waves beat into the boat," and they awakened the sleeping Christ crying out, "Teacher, do You not care if we perish?"

Maybe Christ is saying to us what He, in essence, said to those disciples: "Why are you such cowards? How little faith you have! I have created, redeemed, and appointed you for just such times as these. I am always with you, working out My will through you. Trust Me; I won't let you down. There is a quiet harbor somewhere at the end of your journey, but for now you are to abide in Me and work for Me in the midst of storm."

What this Gospel lesson is saying is that God truly does care about us and, in the midst of our insufficiency, His grace is sufficient—and it is always available. It is not something we have to earn, merit, or work for; it is *grace*, His great gift of love. While He does not promise to cancel out all the storms of our lives as He did that storm on the Sea of Galilee, He does promise to be with us as we face and endure the storms that whirl about us. We need only, in faith, to recognize and accept His promises and power and to lay claim to His loving, super-natural peace even in the midst of these raging tempests that beset us.

Wednesday   *2 Corinthians 5:14–21 (B)*

Abandoned to the Love of God

"For the love of Christ controls us. . . ."

A good question to begin any day with: Am I controlled by the love of God as He is revealed through the loving Christ? I ought to be because "He died for all, that those who live might live no longer for themselves but for Him who for their sake died and was raised."

Or one might consider the same question concerning yesterday: Was I controlled by the love of God, or did some other desire, passion, lust, or prejudice control my attitudes or actions?

Some of us fell far short of Paul's experience yesterday. We were tempted or tainted by some idol or graven image, or we were led astray by our focus on lesser values, or propelled by self-interest, or we rebelled in the face of adversity or failed to show love among unloving people.

"We are ambassadors for Christ, God making His appeal through us." We are a "new creation," God's redeemed creatures, reflecting God's love in whatever circumstances may come our way. Is this tran-spiring in our lives? Did it happen yesterday?

Yesterday is past and forgiven. Today is another day—and a new opportunity to be what we are in Christ, what God would have us be every day of our lives. This will happen only if we are truly abandoned to the love of God and allow that love to purge away all inordinate affections and self-interests, all lesser values and loyalties, and to be clearly portrayed and demonstrated through us. Our determination alone will not enable us to do this, but the grace of God will draw us closer to this noble goal as we abandon ourselves to His love and determine day by day to make this our foremost objective and allow Him to have His way in and through us.

Thursday   *Luke 9:18–24 (C)*

From Milk to Meat

When Jesus invited His disciples to articulate their feelings concerning Himself, the most encouraging statement came from the lips of Peter, who identified and accepted Jesus as "the Christ of God."

Peter's confession was immature at this point, but it was genuine. Jesus accepted it as such, so much so that He dared at this stage in His ministry to predict His coming suffering and death and to reveal to His followers something of the price they would have to pay when continuing the ministry He had begun. They, of course, had no comprehension of what Jesus was talking about. They were still living on milk while Jesus was pointing out to them the real meat of Christian discipleship.

They were destined to mature quickly in the following months, however, and soon understood well the meaning and extent of Christ's predictions and promises. The very men who fearfuly denied their friendship with Christ or went into hiding when He was indicted and sentenced to torture and execution were the very same men who gladly and courageously embraced persecution and martyrdom as a consequence of proclaiming the risen Christ as the world's Savior and Lord.

I once thought myself quite fortunate in being able to rise above the obvious immaturity of Christ's disciples prior to His crucifixion. I thought them to be rather dull, slow learners, and marveled at the infinite patience of Jesus in His dealings with them. I now confess that, even on this side of the Easter happening, and after a lifetime of trying to follow the Christ, I have barely evolved from the kindergarden state of the Christian faith.

There is still a lot of milk left in my spiritual diet. I, along with Peter, can confidently proclaim Jesus to be "the Christ of God." Contrary to the postresurrection Peter, I am not so confident or eager about denying self, taking up the cross, and risking all to follow Jesus Christ.

Abraham's Offspring

"If you are Christ's, then you are Abraham's offspring, heirs according to promise. . . . You are all one in Christ Jesus."

Paul's declaration may not have been very popular in his day—perhaps not today either—but ought to be gladly acknowledged and heralded by Christians of every race and color throughout the world. We are one family, one kingdom, whatever our national origin or ancestry, our church or denomination. Our baptism into Christ brings us into the family of God.

Our adherence to the Law does not make us or keep us the children of God. The Law is still of value in revealing our spiritual poverty and our absolute need for God's grace, but it can in no way make us right with God. It continues to be the basis and a guide for daily living, but it is never a means of salvation. We are baptized into Christ, who has kept the Law in our stead and freed us from its stringent demands and consequential judgments to freely and joyfully love and serve God as His beloved children and servants.

Our faith in God's acceptance of us, His gift of forgiveness and grace, makes it possible for us to celebrate our eternal union with Him and with all those who belong to Him. As a consequence of that faith and that relationship to God as He is revealed through Christ, we embrace a morality or standard of ethics that is far superior to the Law as interpreted by legalists, ancient or modern. This is the standard or morality of love—God's love for the whole human family—imparted to us and reflected through us to our fellow beings throughout the world in which we live.

When the Nights Are Dark

The prophet Jeremiah appears to bounce back and forth between complaints and praises. He honestly proclaims his gripes as well as his gratitude. He was often depressed and discouraged. And so are we. We feel at times that God has given up on us, that while we are children of His grace, we fail to meet His demands for servanthood, we fail to effectively carry out His purposes in stemming the tide of wickedness overwhelming our world, we fail to proclaim and demonstrate God's love to people about us.

Yet we know, deep within us, that His love for us never ceases, that when our faith falters, He is ever faithful, that He cares for us and will never let us go.

We need to be reassured that the world is in God's hands and, despite the persistent rebelliousness of its children, He will accomplish His purposes within it. It is not important that we see the results of our servanthood; it is important that we trust God and His Spirit within us—and that we wait quietly and patiently for the revealing of His kingdom.

So let come what may—adversity or affliction, enmity or opposition, feelings of defeat, even the ridicule of our peers, we are the redeemed children and chosen servants of our God, and we are His forever.

"Sing to the Lord; praise the Lord!"

Sixth Sunday After Pentecost

Matthew 10:34–42 (A)

Peace or Violence?

"I have not come to bring peace, but a sword."

Our first reaction to Jesus' words in this lesson is one of bewilderment and confusion. We are often tempted to regard this as one of the great paradoxes of the gospels and respectfully pass on to those portions of Christ's teachings that are more agreeable to our frame of mind. "But Jesus elsewhere blesses the peacemakers," we protest. Well, we protest too much. Because divine truth can never be adequately presented semantically—by means of human language—it will often appear to be paradoxical. Jesus did promise peace: "Peace I leave with you; My peace I give to you," He said in John's gospel (14:27). But within the same three years of Christ's ministry He proclaimed: "I have not come to bring peace, but a sword."

While we spent most of our Sunday school years picturing our Lord as a gentle, meek peacemaker, this is not the whole picture. When Jesus dealt with the poor, the ill, the simple-minded, the sinners, the publicans, and the fishermen, He spoke words of comfort and challenge, peace and promise. But when He addressed the sanctimonious, hypocritical establishment of His day, He spoke like a revolutionary. His words were like a sharp sword, slicing into the hides and hearts of those oppressive and self-centered leaders like a knife into soft butter.

Our Lord never prescribed or perpetrated violence. Violence, nevertheless, was the result of some of the things He said and did. He met it head-on, as we must, with love, even to the extent of forgiving the very executioners who nailed Him to a cross.

We cannot avoid or ignore the violent events that transpire about us any more than did our Lord and His faithful followers in the face of Israel's legalism or Rome's paganism. Our responsibility is to put our reputations, jobs, incomes, even our lives, on the line to confront violence with courage and hatred with love.

Dying Daily—Living Forever

Regardless of our past, no matter how abominable our wrongdoings, whether such sins be unconscious or deliberate, our Lord's sacrifice is sufficient and God's forgiveness is complete. This does not, however, cancel out our responsibilities in respect to the present and the future. The fact that we are not totally dead to sin, whatever our intention and determination, is indicated by Paul himself when he stated in his first Letter to Timothy: "I am the foremost of sinners" (1:15). This has become obvious in our own lives as we look daily to the cross to realize anew God's gracious forgiveness. We are, nevertheless, in the daily process of dying to sin. That dying will not be completed until we are set free from these mortal coils, but it continues as we cease yielding to self-interests and self-concern, cease seeking our own gratification at the expense of others, as we become increasingly successful at overcoming our lusts, covetousness, bigotry, impatience, apathy, and whatever else clouds our relationship with God and fellow creatures.

We have, in effect, been crucified with Christ and raised with Him from the dead. We are new people, focused upon new goals, compelled by new motives, committed to new objectives. We have been reborn. All things have become new. Having been delivered from sin's destructive bondage and having received God's love and the gift of everlasting life made available through the resurrected Christ, we are now free to love and accept ourselves and to dedicate our lives to loving our fellow persons as ourselves.

We die daily—to the control of sin and self-centeredness; we live forever in loving service to God and our brothers and sisters in the human family.

The Power of Faith

Christianity is a faith religion. No other religion in the world makes so much of faith. "Abraham believed God," we read concerning the father of believers, "and it was reckoned to him as righteousness" (Romans 4:3). "Behold, God is my salvation; I will trust, and will not be afraid," proclaimed Isaiah (12:2). "Let not your hearts be troubled; believe in God, believe also in Me," stated Jesus (John 14:1). "Daughter, your faith has made you well," He said to the woman of our lesson, and when hearing about the death of Jairus' daughter, "Do not fear, only believe."

Many of us who profess to follow Christ have never really grasped this, the prime essential of the Gospel. We press upon Jesus Christ as did the crowds who gathered to witness His miracle-working power, but we often fail to embrace Him in a reckless, all-out, totally trusting faith. We believe in God; we pray when we are desperate; we try to follow the example of Christ, yet we hardly know what it means to allow this Christ to be living and active at the very center of our beings. We come to Him; we hear Him speak to us through the Word; we express our needs through the liturgy and the prayers; we proclaim His praises in the hymns we sing; we indeed touch Him in the Eucharist— and yet we are still assailed by guilt feelings, plagued with weaknesses, defeated and overcome with failures, incapacitated by tragedies, and very much in doubt about the outcome of it all. The reason? Perhaps our touch has not really been the touch of faith. We may be jostling Christ rather than embracing Him.

We believe, O Lord; help us with our unbelief!

Wednesday   *2 Corinthians 8:1–9, 13–14 (B)*

From Rags to Riches

"For your sake He became poor, so that by His poverty you might become rich."

When we think about the amazing grace of God as demonstrated by His Son, Jesus Christ, who enriched our lives through His willingness to embrace poverty, we then see something of the course He has laid out for us. In the measure that God pours out His riches upon us, we ought to channel them into areas of need about us. We are not created to be reservoirs that accumulate, but pipelines that direct and conduct the flow into poverty-stricken lives about us. As we are the recipients of divine gifts through our Spirit-filled parents and peers, so we are the transmitters of such gifts to the human family with whom we have contact. This is the way of God in our world today, and it is thus that He advances His kingdom through His children. He intervenes in the lives of the poor and oppressed through His interveners. We are such interveners; we can limit God's flow of power and wealth into other lives by our selfishness or bless and increase that flow by our sacrificial acts of love.

How privileged we are to be His stewards and trustees in the great task of making His love known and experienced on this planet! There is a spiritual principle here with which we can well afford to experiment: The one who gives much receives much, and the one who holds fast to what he or she possesses has very little to give to others. It is the latter person who is truly poverty-stricken.

Let us love generously; we have nothing to lose but our self-centered notions of what is of true value and worth. We have everything to gain and the guarantee that we will be rich indeed in terms of those things that really count in this life and the next.

Thursday   *Luke 9:51–62 (C)*

Followers or Fellow-Travelers?

There was no lack of fellow travelers dogging Jesus' footsteps, but He was not pleased with this kind of popularity. It therefore became necessary for our Lord to call forth out of this group a band of "inner circle" disciples, men and women who would follow Him out of love and loyalty, selflessly and sacrificially.

There were several "takers," those who responded enthusiastically to Jesus' invitation, but few who could pass the test and measure up to His prerequisites. "I will follow You wherever You go," exuberantly exclaimed one young man. Instead of opening His arms in glad welcome, Jesus deliberately discouraged this fine young fellow. He recognized the enthusiast's words as the words of one who had not counted the cost, and Jesus wanted it clearly understood that there is a battle to fight, a price to pay, a cross to carry, a life to lose, in the business of following Him.

Jesus' message to all of these potential recruits was an emphatic declaration that His claims upon them are paramount, that when He invites or commands, obedience must be instant and absolute, with no interventions, reservations, or postponements.

Our Lord's message to us is disturbing as well as challenging. It indicates that we who call ourselves by His name must throw out our adulterated concepts of discipleship and become authentic in our Christian lives. There is nothing easygoing about Christianity—the kind of Christianity that Jesus lived and proclaimed. It is costly and demanding. It promises not softness but suffering, not comfort but challenge, not safety but sacrifice. There is peace; there is also persecution. There is security, joy, and abundance; there is also blood, sweat, and tears.

May God grant to us the grace to live valid Christian lives.

Free to Love

While we live under law (the standards, the morality that makes it possible for us to be a society and to act and interact as a community of people), our relationship to God is not dependent upon the Law or upon the rules and regulations inaugurated by men. Having submitted to the redeeming love of God, we have been set free from the Law's demands as a means of salvation to embrace a higher law, a higher morality, the morality of love, which ought to guide our lives and issue forth from them as a consequence of God's love and indwelling. Whereas we are responsible for keeping man's laws that do not come in between us and God's higher law and purposes, our eternal salvation does not come through such obedience.

Christ has set us free—to love. It is in this freedom that we are enjoined to lovingly relate to one another, to share with, to serve, to support one another. Thus freed from the need to gratify our fleshly concerns, we can invest in the physical and spiritual needs of others. In this freedom we can shed our anxieties, our guilt feelings, even our concern about our identities, and freely, joyfully, haphazardly give of ourselves in loving service to the human family.

Let us always be aware of subtle temptations to regress into periods of self-concern and self-service. They are always with us, these tendencies and temptations, and we know what happens when we court them and ultimately yield to them. We have been set free from these shackles that bind us, for a deeper investment of our lives in the service of others, a determination, by God's grace, to put the needs of our fellow persons even before our own.

Christ has set us free to love. It's a freedom we need to exercise daily at home, at school, at work, and elsewhere—if we are to grow in our Christian lives.

Run for Your life

Elijah was on the run. He had stood up against the ungodly forces of Ahab and Jezebel and had revealed the far greater powers of his God over the followers of Baal. The victory was bitter-sweet; it did not accomplish what he expected; the ruling powers did not turn to the

Lord, and now Jezebel was out to get Elijah. He was frightened, and he took refuge in a cave. But not for long. He met God there. "What are you doing here, Elijah?" (v. 13). Elijah poured out his complaints: The whole world, or so it seemed, was against him; he alone remained faithful to the true God; he was afraid that he might even die at the hands of the enemy.

We who are pastors have often felt a little like Elijah on Monday morning. Sunday services appeared to go well. We felt that God spoke through our preaching and our listeners were moved by the Spirit. At least we did the best we could. But nothing of any consequence happened, and we take our Monday-morning refuge in our caves of despondency and despair.

It may be that Saturday morning is your day to crawl into a cave or a corner to moan out your complaints. Whatever the day, it happens to all of us at times. We sincerely try our best to do what God would have us do; but nothing of consequence happens, and we are defeated and despondent.

We discover, sometimes to our amazement, that God meets us there. It may not necessarily be a consoling meeting. He may tell us, in His "still, small voice" (v. 12), that the consequences of our ministry during the past week are not to be our primary concern; He will take care of them. And then He may well order us out of our cave to get on with the job of advancing His kingdom. There is another day, another week, ahead of us. We are not promised great victories, but are commanded to sow small seeds. All He requires is that we be faithful to Him; He will be responsible for the results.

Seventh Sunday After Pentecost

Matthew 11:25–30 (A)

Invitation to Fulfillment

We read in the first book of the Bible that God "breathed into his nostrils the breath of life; and man became a living being" (2:7). Man and woman were created in God's image, spiritually, but lost that image and became disjointed, distorted invalids. Thus the breath of creation was followed in the New Testament by the breath of redemption and then of sanctification: "And they were filled with the Holy Spirit." This means that a human being plus the Spirit of God equals a total, complete, fulfilled person, and it is this that gives identity and meaning and purpose to the individual lives of men and women.

This is the kind of life and experience that our Lord calls us to. In this Gospel lesson He extends the invitation to this fulfillment. Our lesson begins with Jesus' prayer of thanksgiving that this invitation is extended to "babes" in terms of wisdom and understanding. This makes every one of us eligible. "Come to Me, all who labor and are heavy laden, for I will give you rest," said Jesus. The Holy Spirit must motivate us for this "coming" by revealing to us our desperate need for God, the sins that stand between us and God. We must recognize that we are sick before we will accept the prescription of the Great Physician; we must realize that the heavy burdens we carry and the labors we struggle through are too much for us, before we lay them upon that One who will carry them in our stead. Only then will we "come," approach and appropriate Him, to receive and to believe, to embrace in faith our God who came to us in Christ.

The invitation and promise of our Lord, however, includes another factor that we must acquiesce to if we are to be total persons: "Take My yoke upon you. . . ." There are many who indeed do "come" to Jesus in confession of sin and acceptance of Christ as Savior—only to avoid or neglect altogether this latter prescription—and then they wonder why their lives are still incomplete and unfulfilled. We are to go all the way with God and accept not only His promises but His "yoke."

What, then, is the "yoke" of our Lord? Need we ask? It is the world, the sin-sick, disease-ridden, catastrophic world about us. It includes its starving, deprived, oppressed, its addicted and enslaved, men and women in need, whatever their color, race, or religion, and wherever they may be found. This is the yoke of our Lord, the yoke He commands us to take upon ourselves. Until we do, we have little or no claim to His promises and may never "find rest for [our] souls."

A Message for Wretched People

Our allegiance is to God through Jesus Christ. Our relationship to Him is based not on what we have done for God, but on what He has done on our behalf. Christ has measured up to God's standards and has taken upon Himself the penalty for our imperfections. We have been declared righteous, perfect in Christ, apart from the Law. We still need laws to direct and protect the lives and destinies of people, but they are incapable of turning sinners into saints.

The ancient yet always relevant Law does portray goodness and justice. It portrays, as well, my utter inability to be truly good and just. I simply do not have within my nature the capability of reaching those high standards. God knows I have tried. He knows, as well, how I again and again so miserably fail. I have the desire, even the will, to do what is right. I do not, in myself, have the power. Thus there is conflict, agonizing conflict, and I am driven to the wall in despair. It is a conflict which, in one measure or another, will persist as long as I live upon this world.

The answer is in Jesus Christ. God through this Christ adopted me as His son apart from the Law. I am set free from the Law's demands, and free from its judgment, free to immerse myself in God's great love, and free to serve Him forever.

This is Paul's testimony. It is mine. It continues to be the testimony of every man and woman who follows Jesus Christ.

Some People One Cannot Reach

There were some people Jesus Himself could not reach. This Gospel lesson deals with what was possibly the second time our Lord preached at His hometown synagogue. And for the second time His message and ministry there was heckled and rejected. His first visit resulted in a riot that drove Him out of the city and might have taken His life save for

God's intervention. The second visit continued to rile the synagogue crowd; they simply could not understand how this man Jesus could speak with such authority and wisdom. After all, was He not just a carpenter, the son of Mary, and a brother to her children, some of whom were still living there? Thereafter Jesus issued the well-known statement often used to this very day: "A prophet is not without honor, except in his own country, and among his own kin, and in his own house."

"They took offense at Him. . . . And He could do no mighty work there. . . . And He marveled because of their unbelief." He left His mark, nonetheless, for He laid hands on and healed a few sick people. Whether it is in our hometown or at some other point along our sojourn, in home or office, Main Street or shopping center, we will come across people whom we apparently cannot reach, who turn deaf ears to our verbal witness and unresponsive hearts to our God-inspired intentions.

So be it. There are some people God Himself cannot reach. We can, nevertheless, leave our mark with them, a witness of love and concern that may eventually find its way into their hearts. They may put down but cannot entirely obliterate the truly good deeds we leave behind. There are times when our deeds of love proclaim more loudly and effectively the Gospel of God's love.

If nothing else happens because of our witness, our actions and deeds may prepare the way for the witness of others who follow in our wake.

Wednesday   *2 Corinthians 12:7–10 (B)*

The Paradox of Paradoxes

"When I, am weak, then I am strong."

Over against the ecstatic high points of irrepressible joy—and we cherish them for ourselves as well as for others—are those balloon-puncturing experiences that flatten us in despair. It may well be that we need both in our lives to keep us close to our Creator and Redeemer. The remarkable thing is that the Spirit of God is often more obvious and more capable of using us during those low, thorn-in-the-flesh points in our lives.

The thing that most often drives us into depression is some pernicious, unconquered fault or weakness in our makeup. We are certainly not expected to revel in our weaknesses; we need to overcome or control these inbred distortions that afflict us and may even harm others around us; but we need not crumble in defeat or falter in despair.

201

They may actually, though indirectly, be the means by which we recognize and learn to rely on God's promised, all-sufficient grace. God is great. He accepts us as we are. He can work out His purposes through us—even in spite of us. We need only to continually submit to Him our whole beings—strengths, weaknesses, and all—and let Him have His way with us.

May God speak to you as He did to Paul: "My grace is sufficient for you, for My power is made perfect in weakness."

Thursday   *Luke 10:1–12, 16 (C)*

Authentic Evangelism

Like the seventy disciples of our Lord's day, we, too, are meant to be thrust out, like "lambs in the midst of wolves," into our secular and revolutionary world. Our immediate assignment may not to be to preach God's Word of judgment or grace to those we meet. Nor are we assigned or equipped to convert people. We are to seek out those people to whom we can relate, who will respond to our friendship. We are to share with them, listen to them. When we have gained their confidence and they begin to share their pains as well as their joys with us, we are to "heal the sick" or to use every means within our power, and the power that God provides, to meet those people and minister to them at the point of their immediate and recognized need. Our God may not transmit through us the power to heal diseases, but we do have the power to show love and concern, and there are resources within our reach to bring people into contact with healing forces. We can help to heal their loneliness, to raise them out of despair, to restore their dignity, or to provide for some of their material needs in order to alleviate their suffering. We are always to seek to relate them to that One who is the Answer to their deepest needs, to proclaim the Good News that "the kingdom of God has come near" to them—that God is here. Jesus went to the cross on their behalf, and they can be set free from their sins and hang-ups and be guaranteed eternal life.

Through our love and concern we can introduce people to and communicate to them the concern of a loving God—and the power He offers to bring healing and enrichment, meaning and purpose into their lives. They have probably heard the message before. Now, as never before, they may see it demonstrated before them in our love and concern for humanity. Now, as never before, they may be moved to respond to it.

Evangelism is our task; this ought to be our method. There are risks involved, and we may never see the results of our witness to most of those within our arena of responsibility. God never promised visible results, only an open door, a harvest field of opportunities. May He find us faithful and obedient to our calling as His ministers and servants!

Friday   *Galatians 6:1–10, 14–16 (C)*

Front and Center

"But far be it from me to glory except in the cross of our Lord Jesus Christ."

Paul certainly rejoiced in the resurrection of Jesus Christ, but he "gloried" in the cross of Christ. The cross is not something we experience once and for all and then leave behind to concentrate totally upon the resurrection. Without the resurrection the cross would be of little significance. Likewise, without the cross of Christ there would be no resurrection. Both are essential to genuine Christianity and effective Christian living. An overemphasis on the cross apart from the resurrection might promote a negative, joyless, powerless experience and witness. An overemphasis on the resurrection apart from the cross might result in unrealistic, ecstatic, humanless, heaven-bound antics that would offer a very inadequate witness to the world about us.

We need to pass by the cross on Calvary's hill before we proceed to the empty tomb, and this is a daily experience for God's redeemed children and chosen servants. Pentecost is the consequence of both the cross and the resurrection of Jesus Christ. Apart from either one of these significant events the pentecostal experience is not possible, and any attempts to bring it about or fake it will meet with ignominious failure.

We daily leave our sins at the foot of the cross; it is there that we die to self-interests and claim anew divine forgiveness. We commit ourselves to the power of the resurrection; there we are made new creatures and are guaranteed our ultimate resurrection as the eternal sons and daughters of God. It adds up to Pentecost, the indwelling of the crucified and resurrected Lord Jesus Christ and the power of His Spirit to enable us to be Christs-incarnate in our broken world.

"We preach Christ crucified," said Paul (1 Corinthians 1:23). It is only when we do this that other significant truths concerning God's life and purposes and gifts for His children will fall into their proper places.

The Prophets Among Us

If Ezekiel should materialize and show up in the pulpit of your church one Sunday morning, what might he say? It might go something like this:

"God will soon gather together His kingdom throughout our world. There are some of you here who are not yet a part of His kingdom. You are deluding yourselves into believing that you are God's children. You make your confessions and professions and assume that your religious exercises are accepted by God; you have not, however, put aside your materialistic idols and committed yourselves to His purposes. You seek to use Him for comfort and good fortune and some guarantee of immortality, but you have not allowed Him to use you by revealing and demonstrating His redeeming love among the peoples of your world. You continue to live to and for yourselves. While God has through Christ borne the cross for you and through His suffering has set you free from sin's bondage, your response to His grace has not resulted in your taking up your cross on behalf of others. Your religion is an intensely self-gratifying activity, and regardless of the slogans you adopt and the convictions you subscribe to, you are in dire danger of being excluded from the kingdom of God."

Does your pastor ever preach like this? Is it possible that he is inspired by the same God that spoke through Ezekiel of old? There are prophets among us today—and he may be one of them.

Eighth Sunday After Pentecost

Matthew 13:1–9 (18–23) (A)

The Search for Disciples

They didn't have computers or vocational testing in Jesus' day, but our Lord utilized some very effective methods in selecting and training leaders for the building of God's kingdom. One of these is presented in this Gospel lesson, initiating what we know as the parabolic method of teaching.

Jesus began His ministry following His baptism by attracting men to Himself and challenging them to loving service. Now it was time for our Lord to separate the men from the boys, the followers from the fellow travelers, and to concentrate on equipping His devoted disciples for the great work that lay before them. The great majority of the huge crowds that emptied towns and villages to see and hear this One called Jesus were curious sign-seekers, looking for spectacular feats. Many brought their sick to be healed; others wanted Jesus to become their king, who would make Israel a free, abundant, and powerful nation. There was a small group, loosely attached disciples, who followed Jesus from time to time but were in question as to their future loyalty toward Him. Then, of course, there was the nucleus, the twelve, who were the closest to Christ in love and loyalty.

Jesus was not yet to abandon the multitudes, but He was beginning to concentrate upon the few. His teaching in parables was a device for the achievement of this end, selecting and stabilizing the loyalty and love of these men who would be so important to the church and the advancement of the kingdom in the near future. He continued to preach, but in such a way as to reveal or obscure the truth. To the curious, the sign-seekers, the shallow and superficial, His teachings would be obscure or hidden. Not seeing a good show, tiring of His magic, no longer being entertained by His activities or receiving any material benefits from Him, they would drop out and look for someone else to follow. To those, however, who hungered and thirsted after righteousness, who persistently sought for truth, His teachings would gradually be revealed and made known.

Jesus was, and is to this very day, searching for disciples. The primary goal of the church today is to search for, call, and equip disciples. May our response be the response of Isaiah to God's call to him: "Here am I! Send me" (6:8).

Monday *Romans 8:18–25 (A)*

Our Sufferings Versus Glory-to-Be-Revealed

Paul had no illusions about the Christian faith being a primrose path or a perpetually ecstatic experience. Lest we be phony in our representations of the Christian life, we need also to be disillusioned about what it means to follow Jesus Christ. It is not a continual mountaintop experience; we have to slog through deep, muddy ravines and around dangerous precipices. Most of us are aware of this by the time we reach some maturity in our growth as Christians. Our testimony becomes that of the psalmist: "Though I walk in the midst of trouble, Thou dost preserve my life . . . and Thy right hand delivers me" (Psalm 138:7). "In the world you have tribulation," said Jesus, "but be of good cheer, I have overcome the world" (John 16:33). We are to "suffer with [Christ] in order that we may also be glorified with Him," wrote Paul in the verse preceding our Epistle lesson.

Even as we rejoice in our secure relationships as God's redeemed and adopted sons and daughters, "we . . . groan inwardly as we wait for adoption as sons [and daughters]," said Paul, and we day-by-day grow into the conviction that present-time sufferings "are not worth comparing with the glory that is to be revealed to us."

Some immature Christians want that "glory" now. The insistence of those who say they have it, that they are presently living within it, contradicts the witness of Paul and the lifelong experiences of unnumbered saints before us. There is some danger that what they have is self-concocted or self-induced, or is promoted by some foreign spirit that seeks to lead them astray.

God does not intend our sufferings; He involves Himself in them. It is His presence in our trials and tribulations that gives them meaning and purpose. Paul enjoins us to enlarge our hope in that which is absolutely certain, to wait with patience for God's total deliverance from all that causes us to suffer. It is soon to take place, and we will be encompassed "with the glory that is to be revealed to us."

Discipleship Means Involvement

People cozy up to the kind of Christianity that is equated with plush pews and pious prayers, even if it involves an offering plate and a weekly pledge. The kind demonstrated by Christ and reflected in His first followers is something difficult to comprehend. Some of us ignore it or relegate it to another age and bypass it. We may even find reason to criticize the occasional St. Francis or Schweitzer who do take our Lord's exhortations seriously and attempt to obey them in some realistic manner.

Discipleship means involvement. Our Lord set the pace, and He expects His disciples to keep it. "As the Father has sent Me, even so I send you" (John 20:21). Jesus indentified Himself with the agonies of humankind. He became involved in their crying needs. To be a disciple of Jesus means that we who accept Him as our Savior must also accept Him as our Lord and Master. To follow Him means that we continue in His course for our lives. We are expected not simply to criticize the distortions of humanity from the pews and pulpits of our sanctuaries, but to become involved in the blood and tears, sorrows and sufferings, of God's creatures in suburb and ghetto, alley and freeway, town and country, wherever they may be found.

The task we are called upon and sent into our world to carry out certainly includes proclaiming forgiveness of sins through faith in Christ. It means, as well, that we stand up with the oppressed against their oppressors, that we try to exorcise the "demons" of life and culture that rob people of their self-respect and dignity, their rights and opportunities, even the demons of pride and prejuduce and ignorance and apathy within us that serve to inhibit the claim of disadvantaged people to the same rights and opportunities available to us.

Discipleship means involvement. As our Lord suffered on our behalf, we are expected to suffer on behalf of others—to lose our life in service to them, only to truly find it anew in the incomparable joy of being a minister and servant of the living and eternal God.

Something to Celebrate

Truly, we have much to celebrate as the sons and daughters of God. We have, through Christ, become the recipients of God's whole treasure-house of spiritual gifts. Even before we were born—before the world itself was made—we were destined to be His children. Christ's death on the cross set us free from the Law's demands. All charges against us were blotted out. Our sins were forgiven. Reconciled to the divine family, we are now an integral part of God's plan to reconcile the whole world to Himself.

It is indeed something we cannot comprehend, but God created us and chose us to be His people, and this was God's purpose and plan from the very beginning. It was made known to us and made possible for us through Jesus Christ. Through Christ and His indwelling Spirit, the brand of God's ownership was burned indelibly into our hearts. With the gracious gift of His Spirit comes the guarantee that all of God's gifts, though at present unseen and little understood, are already ours and will be revealed to us in God's own time.

There is much to celebrate, but let us not forget that it could never have been possible except for the tragedy of the cross. Our redemption, our restoration to God, was "through His blood," the blood of Jesus Christ. The sentiment that God is so loving that He forgives our sins is just that—pure sentiment—unless we recognize that the only ground for such forgiveness is the tremendous tragedy of the cross. Forgiveness, which is relatively easy for us to accept, cost the agony of Calvary. Let us never take forgiveness lightly. All the riches that we inherit as God's children are ours only because we are forgiven, and for that God paid a price—a price that we will never fully comprehend.

Thursday   *Luke 10:25-37 (C)*

And Who Is My Neighbor?

The lawyer was not about to challenge the revered "love God love your neighbor" commandment. He also knew that his colleagues could not challenge his love for God. After all, he said the right words. He went through the required motions. He carried on a very respectable kind of life. But the "love your neighbor" part of the commandment stopped him cold. This was where the authenticity of his faith could be challenged. He had only one recourse: "Who is my neighbor?"

I don't know if Jesus' answer was a surprise to the lawyer, but His recital of the parable of the Good Samaritan is a revealing and judgmental condemnation upon much that goes under the name of Christianity today. It also tends to make so much of my professed or assumed piety appear to be something less than authentic. As long as

208

I say the right words and belong to the right church, my faith cannot be proved or disproved by mortal man. But the parable of the Good Samaritan pins me to the wall and demands that I "put up or shut up." There is no question as to the why and what-for of my salvation. It comes from God; it comes as a gift of His love. It is not enough, however, to say the right words like "I love You, Jesus," or "I accept You, Christ." There must be total committal, a placing of myself at God's disposal, the presentation of my body as a living sacrifice. These are not mere words; it is an act of the will. And the only way I can act in this manner towards the invisible God is to commit myself to the needs of my visible neighbor.

"Who is my neighbor?" Jesus gave the answer—loudly and clearly. Every human being is my neighbor—and that without regard to color, background, or social status. Christ's overall command to the church is to preach the Gospel to every creature. The personal requirement for every Christian is to love one's fellow beings. And God's insistence is that we love them—not with sentimental or dutiful words, but with Christ-impelled actions.

Friday   *Colossians 1:1–14 (C)*

A Time for Gratitude

"He has delivered us from the dominion of darkness and transferred us to the kingdom of His beloved Son."

How grateful we are to God for what He has done for us, for the clear revelation of His love through His Son, our Savior and Lord, Jesus Christ! Through this Christ we have experienced forgiveness and redemption. By way of this Christ we have been set free from the bondage of darkness and despair. In this Christ we become the very heirs of God and share in the inheritance promised to all His sons and daughters from the beginning of time.

He is full of God, this Jesus, God-incarnate. The Word became flesh, and manifests all the glory and beauty, the splendor and majesty, the love and grace of the Godhead—as St. Paul emphasizes in the verses following our reading. We can know God only as He is revealed through this Christ, and so Christ then becomes for us that One who puts it all together, the Head of the body and of the church, our Lord and Leader, our Shepherd and King.

This is the Christ to whom we have committed our lives. This is the One we will worship and follow today. Let us begin this day with gratitude.

Be a Prophet

"I am no prophet," said Amos, and yet he most certainly was. "Speaking up for Christ is not only the history, but the whole future of the Church," said Dr. Oswald Hoffmann. "Paul listed a first gift of the Spirit as prophecy, which is proclamation. This means witnessing to the good name and good news of Jesus Christ." In a very real sense, we are all prophets or proclaimers. "But I am a herdsman, and a dresser of sycamore trees. . . ." "But I am just a housewife, or farmer, or nurse, or businessman. . . . I am no prophet."

Prophesying refers to proclaiming. This has often included revelations concerning some future judgment or event, but is not limited to that. The Word of God is to be proclaimed. In the Old Testament this was usually expressed in terms of proclaiming the law of God. Jesus measured up to the Law on our behalf, and He proclaimed and commanded us to proclaim the glorious Word of God in respect to His redeeming love, His bounteous grace toward His human creatures. Nor is prophesying only a matter of preaching. It is primarily bearing witness to something great and wonderful that has happened in our lives, to what God through Christ has done for us.

There are people in your daily course through life to whom you cannot preach. Yet you can leave with them a prophetic witness—or prepare them for it in your acts of love and concern toward them. As important as your vocation may be—and they all may be sanctified by God's presence—even more important is your call to be a prophet, a witnesser, a proclaimer, a demonstrator, a vehicle and channel of the blessed Word of God. You are not "just a housewife, or farmer, or businessman . . ."; you are a prophet! "So—proclaim wherever you are!"

Ninth Sunday
After Pentecost
Matthew 13:24-30 (36-43) (A)

The Christian in Our World Today

The parable which makes up this Gospel lesson paints a picture of perpetual conflict. The world is a battleground where the forces of good and evil are in constant warfare. There are moments when evil appears to have the upper hand. The atrocities that take place about us have us frightened and insecure. The agony of our own inner beings as we do battle, sometimes unsuccessfully, against the rebellious, selfish taints and tendencies of our humanity, leaves us confused and frustrated. We are involved in struggle—fierce, vicious, unabated. The outcome, according to our Lord's analogy, is not in doubt. When the day of harvest arrives, God will supernaturally intervene and the forces of evil will be eternally defeated.

We long desperately for the day of harvest, when evil shall be no more and we shall know and experience the meaning of ultimate and eternal victory. Jesus does not tell us much about the "why" of struggle, of evil's presence in our world and in our beings. Perhaps this struggle is a necessary part of our redemption; perhaps this crucible experience, with all of its anguish and agony, is essential to our Christian maturity and development; perhaps there is no other way of learning total surrender to and dependence upon God.

The law of all nature—that life is given and enriched through struggle and travail, pain and agony—is no less true in our spiritual lives. It is our task to learn how to exist within this struggle, how to turn failures into successes, how to develop and mature within the throes of conflict and find therein a measure of joy and effectiveness. And it is here, in the midst of daily conflict and struggle, that we are called and equipped to advance the kingdom of God and to contribute to the great harvest God has promised.

211

Praying in the Spirit

Prayer is really a spiritual act; it is no wonder that "we do not know how to pray as we ought." It is only when the Spirit of God within our human frames communicates with God, who is spirit, that there can be effective communication between our dimension and that of our invisible God. Human semantics is a very inadequate and imperfect instrument or vehicle of communication between the human and the divine. Therefore, in the act of prayer, sometimes with words, most often through prayers we cannot even utter, the Spirit expresses for us that which is unutterable.

"Do you not know that your body is a temple of the Holy Spirit within you, which you have from God?" queried Paul (1 Corinthians 6:19). There are both conscious and unconscious aspects to our personalities. We are responsible for the conscious aspect, and that means a continual subjection of our bodies and minds to the power of God's Spirit. If that is under His control, we can be assured that those matters of which we are not conscious are in the hands of God. It is then that God listens not only to our fumbling words, but hears the prayers of His Spirit within the temple of our bodies. Our words are fallible and error-prone; not so the unutterable groanings of the Holy Spirit. Our prayers are not always answered or accepted, because they are often motivated by self-interest; not so the prayers of the Spirit within us.

Our primary concern must be to keep our "temples" clear and clean of anything that may defile them so the Spirit may "help us in our weakness"; then there will arise from our innermost being those intercessions of the Spirit that God does hear and respond to because they are "according to the will of God."

The Lord Will Provide

One of Jesus' most striking miracles, particularly in view of the large numbers of individuals affected, is the feeding of the five thousand, related in the verses immediately following our Scripture reading. In some ways the miracle is a very strange one. The religious leaders of Christ's day were planning a way to get rid of Him. On the other hand, there was a movement afoot, probably known and encouraged by the disciples, to compel Jesus to come forth and declare Himself as king of Israel. Now, as if to accentuate His popularity and standing with the people, He performs this amazing miracle which could only serve to fire up their enthusiasm and intensify their desire to crown Him as their king.

This was not, of course, our Lord's purpose in this miracle. If we were to ascertain just what His purpose might be, we would have to begin with Mark's assertion that Jesus "saw a great throng, and He had compassion on them." His concern for them led to His efforts to teach them, to draw them to Himself and the life He had come to impart to God's human creatures. That, in turn, led Him to reveal His power to meet people's needs in the feeding of the five thousand.

It was not essential that He feed this multitude before Him. It was not a matter of their starving. Yet Jesus took special care, drawing on supernatural power and provision, to feed this mass of humanity that had been following Him and hanging on to His every word.

It is a beautiful expression and example of God's concern for His creatures. The Lord will provide. This is not a trite phrase; it is eternal truth which we have experienced over and over again. It is God's desire that we continue to rely on His promises, to demonstrate the audacity of faith that expects great things though there be nothing visible upon which to build. This is far more reliable than creeping common sense that adheres to facts which are mere shadows and forgets the chief fact, that we have an almighty God and Father, Helper and Friend, at our side who is at all times concerned about our material needs.

Wednesday   *Ephesians 2:13–22 (B)*

We Belong to One Another

Every human being is the object and beneficiary of God's gift of eternal love. Only those who by faith lay hold of this divine offering, however, who accept and live by this saving grace, can discover and experience the salvation that God has prepared for His creatures. Whereas God's love is a gift which cannot be merited by human efforts to aspire to divine standards, God's deliverance from sin and self-service sets us free to give our lives to good works by way of loving God and communicating His love to humanity about us. This is one of the very important purposes of our salvation, that we might serve God and people and thus fulfill the destiny for which we were created.

It is God's love as manifested in Christ that makes us equal, in God's eyes, with all persons and makes all persons equal with us. We differ

213

in many ways: intelligence and talents, training and temperament, background and opportunity. Under God, however, there is no distinction. His all-compassing love levels all barriers and accounts every human creature of equal value and worth.

There are no "foreigners or strangers" (TEV) in God's family, only brothers and sisters. And all of us are the members of one body, the body of Christ, and are commissioned to work together in carrying out His purposes.

Thursday   *Luke 10:38–42 (C)*

The Perils of Distraction

Two statements are recorded concerning the attitudes and character of two friends of Jesus, Martha and Mary. The first is a *comment from Luke*, the author of this Gospel lesson. "But Martha was distracted with much serving," he wrote. He was suggesting, perhaps, that Martha was so taken up with the bustle and hustle of service that she neglected the quietness of worship. She was so busy giving that she was not open to receiving. She may have been unaware that there cannot be effective outflow unless there is intake.

Whatever may have been the import of this comment concerning Martha, it stands as a commentary on the state of affairs in our world today. Men and women, created and called to serve God, have become slaves to their jobs, their property, their lusts; they are victims of distraction.

The second statement is a *commendation from Christ*. "Mary has chosen the good portion," said Jesus, "which shall not be taken away from her." "One thing is needful," Jesus said to Martha. This is what He would say to us today. Probably the most difficult task of the church is to convince men and women in this age of distraction that "one thing is needful." Rather than proclaiming "I believe in God Almighty," people today are indicating that they believe in the almighty dollar, the necessity of financial security, the lust of the flesh, the importance of comfort, and in getting for themselves all they can get out of this life.

We are to be servants in our world. We are such by Christ's call and assignment. This assignment begins at the feet of Jesus, and it returns us periodically to that place of quietness and strength. It is here that we get in touch and keep in tune with God and His purposes. It is in the fellowship of saints around the Word and the Sacrament that we are perpetually renewed and revitalized. It is from there that we are launched out into our Monday-through-Saturday journeys into our discordant world to serve humankind through our earthly calling and to transmit some small touch of divine love and power to despairing, suffering, lonely people who cross our paths.

Friday   *Colossians 1:21–28 (C)*

Suffering for the Sake of Others

It appears to be very important for many Christians today to have leaders with striking personalities. They must possess many gifts or some kind of charisma that attracts and holds their fans. These especially endowed leaders must, in turn, draw their strength and encouragement from the adulation of their followers.

Whereas Paul was certainly a gifted and learned man, he was not known for his charm or followed because of his exciting personality. He "rejoiced in [his] sufferings for [our] sake." It was certainly not his personality that gathered members for the church, but the real presence of Christ coming through him.

In our immaturity we may be tempted to indulge in a sort of personality cult and latch on to leaders who entertain and stimulate and appear to have immediate answers to our every question or problem. When we grow up a little, and this often in spite of such leaders, we begin to recognize what real leadership is all about. The kind of leaders that truly communicate the Gospel may not be carbon copies of Paul, but they will demonstrate a willingness to suffer for the sake of the Gospel —to "complete what is lacking in Christ's afflictions for the sake of His body, that is, the church."

If we are followers, let us be aware of whom we follow. If we are leaders, and most of us are at some point in our lives, let us forsake self-aggrandizement and emulate Jesus Christ. We are to be the servants of those we lead, and share gladly in their sufferings in order that the grace of God may be channeled to their lives through us.

Saturday   *Jeremiah 23:1–6 (B)*

Responsible Leadership

"Woe to the shepherds who destroy and scatter the sheep of my pasture!" says the Lord.

It is often difficult to discern the false shepherds who presume to speak for the Lord throughout our world today. Those who preach a gospel other than that which reveals Christ and His cross as the cornerstone of true faith are certainly to be shunned. There are, however, those who do preach in His name and yet are unwittingly drawing people out of the institutional church. Some of them, by means of the electronic media, are creating invisible congregations that turn away from local Christian groups, wherein they might be able to mature into responsible Christians, and tie on to media personalities that promote a polished, popular, and exciting kind of religious presentation. While we can't fault all of the teachings these electronic shepherds expound, we question the final results and wonder if they are dividing and scattering the Christian flock rather than building up the kingdom of God.

"The Lord is our righteousness." This is truly the Gospel, the Good News, proclaimed as far back as Jeremiah. It is this that was revealed through Jesus Christ, who became the righteousness of God for us, and by way of the cross and His resurrection made possible the gift of God's righteousness to us. Any shepherd who promotes any other righteousness or any other way to get right with God is a false shepherd. This may also be true of any shepherd who knowingly or unknowingly promotes his or her own image and abilities rather than the righteousness, grace, and purposes of God.

Tenth Sunday After Pentecost

Matthew 13:44–52 (A)

Thy Kingdom Come

Up to this point in Jesus' ministry His contemporaries' concepts of God were confined to the rich Old Testament Scriptures that recorded His great acts of deliverance on behalf of Israel and proclaimed His promises of ultimate liberation from their bonds of oppression. They were united in their worship of the one true God and the hope that Israel would one day be restored in all her glory as a great and powerful kingdom.

Jesus had come to reveal to this world what the true kingdom, God's kingdom, was all about. It was a new kind of kingdom, a spiritual kingdom, one not of this world, one that would include people of all nations and races, one that would be fulfilled or fully revealed in a time and dimension beyond this three-dimensional world.

The kingdom parables are the attempts of our Lord to portray such a kingdom. The three parables of this Gospel lesson point up two things about this kingdom of God.

First, *the kingdom of God is expensive.* ". . . like treasure hidden in a field, which a man found. . . . he goes and sells all that he has and buys that field," or "like a merchant . . . who, on finding one pearl of great value, went and sold all that he had and bought it." It cost God the tragedy of the cross; it costs us our very lives. We are to deny ourselves and take up crosses and follow Christ.

Second, *the kingdom of God is exclusive.* ". . . the angels will . . . separate the evil from the righteous. . . ." Not all religious people— even those within the fold of the average congregation—are in the fold of God. Only those who in faith follow Jesus Christ and confess their faith in Him are included in the kingdom of God; all others are excluded.

The kingdom is here. It abides among us. We enter it through Christ —at our baptism. If any have strayed from that kingdom, God grant that in faith they may reenter its portals even today.

217

God and Our Difficult Circumstances

"We know that in everything God works for good with those who love Him, who are called according to His purpose."

The miracle-working power of God becomes obvious, not in His intervention between us and our sufferings, though some of us can bear witness to such apparent divine interventions in our lives, but in the amazing way in which "God works for good with those who love Him. . . ." We can all testify how some of the terrible things that have befallen us became events or instruments which truly did work for good—drawing us closer to God or serving to accomplish His purposes in and through us. Paul believed that God was with him and would work through him whatever the circumstances that pressed in upon him, and he therefore exhorted us to "give thanks in all circumstances" (1 Thessalonians 5:18).

Of this we can be sure: God is with us whatever happens on our daily course through this life. Not only that, but He is able and ready to work out His purposes in and through even the tragic episodes of our lives. When we hurt, God hurts; such is His love for us—even if He does not intervene to shield us from such tragedies. He promises to stay close to us, to help us to cope, and to use our sufferings as well as our joys to accomplish His purposes in and through our lives.

A Remarkable Love-Offering

There is a beautiful incident within the feeding-of-the-five-thousand episode that was remembered and recorded by John alone. Between the famished five thousand and heaven's supernatural provision was a little boy with five barley loaves and two fish. He had brought a lunch with him on this exciting day. He did a selfless, generous thing. He offered his lunch to Jesus to do with as He pleased. It was a profoundly significant act, for it is here, in this simple little incident, that we come across something of the meaning of the cross and of our commission as followers of Jesus Christ. The bridge between God's abundant provision and the world's desperate needs is the sacrificial love-offering. It was made by God Himself, who through Christ descended from His throne of glory, stooped to the humiliating level of our sin, took upon Himself our guilt, and suffered the wages of sin on our behalf. The lad gave all he had; Jesus accepted and blessed this tiny gift, and fed five thousand hungry bodies.

Today you and I, as individuals and members of Christ's body, the church, stand as God's representatives and agents between this world's poverty and heaven's abundant provision. This is our commission, and God holds us, along with the church at large, responsible for channeling His eternal grace to those who are in need. We may appear to be, and often feel ourselves to be, as insignificant as the little boy with his fish and buns, but we are not insignificant to God, and by His grace we will become channels and communicators of His life and love to our fellow persons about us.

Wednesday   *Ephesians 4:1–7, 11–16 (B)*

Help Us to Grow Up

If Christ is our Lord and Leader, we had better set our sights on His prerequisites and standards for our lives and strive to measure up. "Our life in this world is [to be] the same as Christ's," writes John (1 John 4:17b TEV). For one thing, it means that we be kind, gentle, and loving to one another. Why is there so much bickering among the children of God? We are all members of the same body and are motivated and guided by the same Spirit. Yet, like jealous, covetous siblings, we fight among ourselves, jostling, crowding each other, seeking position or honor above the other.

Our gifts, whatever they be, come from the hand of God. They are not designed to give honor to one over another but, together with all who make up Christ's body, to carry out His ojectives and advance His kingdom throughout the world. They are granted to us, not to make us more important—we already know our identity in Christ—but for the purpose of serving the human family about us.

It is time we stop acting like spoiled children, pouting, griping, criticizing, stepping on one another, insisting on our way, or scrambling for some power or position that will boost our ego. We ought to grow up, being grateful for our status as God's ministers, whatever our parish or arena of service, and relate to one another in truth and love. Only then, as the body of Christ, will we be truly effective in our community and world.

God, help us to grow up!

Recipe for Joy

Most of us are learning that we will never discover true happiness if such by itself becomes the primary intent and purpose of our lives, that gleaming gems crumble into worthless dust if we center our ambitions and aspirations on them alone. It is only when we focus our lives upon goals and objectives that are far more important than personal happiness that we are surprised by joy. This is the kind of joy that Jesus offers—the kind that is often "sorrow unmasked" and that fills up those agonizing cavities carved out by long hours of suffering.

Jesus revealed His recipe for joy in His exhortation to "ask . . . seek . . . knock. . . ." It is really the process of finding God—or being found by God—of discovering and being restored to His orbit for our lives by submitting to His saving grace as revealed through the Christ. It is a reliable recipe backed by an infallible guarantee. "For every one who asks receives, and he who seeks finds, and to him who knocks it will be opened," said Jesus. This is the guarantee that is offered by that One who hung the planets on nothing, who created the waters, the land, and the air, who calmed the tempest, who healed the sick and made the blind to see, who raised Christ from the dead, who sent His Spirit to indwell the hearts and lives of His children. And there is no force in all the world that can prevent the fulfillment of this, God's promise through Christ, save the force of our own wills and our rank indifference or stubborn resistance to His divine gifts of mercy and love which He presses upon us.

"Ask . . . seek . . . knock. . . ." not for the things of this life, but for that which God wants to give us. It adds up to total commitment—in scorn of consequences. This is the way to that joy which cannot be stifled or stymied by the tragedies and sorrows, the failures and setbacks, that may come our way.

This is, truly, our Lord's recipe for joy.

A Time to Grow

To be mature as Christians means that we continually grow in the faith into which we have been baptized. It is not sufficient to verbally and emotionally receive Christ. We are to be perpetually open to God as He is fully revealed in Christ and as He continues to instruct and establish us through His Spirit. As we cannot know God save through Christ, so we cannot hear God speak or carry out our allegiance to God unless we listen to Christ's words and follow His leading in our daily lives and activities. If there is anyone who claims to have found God apart from Christ or who insists that he can determine and follow God's will apart from our Lord's revelations and proclamations, he is a usurper, a false prophet, and ought to be resisted and avoided.

We must be aware of those legalists about us who attempt to cramp God into some ethical formula that they pass out as a requisite for God's acceptance and salvation. Their man-made religions are popular with multitudes of people because they assume to provide handles or rungs on a ladder by which human beings can ultimately approach and please the Deity. They are preaching Law, not grace, or mostly Law with a smattering of grace. As attractive as may be their declarations and as devoted as may be their religious activities and promotions, they are proclaiming a false gospel.

"And you, who were dead in trespasses . . . God made alive together with [Christ], having forgiven us all our trespasses, having canceled the bond which stood against us with its legal demands; this He set aside, nailing it to the cross."

Meditate on this—and take time to grow.

Saturday   *1 Kings 3:5–12 (A)*

The Acceptable Prayer

"Ask what I shall give you," the Lord said to Solomon when he was about to begin his duties as king of Israel. It may well be that this is the key to an effective, God-pleasing prayer life. We are indeed to "ask . . . seek . . . knock . . . ," but the prayer that God responds to is the prayer for those things that He wills to grant us. As little children our requests, or prayers, to our parents dealt primarily with the things we wanted—food, drink, sweets, something exciting to do, help in doing the things we wanted to do. Many of our prayers to God are basically still on that childish level. Mature prayers by mature Christians are sincere requests for a continual openness to God to receive what He desires us to have.

Solomon's prayer was a mature prayer. More important to him than riches or long life or victory over his enemies was the wisdom he needed to guide and rule over his people. His prayer for this was pleasing to

God, and Solomon was granted what he humbly requested. He also received many things that he did not request in his prayer.

If God knows our needs and what He wants to give us, why is prayer nevertheless useful and valuable? Probably because we are not ready to receive what He knows we need and what He desires we should have until we get to the point of asking for it.

God will hear our prayers, no matter how childish they may be; yet He ever seeks to bring us to the place where we, in turn, seek the things He wants to grant us. While we accept the fact that "prayer changes things," closer to the truth is the fact that prayer changes us and then we begin to change things.

No matter what our age may be, physically or spiritually, we still need to repeat the request made by the disciples in one of our Gospel lessons for this week: "Lord, teach us to pray."

Eleventh Sunday After Pentecost

Matthew 14:13-21 (A)

Now You Do It!

The feeding of the five thousand revealed our Lord's compassion and concern for the great throngs that followed Him. It also presents to us a tremendous commission. It portrays, on the one hand, the desperate *need of the world*. The hungry multitude about Christ represented need, and one does not have to look very far beyond one's own nose to see that the thing most common to all people is need—of one kind or another. There are hundreds of millions throughout our world today who are in need of the most fundamental elements of physical existence—food, clothing, medicine, shelter, security, freedom. There is within all humanity the need for inner assurance and serenity, for meaning and purpose in life.

On the other hand, the miracle in question portrays the mighty, eternally sufficient *provision of God*. Our Lord's first action, in the face of the oncoming crowd, was to turn to His disciples as if to lay the responsibility of feeding the crowd on them. "We have only five loaves here and two fish," they said to Him. "Bring them here to Me," said Jesus, and taking the loaves and the fish, "He looked up to heaven, and blessed, and broke and gave the loaves to the disciples, and the disciples gave them to the crowds."

Jesus gave these people what they wanted: a miracle to thrill them and bread to fill them. But He who sustained physical life with mere bread was here for the real purpose of giving people eternal life with that Bread which came from heaven, the Son of God Himself. He would have these people and us understand that the provision of God is more than enough to fulfill every need of every man, woman, and child and that He is God Himself come to earth to bring that ample, divine provision to needy hearts and lives.

This is the reason that we who have received that Bread are here today. We are called and committed to bear witness to God's provision and to channel and distribute it to the desperate needs of His children throughout our world.

223

Eternal Security

Nothing, nothing at all, can come between us and our loving God. Our feelings of guilt and depression may rise up to haunt us, but they in no way alter God's redeeming and accepting love. Not, that is, unless we acquiesce to such feelings and neglect to hear and abide by God's Word. The tragedies and conflicts of this life will discourage us, but they can in no way change God's attitude or stifle His love for us. Failures and defeats may trip us up, but they do not affect our relationship to God.

Our boat will rock; the earth will tremble. Revolutions will shake up governments and institutions. Our traditions may be nullified, our convictions threatened. Every temporal security may crumble. But God's love and reconciling grace are forever, and He will never let us go. If our allegiance is to God and our faith is fixed on Him, the very atrocities that seek to destroy us become the means by which He carries out His will in and through us.

Nothing, absolutely nothing can separate us from the love of God as revealed and proclaimed and demonstrated through Jesus Christ. We are the sons and daughters of God, His servants and disciples forever.

When Life Has Meaning

"What is life for?" questioned Leo Tolstoy, that famous Russian writer of the last century. "What is life for? To die? To kill myself at once? No, I am afraid. To wait for death till it comes? I fear that even more. Then I must live. But what for? In order to die? And I could not escape from that circle." "Why was I ever born?" Job asked in the midst of his excruciating sufferings. Job was discovering, as many of us do in this vale of tears, that the most atrocious and destructive type of suffering is that in which the victim realizes no meaning or purpose in his suffering.

The primary purpose of our Lord's sojourn on this planet was to point out life's meaning, to reveal order and purpose in life's activity, and to direct men and women inextricably entangled in nets of their own making back to the orbit and destiny for which they were created—the eternal purposes of God. He first had to break through the thick crust of materialism that numbs most of God's creatures to eternal and infinite values. "Do not labor for the food which perishes," He exhorts. He is not condoning lethargy and indolence, but is rebuking the excessive attention we place on labor designed to fill one's belly and increase one's wealth of possessions at the sacrifice of spiritual and eternal values. "Do not labor—do not place the focus of your life or set your ultimate goals upon bread or material worth or anything which may perish within the moment or the hour." Reach out, instead, "for the food which endures to eternal life, which the Son of Man will give to you." And then Jesus points this up by saying: "This is the work of God, that you believe in Him whom He has sent."

When Jesus becomes the Bread of Life for us, we become bread to others about us. We become, with God's gifts of grace, a generating, power-giving source of life and energy for our brothers and sisters in the human family. This, then, becomes our purpose in life and gives present, perpetual, eternal meaning to life.

Wednesday   *Ephesians 4:17–24 (B)*

Exercise in Holiness

Having become God's children, we are enjoined to live as God's children. As in a human family, this involves a certain amount of discipline. As a preacher's son, I was supposed to disassociate myself from the world in respect to those things considered at the time to be unchristian—movies, card-playing, smoking, dancing, etc. There are many who still feel that external discipline in matters such as these is necessary to their Christian growth and witness. We have no argument with them—until they attempt to measure all Christians in accordance with their particular convictions concerning Christian ethics.

Nor do we have an argument with Paul's "Put off . . . put on" injunctions in respect to the necessary internal discipline required of all of us if we are to grow and mature in the Christian faith. It is a daily discipline, and such discipline involves an incessant struggle—in some cases a very painful one. To replace griping with gratitude, lust with love, anger with kindness, selfishness with selflessness, pride with humility, insensitivity with concern, all this, and the gradual acquisition of those qualities and attributes exemplified by Jesus Christ, demands a lifelong determination and discipline. Any real victories come by the grace of God, and total victory in all these matters will be realized only after we leave the body to be with God Himself.

Paul encourages us to enter into this daily discipline and exercise in holiness. Failures must not deter us, only challenge us to keep going, to keep the faith, to "be renewed in the spirit of [our] minds." We will lose some of the battles along the way, but we will ultimately win the war. This is the promise of Jesus Christ, who has already won that war on our behalf.

Thursday   *Luke 12:13–21 (C)*

Security Can Be Dangerous

"Take heed . . . beware . . . for a man's life does not consist in the abundance of his possessions."

We are not about to put down security. Some of it is good; a certain amount of it is necessary to human happiness. We need to be reminded, however, that security can be dangerous—and even damning—if our sense of security is pinned, like a donkey's tail, on the backside of ephemeral and tangible objects, or upon those material blessings inherited through the toil of others who have gone before us.

While many people still identify sin with the glaring headlines of scandal sheets, we discover it to be anything and everything—materialistic, sensate, or mystical—that causes us to draw our life's energies from anything less than God, that the sin that damns involves the person "who lays up treasure for himself, and is not rich toward God."

It becomes needful for us to take the danger and destructiveness out of our worldly security by seeking that which is truly meaningful for our lives. It must begin with reappraisal or reassessment of our life's goals; "for where your treasure is, there will your heart be also," said Jesus in the Sermon on the Mount. This is followed by repentance, a recognition of our folly, its renunciation, and a return to the love and grace of God. Repentance must be combined with refocus, a determination to "seek first [God's] kingdom and His righteousness" (Matthew 6:33). There is nothing inherently sinful in the things of this life. The tragedy evolves when the acquisition of such things takes precedence over God and spiritual values. So we must refocus, put things in their proper perspective, lest we lose out altogether on divine meaning and purpose and its resultant order and joy for our lives.

There is still time to heed the warning of our Lord, to stop short in our pursuit of this world's abundance, and to rededicate our efforts and energies, cares and concerns, love and loyalty to the program and purposes of God.

We Are Really Alive

I wonder if we understand it, that we truly are the people of God, that He loves us and chooses that we be His people. Now we are really alive! As Christ was raised from the dead, so we have been brought from death to life and shall live forever. We ought daily to set our hearts and fix our minds on this fantastic truth. Faith means that we begin to live and act on this truth, that this really happened, whether we feel it or not.

There are, however, still some things within us that must not be permitted to control our thinking or activities. They are those things that come between us and God and are capable of causing harm to our fellow persons. Still rising out of the darkness to haunt and tempt us are the shadows of lust and greed and covetousness and hostility and deceit. They are like booby traps; they can destroy us and anyone close to us. We must, by God's grace and His power at work within us, blast these insidious demons out of our lives; and we must do it again and again, for they die hard, these agents of death.

It is thus that we grow in faith, allowing the Spirit of God to captivate and subordinate every aspect of our lives under His purging love. We learn how to plug up the loopholes in our lives by allowing God to flood our hearts with His love. We commit ourselves to exercising that inflowing and outgoing love by reaching out to others in concern and compassion.

It's a great life; let's get on with it!

Chasing the Wind

When our vision of God dims and the bright lights of our sensuous, materialistic world seem suddenly attractive and inviting, it may be well to consult with the writer of Ecclesiastes. He had it all and tried it all, wealth, position, pleasures galore; and it turned to dust in his hands. And so it would in our hands—especially now after we have tasted of God's out-of-this-world blessings and have had small glimpses of the glory yet to be revealed. We are often discouraged by the frustrations of Christian living and the hard realities of what it means to follow Jesus Christ in our kind of world.

While painfully struggling at times, and failing often to be what Jesus would have us to be, we *are* growing toward that image, and are looking even higher to the promise and joy of eternal union with our Creator and Redeemer.

Twelfth Sunday After Pentecost

Matthew 14:22–33 (A)

"You Gotta Believe"

Deeply impressed by my reading of the autobiographies of men and women of great faith in my early years, I have occasionally challenged God to move a few mountains in my life. Then I came across a little piece by Marjorie Stump that brought some sort of reality into my praying. Her poem points out that we would enjoy doing a useless act like walking on water but are not so eager to help with a messy job like feeding the multitudes.

The crowd-gathering religions today, as well as in Christ's day, are for the most part satisfied with the spectacular and the fantastic, the walking-on-water, feeding-the-five-thousand, healing-the-sick, turning-water-into-wine aspects of religion, and there appears to be little relationship between that and the "faith of our fathers, living still, in spite of dungeon, fire, and sword."

Jesus was in the process of creating and nourishing faith in His disciples, the kind of faith that stirs up the daring within the soul, that goes beyond the limits of what is reasonable and rational, and flirts with the risk and gamble of new ventures, that turns its back upon one's well-laid plans for future security and well-being and dares to tread the fringe of danger for the benefit of others. It is a vibrant, living, daring, sacrificing faith, a faith that does not burn out, that does not falter when one begins to sink beneath the waters, but lays hold afresh on the proclaimed and dramatized saving love and grace of God and rises again to joy and service.

"We gotta believe"—not in some vague, positive-thinking type of religion, or in a god who titillates us on demand, but in the God of our fathers, our Lord and Christ, who created and redeemed us and made us His own, who provides us with all we need to be what He would have us to be and do what He would have us to do. We must believe and act like it—not only in spite of evidences, but in scorn of consequences.

Grant me, O God, this kind of faith.

How Much Should One Love?

It is probable that few of us can love as much as Paul loved his people. How many of us "could wish that [we ourselves] were accursed and cut off from Christ for the sake of [our] . . . kinsmen"? Not only did Paul offer up his life for the sake of Jew and Gentile alike, but he was willing to be cut off from God's saving love—to submit to eternal damnation—if that would result in the salvation of the Jews. We are able to love those who love us, and are learning something about loving those of other races—even our enemies—but we dare not claim the love that Paul had for his brothers and sisters.

Yet Paul reveals in some measure the content and quality of Christ's love for us. Jesus submitted to death on the cross in His love for us. He enjoined us to love others even as He loved us. It is obvious that we have a long way to go. While we may never reach the quality and intensity of love Paul declared for his people, and certainly won't attain the heights and depths of Christ's love for us, this is the goal we ought to be reaching for.

Recognizing, as did Paul, that salvation comes only through Christ and that we can in no way save others by being damned in their stead, we should be compelled by God's eternal love for us and all His creatures to spend and expend all we are and have in order that others about us may hear about and desire to receive God's saving grace. God grant that we may experience "unceasing anguish" for those who have thus far rejected or ignored Jesus Christ. Let us be aware that it can in no way match the anguish in the heart of God Himself over those who turn away from Him as He is revealed in Jesus Christ.

The Meaning of Believing

"No one can come to Me unless the Father who sent Me draws him," the Savior said.

We would hope that the average church member today is not as shallow in his or her concept of the Christ as were those who gathered about Him on this occasion. Is it possible to be united with Christ in baptism, to make weekly confessions and go through the motions of worship, and yet fail to comprehend what it really means to believe in Jesus Christ? Don't we all attempt to take the all-wise, everywhere-present God of the Bible and press Him into the confinements of our small thinking? Like a pilot grabbing for his parachute when the motor of his small plane conks out, don't we grab for some comfortable concept of God, for a piece of the Divine, and state emphatically that we believe in God?

A right relationship to God, an authentic faith in Jesus Christ, is really a two-way street. He gives us His all—even though we have nothing to give but our depraved, sin-ridden hearts. This takes place at our baptism. When we become aware of God's covenant made with us through Jesus Christ and appropriated to us at our baptism, we are consciously to embrace His forgiving love and recognize our adoption as His sons and daughters and our appointment as His servants and disciples. We "eat" and "drink" Him; we identify with Him; we take Him into the very center of our beings. We become one with Him through Christ. His life becomes our life; His love becomes our love; His purposes become our purposes, His goal our goal. Redeemed by His forgiving and sanctifying grace, we become energized and empowered by His indwelling Spirit to be His vessels through which to communicate His love to a fractured world, and we who "eat" of that Bread which was broken for us become broken bread to the hungry lives of men and women about us.

Isn't that what it means to believe in Jesus Christ?

Wednesday   *Ephesians 4:30–5:2 (B)*

Participators and Imitators

We know that we are the children of God. It follows, then, that we are responsible to Him—to emulate Him, follow Him—to soar within His orbit for our lives. It is only as we participate in what God has done for us through Jesus Christ that we are enabled and expected to imitate Him as well. As God, through Christ, demonstrated His love for us, so our lives, controlled by His love, are to demonstrate such love toward people about us. It is this that ought to determine our daily conduct. The way we speak or act, the company we keep, whatever we do—whether working or playing, resting or recreating, eating or sleeping—needs to be measured, not by what most pleases us, but in terms of

231

what is pleasing to God and what is most beneficial to our fellow persons.

The fact is, we are under new management, new orders. Our primary task is now to reflect, administer, communicate God's infinite love to a distorted and disjointed world. While self-surrender underlines our relationship to God, self-disclosure should characterize our relationship toward our fellow persons. We are to "be kind to one another, tender-hearted, forgiving one another, as God in Christ forgave [us] . . . and walk in love. . . ." It is this that constitutes the ethics of a Christian. With God's help, and because of His great love for us, let us learn how to invest in one another. This is the key to genuine and everlasting joy whatever the circumstances that crowd in upon us.

Thursday   *Luke 12:32–40 (C)*

Divine Words in a Dark World

"Fear not, little flock, for it is your Father's good pleasure to give you the kingdom," said Jesus. These are words of consolation—words that offer an exceedingly reliable prescription for joyful and secure living in a very dark and uncertain world. Jesus did not guarantee earthly security or freedom from all things that might cause pain or sorrow; yet He said, in effect, that we have nothing to be afraid of. As God's children and servants we are blessed with God's divine words and promises in a dark world. We shall not be afraid.

Jesus also speaks words of exhortation. We are enjoined to *sell*, to take our clutching fingers off that which we classify as ours—our possessions, our talents, our very lives. In order to inherit the riches of eternity, we must willingly and gladly disinherit earth and its lesser values. Christ must come first in our lives—or He doesn't come at all. We are enjoined to *give*. What good we have received is from God. This does not make it our sole possession. It is ours to enjoy; it is also ours to give away. It is meant to meet some of the needs of people about us. When we neglect to give, we become dead-end streets, stagnant pools. Where there is no outlet, there ceases to be inflow. He enjoins us to *invest wisely*—in the "treasure in the heavens that does not fail." This investment of lives and possessions must be in the hungry that need feeding, the naked that need clothing, the sick that need healing and comforting, the souls that need saving. It is the kind of investment that will pay off in this life and in the life to come.

The Day Before Us

"And he went out, not knowing where he was to go."

It is difficult for some of us to face a new day without preconceived plans as to what our errands and actions are to be. It appears that a well-ordered life is a distinct virtue in our times and should not be ignored. But maybe we should experiment with the kind of faith Abraham demonstrated when he "went out, not knowing where he was to go." Abraham obviously scored high with God in obeying His command to "go" without insisting on some revelation as to where he was to go or what God would have him do. Nor should we insist on such revelation. God reveals Himself to us; He seldom reveals much more. The God-given ability to believe in Him for our salvation includes the ability to trust Him to lead us and accomplish His purposes through us on any day of any week.

Whereas our great God grants to us the ability to have faith, it is necessary for us to utilize and exercise this ability. It means that we focus upon the infinite grace of God, accept His forgiving love won for us by Christ and proclaimed through His Word, and in scorn of consequences place our lives and fortunes in His hands. Without faith there is no way of relating to God. With faith, and its resultant commitment to Christian discipleship, there is joy and meaning, risk and excitement, love and freedom, purpose and objective for every son and daughter of God.

Have a good day!

Strength for the Journey

There are times when even stout hearts will faint and strong men and women will falter. As with Elijah, this could even be a sort of post-victory depression or a letdown after an active and reasonably successful week out in the Monday-through-Friday arena of one's life. Most often it is a desperate feeling of discouragement and failure. Elijah wanted to die; he was so frightened and despondent. We have had days like that in our lives. We consider Elijah rather fortunate in that he had a visit from an angel who baked him a cake and provided him with drink. In our pain and misery we wonder if there might be an angel or two about to aid us in our distress.

Usually not, but we have something far better, for God Himself is with us, whatever the difficulties that befall us. He has filled us with His Spirit and, even when our bodies are wracked with pain and our minds clouded by despair, He is with us always and will take the journey with us, no matter how difficult the course we travel. "Arise and eat, else the journey will be too great for you," the angel said to Elijah. "And he arose, and ate and drank, and went on in the strength of that food," we are told.

"The cup of blessing which we bless, is it not a participation in the blood of Christ? The bread which we break, is it not a participation in the body of Christ?" wrote Paul (1 Corinthians 10:16). "Drink of it, all of you," said Jesus, "for this is My blood of the covenant, which is poured out for many . . ." (Matthew 26:27–28). There is indeed refreshment for God's children as they slog their way through the wilderness of this life. It is offered in the Word that will be proclaimed tomorrow, and it is granted in a very special way through the Lord's Supper. God does not send us angels; He Himself comes to us through Jesus Christ by way of the Word and the Sacrament, and He comes to bring light into our dark despair and to affirm and strengthen us for the journey ahead.

Now rise up and move on; God is with you!

Thirteenth Sunday After Pentecost

Matthew 15:21–28 (A)

Why Is God So Stubborn?

Why is God so stubborn? It is a question many of us have entertained at one time or another. There are those times when we have felt that God is downright obstinate and seems to be cold, indifferent, insulated, or unrelated to our aches and agonies. He not only allows us to get into complexities and entanglements we have no intention or desire to get into, but He appears at times to be totally oblivious to our struggles and conflicts. We agree that God is in His heaven—lest one be accused of blasphemy or heresy—but there are occasions when He seems to have abdicated our chaotic world.

Why is God so stubborn? Perhaps it is because He loves us so much that He insists on giving us the very best in life. There are times when the only way God has of introducing us to the best is to allow us to prick ourselves on the thorny bushes of this existence, or run amok in its blind alleys and dead-end streets, or flail helplessly on its quicksands of ultimate disillusionment and disaster. When we desperately long for deliverance, as did the Canaanite woman, we have taken the initial step in preparing the way for God to grant the miracle of sufficient grace to bear our afflictions or to live fruitfully and effectively with our problems.

It is not enough that we bring our problems to God. We must bring ourselves to Him—yield over to Him the reins of our lives, place before Him all that we are and have. Then miracles will happen in our lives.

Monday   *Romans 11:13–15, 29–32 (A)*

God's Mercy Toward His Disobedient Creatures

Paul suffered much anguish over the unwillingness of his fellow countrymen to receive God's mercy as revealed through the Christ. He points out that it was their rejection of Jesus Christ as Redeemer and Savior that compelled him to focus the primary emphasis of his ministry upon the Gentile world. He was living in the hope that the Gentile acceptance of God's mercy as portrayed and proclaimed through Christ and His disciples would, in turn, be a blessing to the Jews and encourage them to receive God's loving mercy and everlasting salvation.

Of this we can be sure: Even if His beloved creatures turn away from Him, God does not reject them. Whereas divine love can be resisted, as it cannot be forced upon the objects of such love, yet those objects continue to be loved. Even while we may eventually give up on those who shun our attempts to introduce them to Christ, God never gives them up—at least not in this life.

We are obviously not able to comprehend the vast depths of the kind of love that continues to pursue these runaway children until they are found and returned to the fold. How grateful we ought to be that God persisted in His search for our souls! How eagerly and diligently ought we to unite with Him in His persistent search for the lost and wandering, the willful and rebellious souls of men and women, Jews and Gentiles, about us! It was, in part, because of the rebelliousness of God's originally chosen people that the Gospel came to us and enabled us to be numbered among the "chosen." While we celebrate God's amazing and never-ending love for His human creatures, let us live and act in such a way that we may communicate that divine love to all people and draw them into the kingdom of God.

Tuesday   *John 6:51–58 (B)*

Maybe Our God Is Too Small

Jesus' contemporaries, flabbergasted by what they had just witnessed in the feeding-of-the-five-thousand miracle, were about to believe that this Jesus really was the promised Messiah and to start a Christ-for-king movement that would put Him on the throne and establish Israel as a great and powerful nation once more. Jesus then set about to disabuse their foolish, fanciful notions of His Messianic ministry and attempted to tell them something of what it really meant to believe in Him, to embrace Him as their Messiah, and follow Him as their King.

As with the people of Jesus' day, so our concept of what it means to believe in, worship, and follow Jesus Christ is often too small, too immature. What our Lord is saying, in today's terms, is that the key to authentic Christianity is faith and commitment. The disciples never really understood this until after Christ's resurrection; some of us still have to discover it. The faith and fervor of those first followers of

Christ, the devotion and drive manifested in the waking hours of the church, are hard to come by in our generation. The Christianity that some of us have been a part of is a kind of streamlined, plush-lined facsimile of the real thing, a kind of defensive, crawling-into-our-holes-to-lick-our-wounds Christianity, an escapism, a running away from reality, a place of refuge and hiding. The soft faith that characterizes the religion of our day is obviously not sponsored by Christ but is the invention of the minds of men and women who want the pearl without paying the price, who don't really understand that there is a price to pay, a battle to fight, a life to lose, in the great business of following Jesus Christ.

We make our God too small. We simply cannot confine Him to small thinking, to unwilling and unloving hearts. If we receive Him, it must be as He is, in all that He is, as His Word declares Him to be. It must be totally, intimately, conclusively—with all that we are and have. Only then will our great God be almighty and omnipotent in and through our lives.

Wednesday   *Ephesians 5:15–20 (B)*

Carefully and Gratefully

"Look carefully then how you walk. . . ."

When we are blessed with a new friend, or obtain a new job or a new car or a new home, we are generally very careful about how we treat this individual or those things. We "walk" carefully, for they are of great value to us. It may be that we are not nearly so concerned about that "pearl of great price," that divine gift and eternal relationship which is of infinitely greater value than anything of which we can conceive. We tend to take God for granted and therefore become careless and irresponsible in respect to our relationship with Him. This has to do, as well, with our responsibility in respect to our relationships with our fellow beings, the servants and ministers of God. We are careful about the things we love the most; it follows, then, that if we truly love our Lord, and our brothers and sisters in the family of God, we will "look carefully . . . how [we] walk."

While we walk carefully, we are enjoined to live gratefully. It is difficult to understand how even Christians can "always and for everything [give] thanks." But we can learn how to be grateful to God, to live thankful lives, irrespective of dire happenings, realizing that even the painful, tragic things that come our way can be used to carry out God's purposes in and through us.

We have something of infinite, incalculable value in our relationship to God and His children; let us be careful and grateful.

The Radical Christ

We spent many of our youthful years regarding Jesus as a gentle, meek peacemaker. We subsequently came across portions of Scripture that picture Him quite differently. "Do you think I have come to give peace on earth? No. . . . I came to cast fire upon the earth. . . ."

Jesus did promise us His peace (John 14:27). He promised, as well, that those who labored for His kingdom would face division, conflict, and persecution. He led the way to the scaffold; most of His disciples followed closely behind. And He has left us with the assuring word that we need not be afraid when we face the courts that seek to snuff us out. He has gone before us—but only to return in order to embrace us and love us in the midst of earthshaking events, staying close beside us all the way.

The point is, the Christian life itself is a revolutionary life, a life fraught with conflicts. It has been such from the beginning; it shall be as long as life on this earth continues. Those people who float peacefully by, totally content with their religious experience, oblivious or impervious to the conflict-ridden world about them, desperately holding on to their precious ecstasies or God-in-a-box concepts until Jesus comes to take them to heaven, those people may be on the wrong ship—or are dry-docked in some harbor when they should be sailing the storm-tossed seas of reality where God's servants and fishers-of-men-and-women-and-children are supposed to be.

When we reach out to embrace the peace of a right relationship with God, we must also reckon with the conflicts that come as a consequence of that redeeming, healing, joy-giving relationship; for we are the followers of the radical Christ in a revolutionary world.

The Faith That Keeps Us Going

Faith is in itself a gift of God. It is not something we can manufacture. And yet, one of the most powerful incentives to have faith, to trust God, to believe in His gracious promises, is the faith of those who have gone before us.

It ought to be enough to enable us to cut loose from our inordinate attachment to earthbound securities, to cast off our foolish doubts, and to let go, let God, and let the chips fall where they may. While our Lord is no longer visibly present, we have His Word and His example, and the example and experience of countless saints, to nourish and mature our faith.

If we expect only sweetness and light, thrills and ecstasies, as the consequences of our involvement with God and His purposes, we have a wrong conception of what faith is all about. There is an element of risk, a measure of pain, involved in our walk of faith. Faith, no matter how intense, does not shield us from the episodes that wound us or the failures that flatten us in despair. But faith is capable of embracing suffering and despair and molding and maneuvering these into instruments that mature us and make us more sensitive to the hurts of others, even while we learn how more graciously to accept the hardships and difficulties of this life.

Rather than floundering and folding in the midst of every turbulence that engulfs us, we can, by the grace of God, learn how to stand firm against the storm and walk steadily among the vicissitudes of daily living. May our great God, who is always with us and within us seeking to work out His purposes through us, grant us this measure of faith as we face the day before us.

Saturday   *Jeremiah 23:23–29 (C)*

Beware of Dreamers

"Let the prophet who has a dream tell the dream, but let him who has My Word speak My Word faithfully."

Our Lord's indictments against the many false prophets of Jeremiah's day are applicable to our generation as well. Scores of cults are led by false prophets who base their credentials on some dream. While they may use our Bible to pad their presentations, it is most often some out-of-context portions that are utilized to support their allegations and promote their purposes.

Dreams and visions are not all bad; some may even be useful; and there are indications that dreams have been effectual in relaying divine messages to a dark world. When, however, they are placed above or on a par with God's Word as revealed through Christ and related through the Scriptures, they cannot be trusted and may lead one down the road to disaster.

The dreamers about us are not confined to cults or sects. As the people of Christ's day looked for supernatural signs, even Christians in long-established churches are sometimes tempted to reach for magical dreams or visions to spice up their faith or to satisfy their sensual and emotional hungers or their need for temporal security and serenity.

Whether we be preachers or God's servants in the marketplace or on Main Street, we who have heard God's Word are to "speak [His] Word faithfully." That Word is not always a comforting Word; it sometimes jars and provokes, even as it did the Israelites in Jeremiah's time. Nevertheless, it eventually and resolutely leads us to eternal truth and joy. God forbid that we replace it or confuse it with the silly dreams and proclamations of self-styled prophets!

Fourteenth Sunday After Pentecost

Matthew 16:13–20 (A)

A Genuine Confession

It is quite probable that Jesus was discouraged over the responses of the many who had heard Him preach and who witnessed His miracles such as the feeding of the five thousand. Like people who flock to certain churches today that offer healing or mesmerize their audiences with mind-blowing antics that are geared to crowd-gathering, there were crowds who pressed in upon Christ because He could perform the kind of magic that pleased them or fed them or healed them. They were quite willing to vote Him into office as king if that could be arranged.

Jesus took His most loyal followers aside to question them concerning their attitudes in this matter. He invited them to articulate their feelings toward Him. The larger group of followers that showed some interest in Christ compared Him to Elijah or John the Baptist or some prophet come back to life. From the inner circle of followers, through the lips of Peter, came a more encouraging confession: "You are the Christ, the Son of the living God." It was a true confession, probably immature at this point; nevertheless it was genuine, and Jesus accepted it as such.

Then Jesus gave His disciples a small glimpse of His plan for them in the future. Using the word "church" for the first time in this Gospel, He informed Peter and the other disciples that they would be the foundation blocks of the future church.

Now we are the building blocks of the church and the kingdom of God, and we build on "Christ, the Son of the living God." No other confession will do. May it be a genuine confession even if it is, as in the case of Peter, still immature. As Peter developed in his comprehension of Christ's person and purposes and his own committal to Him, so we will grow and mature as sons and daughters of God and disciples of Jesus Christ.

241

When There Are No Answers

"How unsearchable are His judgments and how inscrutable His ways."

This is Paul's response to our unsolvable problems. In his case it was the problem of his rebellious and apparently rejected countrymen who refused to believe in Jesus Christ as their Savior and Lord. The lack of an answer to the problem, his inability to fully discern God's mind or future action toward the Jews who rejected God's Son, threw him back on the wisdom and judgments of God. He was able to rejoice in knowing that God's ways are right and His judgments are perfect.

If we are worshiping a God who reveals all the answers to the problems and conflicts of our lives, we are worshiping something less than the true God. Beware of those religious leaders or religions that have the answers to everything that confounds us; they indicate that they tend to confine the wisdom and judgments of God to their own small minds. Our God is far greater than that—and so are His thoughts than our thoughts and His ways than our ways. Some of God's mysteries may gradually unfold when we become more mature in knowledge and insight. But most of His mysteries will remain such to us as long as we abide on this planet.

We can, however, rejoice as did Paul, "For from Him and through Him and to Him are all things." We will never fully know our God, nor the answers to all our problems, but He knows us. We can well afford to trust Him—and praise Him.

The Gospel that Offends

"After this many of His disciples drew back and no longer went about with Him."

The Gospel of Jesus Christ does, indeed, offer comfort. Something we may hesitate to accept and may find difficult to proclaim is the fact that the Gospel also offends. Many are ill at ease with its paradoxes and demands and make foolish attempts to reduce the Christian faith to simple and often maudlin categories that they can handle without too much pain or discomfort. Others find it downright offensive; it demands too much, and they seek elsewhere for spiritual solace. Christ's preaching resulted in sifting out the fellow travelers who followed Him for material or political benefits. Jesus ignored their earthbound concepts and invited them to "eat" and "drink" (see the verses just before our reading), to identify and become one with Him, to commit themselves totally to Him and His purposes. The crowd melted away, and Jesus was left with His original following of twelve men.

Anything that strikes at the very core of our self-centered lives is bound to cause offense. We recognize our sin and are driven to the offense of the cross. We yield, sometimes very painfully, to God's forgiving love. Then we meet up with the offense of yielding control of our lives to Jesus and His purposes, dying daily to sin and self-centeredness to live for the sake of others. Offense will dog our footsteps until there is a genuine surrender to the blessed will of God and to servanthood as His ministers in our world. Thus we discover God's orbit for our lives, and offense is transformed into abundant joy—even in the midst of suffering and persecution.

"Lord, to whom shall we go?" said the disciples. "You have the words of eternal life. . . ."

Wednesday   *Ephesians 5:21–31 (B)*

Our Interpersonal Relationships

"Be subject to one another out of reverence for Christ."

Some of us may have a problem with Paul's injunction to wives and their relationship to their husbands. This particular text was read at my wedding, and in the early years of my marriage I occasionally reminded my spouse of the significance of these words. She, in turn, challenged me to love her as Christ loved the church. It is my opinion that Paul, who was certainly upgrading wife-husband relationships in his day, would say some things a bit differently if he were writing letters to our churches today.

Whether we think of marital or family relationships, or our relationships to one another as the sons and daughters of God, Paul most certainly points up Christ's injunction to love one another. A byproduct of that kind of love has to do with our concern for and consideration of the needs of the other even above our own needs. This is the responsibility of husbands and wives, sisters and brothers, parents and children, and is to be the dominant note in our relationships with all of God's children.

Subjection or submission of one to another is a two-way street. I often subject myself to my wife, sometimes reluctantly, in those matters where she is gifted and qualified to make decisions. She, by the same token, subjects herself to me and to what I feel is important in our relationships to one another and to God's purposes in our lives. This is the fruit, and a necessary aspect, of our love. Both of us are slowly learning how to subject ourselves to the needs of others about us. This is in response to and is the consequence of God's great love for us. And this is what belonging to the family of Christ is all about.

Feed our love for one another, Lord, with Your love for us.

Thursday   *Luke 13:22–30 (C)*

When Label Becomes Libel

Most of our daily activities, from morning to night, are guided by labels of some sort, whether we be eating, driving, working, or learning. When something is purchased under a particular label, but turns out to be far different than the label led one to suspect, then the label projected a lie.

Jesus says, in effect, that it is quite possible to wear the label of Christianity without living its life, to don its uniform without fighting in its battles, to claim its benefits without carrying its cross.

We stand convicted—many of us at many times. We may have worn the label; it may, at times, have come out as a libel. There has been considerable foliage, but too little fruit. We may have faithfully and piously carried out our religious exercises in the sanctuary only to demonstrate our selfishness and self-centeredness in the home, the office, the marketplace. "Not everyone who says to me, 'Lord, Lord,' shall enter the kingdom of heaven," Jesus said on another occasion, "but he who does the will of My Father." (Matthew 7:21). Profession apart from genuine expression is just so much moist air. It may dazzle and awe a few people; it doesn't get through to God.

To take the libel out of our label we need constantly to recognize our call to servanthood, the necessity of divine grace in the carrying out of that servanthood, the importance of a perpetual and total commitment to the living Christ as Savior and Lord, and the courage to live and act as He would live and act in our circumstances.

Grace Rather than Fear

We have, at times, tended to become rather chummy with God, to regard Him as "the man upstairs" or a kindly grandfather in the sky, a big brother of sorts, and to subscribe to Him a familiarity, and indulgent nature, that tolerates our idiosyncrasies even while He tries to keep us in line. This is far removed from the God of the Old Testament, whom people regarded with great fear and trembling. There are times when we ought to put a little of that ancient fear of God back into our worship services and daily activities and demonstrate some holy respect for our Creator and Judge.

While we are enjoined to fear or to be aware of the consequences of acting contrary to the will of God, we need never fear approaching God, no more than a child would fear coming to the arms of a loving mother or father. God is ever approachable, and His everlasting grace has forever opened the door of the inner sanctuary where we can confess, confide, and reconsecrate our lives to Him and His purposes. This has been made possible in Jesus Christ, through whom God came to us and is ever available to us.

We who have come to God through Christ have indeed drawn near "to Mount Zion and to the city of the living God, the heavenly Jerusalem, and to innumerable angels in festal gathering, and to the assembly of the firstborn who are enrolled in heaven, and to a judge who is God of all, and to the spirits of just men made perfect . . ." and all this through "Jesus, the mediator of a new covenant. . . ."

Grace has taken over where trembling, terrifying fear once occupied the hearts of men and women in their relationship to God.

A Matter of Response

The Israelites were challenged to make a clear-cut choice. They were to submit to God's will or to go traipsing after the gods of some other nation or tribe. They had nothing to do with God's choice of them to be His people, but they, in turn were able to reject Him.

We have some difficulty with the semantics of the large number of churches or denominations who beseech their constituents to "choose" Jesus, to make a "decision" for Christ. We sometimes wonder if they are aware that we did not choose Christ, but He chose us that we should be the children and servants of God forever. We who were baptized into Christ as infants have no awareness of choosing to receive God's infinite and eternal love. God chose us and gathered us into His graciousness.

Yet, decision of one kind or another eventually becomes paramount for most of us. We inevitably encounter crossroads or rivers to cross in our sojourn through this life. Whether conscious of it or not, we do make decisions. Some of them are in tune with God's Spirit within us; others appear to cloud up or obscure His will and purposes for us. The point is, we are capable of resisting God's will or ignoring the direction of His Spirit. True faith, that faith which justifies, is receptivity—the acknowledgment, reception, and appropriation of God's grace bestowed upon us through Jesus Christ. God grants us His love and forgiveness; we are privileged and enabled to respond to it—or to make the dreadful decision not to respond to it.

It is sometimes a frightening responsibility—this ability to respond. May God grant to us the grace and wisdom to respond today and every day in ways that are pleasing to Him and enriching for us and for others about us.

Fifteenth Sunday After Pentecost

Matthew 16:21–26 (A)

The Centrality of the Cross

Our lives as Christians begin with the cross. It is central; it is essential; it is the center and core, pivot and apex of Christianity. It is because of the cross that Jesus accepts us as we are—with all of our sins, failures, and hang-ups. In this lesson, however, our Lord talks not only of its centrality and essentiality, but of its perpetuity. "If any man would come after Me, let him deny himself and take up his cross and follow Me."

What does this mean to you and me in this day and hour? It means accepting our fellow beings where they are in order that we may patiently and lovingly lead them to where God wants them to be. It means to stoop to the feet-washing level of our neighbor's need in order that we may lift him or her to the glorious heights of God's loving acceptance. It means to identify with humanity about us, irrespective of race, color, or creed—to be truly human in the presence of our human brothers and sisters. It means involvement with the sufferings and sorrows, conflicts and consternations, failures and defeats, of our fellow persons. It means that we bear one another's burdens and share in their despair. It means that we listen—and then put our lives on the line in loving and sacrificial action to bring justice and dignity and opportunity and validity to every human being within our reach or circle of influence. It means that, whenever and wherever possible, we proclaim the blessed Gospel of God's love and grace through Jesus Christ.

It may mean other things as well, but these will certainly demand self-denial and cross-bearing of the disciples of Jesus.

Monday   *Romans 12:1–8 (A)*

God Gives—We Respond

Our great God gives; we are expected to respond to His gracious gifts. This response, according to Paul, is to be the offering of our lives, the placing of ourselves at God's disposal, for the accomplishment of His purposes in our world about us. It means that we turn our hearts, minds, and bodies over to God's ownership and dedicate our abilities to His service.

We have all received God's gifts for this very purpose. They are not given to us to enhance our beauty or assure our worldly security, or even to make us more desirable or respected among the people with whom we live and labor. They are committed to us in order to be committed back to God in and through and by way of service to our fellow beings for God's sake. This is precisely the way in which our God meets the needs of our neighbor—through us and through the gifts entrusted to us.

Not all of us have the gifts that would enable us to administer or preach or finance important projects. But we all have specific gifts and abilities—love, energy, persistence, patience, sincerity, concern, creativity. We are to exercise these things upon one another and on behalf of one another. We are to care for each other even as much as we care for ourselves. We are to allow our God to reach and touch others, even our very enemies, with His care and concern for them through us.

"We are His workmanship, created in Christ Jesus for good works," wrote Paul to the church at Ephesus (2:10). The sacrifice we are to make to God as our response to His saving grace is ourselves. The altar upon which our sacrifice is to be made is the altar of our neighbor's need. Let us celebrate and serve!

Tuesday   *Mark 7:1–8, 14–15, 21–23 (B)*

Worship that Is Acceptable

One day, thousands of years ago, two men brought their sacrifices to their crudely made altars to offer them to God. The first man was Abel; he was a keeper of sheep. His sacrifice was the best of the flock. The second man was Cain; he was a tiller of the soil. His sacrifice was the fruit of the ground. Both men brought sacrifices; both brought of what they had; both offered them to God. Yet there was a significant distinction, one made by God Himself: "And the Lord had regard for Abel and his offering, but for Cain and his offering He had no regard" (Genesis 4:4–5).

While some have attempted to explain the dilemma by referring to the necessity of a blood-offering, which Cain's was not, I suggest that it goes deeper than this. The difference in God's attitude toward the sacrifices of the two worshipers lay in the heart attitudes of these two before God. Cain was going through a religious exercise. Abel's offering was sprinkled with the incense of lowly trust and came from a heart which desired to love God and obey His commandments. It was therefore a joy to God.

Customs and traditions change a great deal, but not the attitudes of men and women before God. There are, on the one hand, the lip-worshipers: "This people honors Me with their lips, but their heart is far from Me," said Jesus; "in vain do they worship Me. . . ." Lip-worshipers are the loose adherents of the Christian movement. They use the church and the name of Christian for their own self-centered purposes. According to one writer, they are "pagans with a fringe on top." There are, on the other hand, those who demonstrate heart-trust. They bring the acceptable offering—the offering of Abraham, who portrayed his heart-trust by his obedience to God; or of David, who prayed: "Create in me a clean heart, O God"; or of Isaiah, who responded to God's call with the answer and committal: "Here am I, send me"; or of Zacchaeus, who responded to Christ's invitation to follow Him with the pledge to give half of his goods to the poor and restore fourfold to anyone he may have defrauded; or of Paul, who "counted everything as loss because of the surpassing worth of knowing Christ Jesus."

Is our worship today acceptable? It is if we come to God as His children and go out into our world as His servants.

Wednesday   *Ephesians 6:10–20 (B)*

Off to the Wars

The Christian walk is never easy. There are enemies to contend with, obstacles to confront, and these are to be opposed and overcome in the power and Spirit of God. Whether these enemies, these spiritual forces of darkness, work through the power structures over us or the numerous loopholes that plague our individual lives, we must learn how to recognize who and what they are and resist them whenever they appear.

If we are to be strong and courageous in the face of enemy forces far stronger than we are, it will necessitate our leaning on or drawing from the power made available to us through Jesus Christ. For one thing, we will have to be intense in our search for truth. Christ has revealed to us all we need to know in order to experience daily God's saving love. Yet we should be open always to ever deeper insights and experiences of His divine love. We are clothed in God's righteousness, gifted with His salvation. Nothing can change that—save our neglect to act upon it. We are to walk in God's path for our lives, the path of loving service to our fellow persons for His sake. We are to fill our minds and commit our lives to His Word and His will for us, and our bodies will act accordingly. We must continually shun the ever-grasping tentacles of the Law that seek to draw us back into its stifling embrace, and walk and run, work and serve, with our faith centered upon that One who made us His own through Jesus Christ.

We are off to the wars. Let us keep awake and be aware—and joyously and freely abandon ourselves to loving God and communicating His love through our love for those we meet along the way.

Thursday   *Luke 14–1, 7–14 (C)*

The Main Course: Humble Pie

The way to God is the way of humility. "He who humbles himself will be exalted," said Jesus. Before God can do anything with us, we must be humbled, repentant, needful before Him.

The way to humility is the way of a broken heart. "The sacrifice acceptable to God is a broken spirit," said the psalmist; "a broken and contrite heart, O God, Thou wilt not despise" (Psalm 51:17). This has been true throughout the history of Israel. From Abraham, the father of believers, to the insignificant tax collector beating his breast in the temple, the sign and seal of God's presence has always been brokenness.

It is the same with us. When God comes near, we find nothing in ourselves to cling to. Our aims and ambitions are transformed into gaping idols. Our merits and manners become like dead leaves before the wind. Our sins and shortcomings blot out the very sun. Before we can be of use to God, we must be broken, crushed, sometimes even to the point of despair. Some people enter into this experience in almost imperceptible ways, under the preaching of the Word or the prick of the conscience. Others need to be frightened by an earthquake or drained dry by some physical disease or emotional trauma. Only then will they recognize their fallibilities and insufficiencies and humble themselves before the almighty, loving God.

It is then that the divine Potter reaches out to gather the broken pieces and mold them into a vessel beautiful and precious in His sight. The way of humility is the way of a broken heart. It is also the way to true significance and worth.

Advice for God's Children

We are to guard carefully our relationships with one another and regard even those who are unknown to us as possible emissaries from God. Every interpersonal relationship is a sacred trust—especially those within the family of faith. We need to remember our comrades who are facing problems and conflicts that are even more severe than our own. Our leaders, as human and frail and error-prone as we are, need our respect and our prayers. When they are compelled to make unpopular decisions that are necessary to God's purposes, let us contribute to their courage and respect by giving them our support. We are to do this joyfully, not fearfully, for we are all God's ministers and must learn how to suffer and rejoice together.

We are all God's emissaries to one another—and through us He shares His grace with the members of Christ's body. We march together through a hostile world as the children of God—reaching out to the wanderers and stragglers by the way to draw them into God's family. There will be a price to pay and pains to bear, but we will be able to cope with these because we have a great God whose love for us never changes and who promises that eternal joy which we even now have found in some measure and which we shall experience fully and eternally when our march has been completed.

"Let brotherly love continue."

We Are His Forever

"If you return, I will restore you, and you shall stand before Me."

We feel at times that God has given up on us, that while we are the children of His grace, we as His servants have failed to measure up to our responsibilities to effectively carry out His purposes in stemming the tide of wickedness overwhelming our world and in proclaiming and demonstrating His redeeming love to the people about us. Yet we know, deep within us, that His love for us never ceases, that when our faith falters, He is ever faithful.

We must daily remember that He cares about us, that He is with us, that He will never withdraw His grace from us. The world is in His hands, and despite the persistent rebelliousness of its inhabitants, He will accomplish His purposes within it. It is not important that we see the results of our servanthood; it is important that we trust God and His Spirit—that we wait quietly and patiently for the revealing of His kingdom. Let come what may, adversity or affliction, enmity or opposition, feelings of defeat or the ridicule of our peers, we are the redeemed children and the chosen servants of our God.

We will fail; we will flounder and fall—but only to arise again and stand before God as His forgiven and restored children and servants, for we are His forever.

Sixteenth Sunday After Pentecost

Matthew 18:15–20 (A)

You Are My Body

"This is My body," said Jesus as He broke bread and distributed it among His disciples. It is possible that He was also saying, in effect: "You are My body; from now on you are to be My visible body in your world. Partaking of Me and empowered by My Spirit, you are to communicate and demonstrate My Father's love and purposes in the world about you. I must now leave you to make the supreme sacrifice, but you will now become My visible body and assume My role in representing and channeling God's saving love to the masses on your planet."

As we partake of the body and blood through the bread and wine today, we need to be aware of three things. The *first* has to do with our own bankruptcy. Pervaded, permeated, and impregnated with sin and self-centeredness, we are incapable of pleasing God or winning His favor. But, by the grace of God, that status has been changed. He has redeemed, forgiven, restored us to Himself, and we are assured of that in the blessed Sacrament.

The *second* is that we must come determined that there is nothing between us and our Christian brothers and sisters—the other members of Christ's body that gather at the Lord's table along with us. Our Lord made this a requirement. We are to love one another, and that means to forgive one another and do everything possible to receive the forgiveness of those we have hurt or offended. This is our real family that we are communing with—more truly so than are our unchristian blood-relatives.

The *third* is that we are to come to the Lord's table as the various members of Christ's body to be assured of His forgiving love and of one another's love, and to be strengthened and encouraged, that we may leave the sanctuary joyful and strong and motivated and ready to apply our lives and energies and specific gifts to carrying out Christ's purposes in our community and world.

If this is our desire and intention today, we are invited to come to the Lord's table to celebrate our redemption, to receive God's grace through Christ, to lovingly bind ourselves to one another, and then to go out determined to enlist our lives and gifts in the service of God—in our family, our job, and in the wide human family about us.

God and Government

We are now God's children. We have been set free from the stern requirements of the Law, even the screaming demands of our self-centered natures, in order to live and celebrate and serve as the sons and daughters of God. We are, however, to live our lives responsibly. Even the secular authorities over us are to be God's instruments through which He governs and directs our lives. When we disobey these, or fail in our obligations to them, we must expect to suffer the penalty for our disobedience.

Nevertheless, our responsibility is first and foremost to God. The authorities we choose to govern us are expected to govern in accordance with His goals and objectives. If their rule is unjust, we must seek to bring justice to all men and women. If they seek to usurp God's will for our lives, we must obey God's will in scorn of consequences. They may be God's instruments, but they can by no means take God's place in our lives and force us to carry out their wishes and objectives if these run contrary to God's will and Word for us. While we must surely honor our governing authorities, God forbid that we deify them in respect to our lives or the welfare of humanity about us.

We have been set free from the demands of the Law in order to relate to and be governed by a higher, more perfect law. It is the law or the requirement of love. We are to love God, and we are to love our fellow persons even as we love ourselves. It is that law which enjoins us to demonstrate true love in our fractured world.

May God help us live for Him and for others rather than solely for ourselves!

The Touch That Transforms

This Gospel lesson gives us a glimpse of the miracle-working touch of Jesus, our Lord and Savior. By His touch eyes were made to see, ears to hear, tongues to speak, feet to walk, hands to serve again. It means more than that. He came to disentangle the broken strands of life, the discordant harmonies of fear and despair and hopelessness. He came, that by His miraculous touch men and women might again be brought into pitch with God and walk once more within divine order and orbit for their lives. A woman was taken in the act of adultery and dragged before Jesus to be judged. By His touch she became a loving and loyal disciple. A tax collector turned from his cheating and robbing to feel His touch and became a warrior for Christ. A hater of Christians who sought them out for imprisonment or execution felt the touch of Christ and was transformed from the cruelest persecuter into the greatest propagator of Christianity this world has ever known.

And things like this are happening every day throughout the world. Alcoholics, drug addicts, criminals, sick, lonely, empty, suicidal people are being touched by the Spirit of God and transformed into His loving and serving sons and daughters.

The touch of the Master has come upon each of us. It first came through His Spirit in our baptism. It became real to us when we decisively and willfully committed ourselves to the Christ of the baptismal covenant. This did not bring with it the dissolving of all our problems or the eradication of all our conflicts, but with Christ's touch came new order and harmony and joy and power and meaning and purpose into our lives. God grant that it will result in the extending of our lives into the unbearable, unendurable conflicts of others about us, where we may become the loving and healing touch of God upon their lives.

Wednesday   *James 1:17–22, 26–27 (B)*

Growing in Faith

We have much to learn as the children of God. The most difficult, perhaps, is to learn how to regard our trials and tribulations, even the tragedies that beset us (see the verses just before our reading), as capable of enhancing and enriching our lives. Whereas God does not send them, He does permit them—or chooses not to intervene between us and the sufferings that afflict us. Yet He can use them to draw us closer to Him and thereby accomplish His purposes in and through us. We need the wisdom to accept these painful happenings with graciousness, even with joy, knowing that whatever they may be, God can transform them from ugliness into beauty, from the plots of Satan designed to destroy into the purposes of God destined to fulfill. The key is a genuine faith in a loving God, a faith that frees us and strengthens us to endure whatever may come our way. We won't win every battle in this incessant war against the powers of the night, but the ultimate victory is, in Jesus Christ, already ours.

There is something else we must learn as God's children. It is not enough to be listeners and proclaimers of the Gospel; we are commissioned to be doers. Christian faith that falls short of loving performance in respect to the needs of suffering people about us falls far short of what it should be. May our faith be rekindled and burn bright with joy and obedience.

Call for Commitment

Jesus constantly called for commitment. He never allowed or expected that His followers would get by with anything less. And it was this kind of preaching that limited His following to a mere handful of publicans and fishermen. "You had better count the cost if you are going to be My disciple," He said. "My purpose for your life must take precedence over your country, parents, mates, children—even your own life. Indeed, if you are not willing to renounce everything you have, you simply cannot be My disciple."

Abraham was called to leave his country and his father's house, that he might be of use to God. Moses was called to turn his back on those who brought him up, that he might be free to serve God. Jeremiah was asked to deny himself many of the greatest joys of life, such as wife and children, in order to follow God's plan for his life. God may never call on us to do what He expected of Abraham or Moses or Jeremiah— or of Christ's disciples, most of whom were martyred for His sake—but whatever His word to us and His will for us, it may be better to make no decision at all to follow Jesus if that decision is to be a halfhearted one.

Our response to God's great gift of love and to Christ's call to servanthood must be commitment. There are risks involved as to our lives and possessions. And there will be failures in our determination to live committed lives; but there is always forgiveness and renewal when we fall, and the grace to get up and try again.

God grant to us the grace to live valid Christian lives.

Our Equality Before God

Our relationship to our fellow beings within the body of Christ is of paramount importance. Our roles as the ministers of Christ, our assignments as His beloved servants, may greatly vary. Some of us are leaders who have been granted positions of authority over others. We ought to be aware that our social or educational status, regardless of what it means to our peers, does not impress our Lord; every one of His children is equally important to Him. And we need to be reminded, from time to time, that with leadership comes responsibility, the responsibility to treat those who work under us as our equals before God, and to love them as such, our brothers and sisters in Christ.

We are, every one of us, the ministers of God. God works through us. We need each other, parent and child, employer and employee, master and servant. We must together submit to the Master of masters, the Lord of lords, our Redeemer and King, our Father and our God. Together we seek to fulfill His objectives and advance His kingdom. We do so as members of the same family, the family of God and Christ.

Saturday *Ezekiel 33:7–9 (A)*

Commanded to Bear Witness

In response to God's grace we have embraced Him not only as our Savior but as our Lord and Master. Our obedience ought to come as a result or consequence of our salvation. If we have received His love, we respond in loving obedience, to servanthood, to sacrificial giving, to speaking Law and Gospel to the multitudes of God's creatures about us. Because we are human beings still tainted by self-centeredness and afflicted by weaknesses, bound to this sin-ridden world by our mortality, we need the challenges, admonitions, and exhortations of Scripture and of our comrades in Christ to stir us from our selfish, fearful slumbers and push us out into our world to serve God by speaking His Word to people and by serving humanity on His behalf.

Seventeenth Sunday After Pentecost

Matthew 18:21–35 (A)

God Forgives—Can We Forgive?

The servant within the parable of our Gospel lesson was graciously released from his impossible-to-pay debt only to sally forth and harass a fellow servant who owed him a small sum. The king had pronounced him forgiven, but that had not altered the resentment and hostility in his heart, and he turned right around to take it out of the hide of his fellowman.

Something of this sort often happens in the Christian frame of reference. Maybe such an attitude is apparent in our inborn prejudices toward other races or social classes, our snobbishness, our looking-down-our-noses at the weaknesses and failures of others. If this is true, does it not proclaim to the world that something is out of kilter in our relationship to God? God has done His part; He has bestowed His love and forgiveness on every one of us. If we, in turn, cannot genuinely portray a like spirit of love and forgiveness toward our fellow persons, it indicates some basic insincerity or lack of receptivity in respect to the forgiveness of our sin. The forgiving and accepting love of God is the basis for our forgiving and accepting and loving our fellow beings. If the first does not result in the latter, that, according to Jesus, puts us at odds with God. "To be reconciled with God," writes Stewart James, "is to see all mankind with new eyes." It is to have the living Christ within, which means to feel towards others as Christ would feel and act toward them.

It is disconcerting to realize how often our unforgiving attitudes toward others are in reality a reflection or a projection of our disgust for ourselves. Our recognition and declaration of our own bankruptcy, and of God's acceptance of us as we are, certainly ought to result in making us tender, acceptive, understanding, and forgiving toward our fellow persons. If we really embrace God's forgiveness, we will be forgiving.

We Are the Lord's

No matter how strong our convictions, or how ecstatic our feelings in respect to our faith, God forbid that we attempt to compress Him into set forms or shapes that we expect others to swallow and digest. God is too big for our little boxes or our personal convictions. Whereas He is most certainly revealed through the Christ, He is not confined to the regulations and revelations that we wrap around Him. What may be good for us in respect to the means and methods of sustaining and demonstrating our faith is not necessarily appropriate for others.

We have no right or obligation to deny or demean another person's experience. Others cannot dictate what we can or cannot do as Christians. At the same time, Christian love will not permit us to unnecessarily hurt or offend them. Our freedom in Christ enables us to respect another person's convictions even if they don't make much sense to us. Few of us will agree on all interpretations of God and His will for our lives. We can and ought to agree on the prime requirements of every Christian—that we learn how to love and care for one another.

"We are the Lord's." Whatever we do, live or die, eat or drink, indulge or abstain, we do as the children of God. May our love be large enough and generous enough to embrace one another regardless of the manner in which we assume to understand or endeavor to worship and serve our God.

Have We Been Identified?

Peter identified Jesus as the Christ, the Messiah, the One who was promised. We have, as Peter ultimately did, identified Jesus Christ as God-come-to-earth and as our Lord and Savior by way of His cross where He died for our sins and the empty tomb from which He was raised as victor over sin and death. We declare with conviction that He is the Way, the Life, and the Truth, and we claim our redemption and salvation through Him.

Now the question is, have *we* been identified? Jesus said it plainly: There must also be a cross in our lives. Does our faith in what God has done for us through Christ and His cross result in our taking up our cross to follow Christ—in giving and losing our lives for His sake and the Gospel's? If it does not, are we truly, can we truly be, identified as Christians?

We are, of course, identified as God's sons and daughters at our baptism, but does that identification hold true today? While God never reneges on that covenant He made with us in our infancy, we can, and often do, as we mature into adulthood. We may continue to make our confessions of sin and faith, but these do not necessarily identify us as the followers of Christ. To be properly identified as such, we must proceed from confession to cross-bearing. It happened in the life of Peter; it is supposed to happen in our lives. We must begin with the cross—the cross of Jesus Christ. It is because of that cross that we are accepted just as we are. It is on the basis of what Christ did for us that we are to deny ourselves and take up our cross on behalf of others and to commit our forgiven and cleansed lives to servanthood.

It is as we do this that we are truly identified as the disciples of Jesus Christ.

Wednesday   *James 2:1–5, 8–10, 14–18 (B)*

When Our Faith Is Genuine

It may appear to be a small matter, but it translates into a gigantic flaw in the lives of scores of Christians. They dare to call themselves believers in and followers of Jesus Christ, and yet they act like outright bigots in their relationships with people who cross their path. If we look carefully—and honestly—we may recognize this to be one of ur problems, that we are at times among those who talk limitlessly about loving humanity but are really very selective about whom we accept as the objects of our love and concern.

We are enjoined to love our neighbor as ourselves. When our judgment of people and our actions toward them are determined by the color of their skin, the cut of their clothes, or the size of their bank account, we are not acting like the children and servants of God. Indeed, we are sinning against God and endangering our relationship to Him when we neglect to give equal respect and value to all of His children around us. We need to reexamine our concepts of morality, to blast out some of the silly notions that apparently influence our responses to life and people, and learn how to be loving and compassionate.

Some of us may still be hooked on the ridiculous notion that religious faith is something to be exercised primarily through the rituals of a worship service. We can be all mouth in terms of confessions and testimonials while the rest of our bodies may be paralyzed by unbelief or disobedience. We need to call a spade a spade, to tear away the fictitious labels and have the courage to confront the painful truth that we can't talk faith unless we have faith; and when we have the faith that Jesus proclaimed and dmonstrated, we in turn will live it and demonstrate it in sacrificial love for the human family about us.

Thursday   *Luke 15:1–10 (C)*

The One Who Was Lost

I am the one who was lost. There is only one antidote for the poison that taints my soul and binds me to the insufficiencies and inadequacies of this existence. It is revealed in Jesus Christ and the Gospel He proclaims, the Gospel that Christ is seeking the one who is lost. Until I realized that I could not escape, that I was lost, it wasn't likely that I would ever be found. The very purpose of Christ's coming, of His cross and the empty tomb, is to find and redeem the lost, to receive sinners, to draw me and others like me back into His orbit for our lives. Where there is no sin, no unsolvable problems or overwhelming complexities, no moral or human weakness, there is no need of a Savior.

It is when I am up against something that is too much for me—when there are problems, weaknesses, sins, distortions in my life that I cannot solve or overcome, when I am truly lost in the wilderness of my failures and insufficiencies—that I become the object of God's search and may hear the divine call of the Good Shepherd and be restored once more to His loving care. It is then that He delivers and heals, forgives and empowers, and draws me into the experience of joy and health and strength and courage that puts point and purpose back into my life and living.

I have been found. I have been drawn back into God's will and purpose for my life. It is a place of refuge in a tempestuous world. But my Lord is still out in that world—seeking those who are lost, the creatures for whom He died and rose again, reaching out, touching, embracing, healing, loving, guiding men and women and children back into His loving will for their lives. And there is where I must be— alongside my brothers and sisters—as the vehicle and instrument through which Christ's Spirit may find others who are lost, in order to touch them with His love and grace and restore them to His order and purpose.

The Law Versus the Gospel

Though it may never have been intended as such, this lesson is a remarkable sequel to yesterday's Gospel lesson. Paul certainly considered himself as one of those who was lost, and this even though he faithfully lived by the Law he once subscribed to and vigorously attempted to stamp out the followers of the Christ who proclaimed Him as the way of salvation. Paul's amazing conversion experience qualified him to say "that Christ Jesus came into the world to save sinners," and he was quite sure that he was the "foremost of sinners."

Our salvation does not come, nor is our relationship to God assured, by our subscription to particular rules and orders, be they traditional or contemporary, that are being peddled as Gospel today. We are saved by faith—by our total acceptance of what Christ has done on our behalf, with a resulting commitment to God and His will for our lives. In a society where crime and corruption, family breakdowns, sexual promiscuity, and disregard for human life are on the rise, in a nation where much-relied-on structures are crumbling, it is indeed tempting to correlate laws and rules and orders with the Gospel of love and freedom that was proclaimed and demonstrated by Jesus Christ. We need to be guided, and sometimes inhibited, by laws and rules. It is when we make them a part of the Gospel we proclaim and live by, that we endanger our faith and promote a system of beliefs that may corrupt the faith of others.

Let us thank God, as did Paul, that we, whatever our past sins and errors, have been restored to the mercy of God and are counted worthy in Christ to be His servants.

The Greatest Miracle of All

"You meant evil against me, but God meant it for good."

I wonder if Paul had Joseph's experience in mind when he wrote, "We know that in everything God works for good with those who love Him, who are called according to His purpose" (Romans 8:28). The greatest miracle of all, in my estimation, is not that God somehow engineers or manipulates our circumstances, but that He is with us through them and in them and can miraculously bring them about or turn and use them to accomplish His purposes in and through us.

To believe that God programs us like some kind of computer, that the tragic happenings in our lives are instigated by Him in order to keep us in line or to mature and equip us for His service, is to reduce the miracle-working power of God and regard Him as a puppeteer of sorts. He thrust us into our chaotic, sin-ridden world and, allowing for some remarkable exceptions, allows us to deal with its gifts of joy and its hours of horror and pain without some supernatural intervention to shield us from its potential ugliness and misery. The miracle is that His children are never without His loving presence or His gifts of strength and courage, which enable them to face whatever befalls them. If we cling to Him, He will bring beauty out of ashes and springs of water out of parched sands—in His own good time and in response to our faith in Him and His promises.

This is what He did in the life of Joseph, miraculously using him as a vehicle of blessing to the people of Israel. It is this sort of thing that He has done and will do in our lives.

Eighteenth Sunday After Pentecost

Matthew 20:1–16 (A)

Idle Hands

"Why do you stand here idle all day?"

Why is it that so many who claim the experience and title of Christian are not carrying out their ministry as the servants and priests of God? They have the calling and the assignment; they are the recipients of God's grace and power through His Spirit; they have a field of service, a parish or arena in which to proclaim Christ through word and demonstrate and transmit His love through word and deed. "Why do you stand here idle . . . ?"

Maybe we need to understand again just what Christianity is. It is not a mere philosophy, a conglomeration of virtues, a system of ethics, but a radical, revolutionary experience. It is not confined to having our sins forgiven, or a guarantee of heaven and eternal life, as basic and necessary and glorious as all this is. It is a losing of our lives that we may find them, a denying of self and taking up the cross and following Christ, a pledging of loyalty and unhesitating obedience to Christ as King and Lord and Commander-in-Chief, a following of that One who commands us to "Go into all the world . . . preach . . . bear fruit . . . love. . . ." It means that, by virtue of our redemption, we become debtors to every human being on the face of the earth until they, too, are brought into the redemption of Christ.

Martin Buber once said: "He who ceases to make a response ceases to hear the Word." So "why do [we] stand here idle. . . . ?" Is Jesus real to us, or is He just a fad, a crying-post, a pious notion? This is our opportunity and our invitation. We need only to confess and renounce our inactive, idle, sinful past, to crown Jesus Christ as Savior, Lord, and King of our lives, and having thus "tuned in" to Him to "turn out" our lives toward the accomplishment of His purposes among our fellow beings.

Alive and Serving

It is truly amazing, and it should be encouraging to all of us, the way God is able to turn the unhappy things that befall us, even our foolish errors and failures, into stepping-stones toward the accomplishment of His purposes in our world. We have much to celebrate. God has not given up on our world. He is here—and sometimes because of us, sometimes in spite of us, He is working out His purposes in our world.

Our greatest concern should be that we may fail to give God our all, and to risk our all, so that His purposes may be accomplished through us. This means that we should be willing to put our lives on the line, to live and, if need be, to die in order to fulfill our commission as God's soldiers and servants. We have nothing to lose and nothing to be afraid of. It is not surprising that we cling so tenaciously to this life. It is all that our natural senses can comprehend. Nevertheless, if we knew what God has in store for us, we would have no fear whatsoever of death and whatever may follow death. We would probably be most eager to leave this vale of tears for the indescribable glories of life eternal.

We are, however, here in the valley and under divine orders. Let us be alive and courageous and joyful and obedient as we faithfully carry out God's commission to us.

The Secret of Greatness

Still thinking of the new kingdom that they visualized, and still assuming that their Master was about to launch a new and all-powerful kingdom with the people of Israel, the disciples conjectured among themselves about who might be the greatest and the most honored among them in the new kingdom Jesus was about to establish. We are perfectly capable of understanding and identifying with the disciples in this instance because we are very much like them. The difference between our world-order and God's order is that our ambitions in terms of this world are usually for being number one or being better than others in some aspect of life. This concept is as American as motherhood and apple pie. It is encouraged in our educational programs, our sports and athletic extravaganzas, in politics, the business world, the entertainment world, the arts. Competition and winning are the name of the game. It has almost become the primary religion of our lives.

Jesus knew what the disciples were thinking—and what we are inclined to feel. He took His disciples aside and said to them and to us, "If any one would be first, he must be last of all and servant of all." This is the secret of greatness in the new order that Jesus came to establish. It happens when we learn how to be servants. We are not here to lead or dominate or simply serve our private interests, but to serve—in our community, in our world—by taking sides with the poor and oppressed against this world's forces that ignore them or seek to manipulate them, by responding to their desperate needs. Those needs are primarily spiritual in terms of hearing and responding to God's Word. They are also physical and temporal, their needs for freedom and justice and daily sustenance.

As with Jesus, so with us, this kind of servanthood involves a cross. For us this means the crucifixion of our self-centered efforts to be number one and the pain and suffering involved in being servants to one another. This is the secret of greatness.

Wednesday   *James 3:16—4:6 (B)*

The War Within Us

There is a war of sorts being waged within us which, if not adequately handled, is capable of creating a war around us. It is initiated by the ever-present inner urge for self-gratification and -glorification. There seems always to be something on the inside that rebels against and even attempts to dethrone the God who created us and claims us for Himself. It began with Adam; it continues within each of us.

More often than not, we yield to those self-serving instincts and desires and thereby crowd the Spirit of God into some small corner of our lives wherein His influence and control upon us and through us is severely limited. The evil force within us, when unleashed, is capable of turning us into the very enemies of God—of rupturing our faith and drawing us back into darkness again.

We cannot totally escape the siren calls of the natural man and woman, and we shall fall prey to those destructive powers if we do battle on their own ground. We can, however, resist these urges and instincts, and resist them successfully, if we do so with the grace that God grants His children. He grants this grace to those of us who submit to His loving intervention in our lives and who give Him permission to conquer, control, and remold our passions into vessels for His holy use.

It is a day-by-day, week-by-week battle, but it is one that Christ has won—and will win for us if we remain faithful to Him.

Thursday   *Luke 16:1–13 (C)*

Accumulators or Stewards?

Christ in this parable relates how some people who are not of His kingdom make use of wealth in ways that secure their existence upon this world. They see to it that some material riches are used for the welfare of others. They are wiser, in their own way, than many of those who claim to follow Jesus.

One does not enter God's kingdom by generously sharing gifts with others—though a person may thereby benefit by the love and devotion of those whom he or she serves. No one can come to the Father except through Christ. However, all who come unto Him and become a part of His kingdom will accept their calling as stewards of God's great gifts and utilize them to bring light and joy into the lives of God's creatures about them. They will find their greatest joy in serving others, because in serving them they are truly serving God.

What we have acquired and accumulated is not ours; all the good things that have come our way have come from the hand of the Father. While they are given to enrich our lives here upon earth, they are also granted for the purpose of enriching and blessing the lives of others. When, however, we make God's gifts the object of our loyalty and devotion, they take His place in our lives and become a curse rather than a blessing and may render us ineligible for that life and kingdom which He has prepared for us. In that event, we are, in the midst of our grand accumulations, truly and eternally poverty-stricken.

Friday   *1 Timothy 2:1–8 (C)*

Let Us Pray

Salvation does not come to us by way of the Law or by our participation in religious exercises, but our acceptance of God's forgiving and

267

redeeming love does place upon us certain responsibilities. We are to live through loving, and that requires that we be nonviolent, peaceful, kind, humble, nonjudgmental, caring, fair-minded, self-giving, and persistent seekers for equality and dignity, freedom and opportunity, for everyone. This may well begin with prayers to God on behalf of every human being—from our leaders and executives in high places to the laborer, the poor, the uneducated, the oppressed.

We are most certainly enjoined to pray for these people. Then we must get off our knees and do whatever we possibly can, by the grace that God grants, to become His means of answering our own prayers on behalf of these people. We need to select leaders who will fulfill the requisites of just leadership. We are to support them in these endeavors, and to do everything possible to feed the hungry and assure equality and dignity, freedom and opportunity, for all.

God knows far better than we the needs of every human being. While our prayers for others offer no new information to Him, they may prepare us to be the vehicles through which He can meet people's needs with His loving grace.

Saturday   *Amos 8:4–7 (C)*

Time to Think

The prophet Amos compared the Lord's speaking to the roar of a lion (1:2; 3:8). Is it possible that this lion has been domesticated for most of us—even those of us who are in the church? In our Old Testament lesson Amos rails against his people "who trample upon the needy and bring the poor of the land to an end" in their efforts to make the best deals they can in buying and selling and the securing of their own futures. Is it possible that the Lord through Amos may be roaring against us?

Most of us are comparably rich in view of this world's masses that struggle so desperately for survival. So often we refuse to accept responsibility for helping them in their plight. We assume that we deserve our good fortune, and we overindulge in food and drink and luxurious living as if we were the favored children of God. Apart from occasional "hunger offerings," we busy ourselves with our small problems and all but ignore the multitudes who are starving to death.

While we have no immediate answers to the problem of the poor and oppressed, we are responsible for doing our best to relieve the conditions that make and keep people poor. Amos was a genius at this, and his words may upset our weekend, but it is time that we and our churches take note of his social analysis and contemplate what we can do about world poverty. How can we remain Christians without relating to the prophet's and our Lord's concern for the oppressed people of our world?

It is certainly something to think about. It may result in our seeking for ways to do something about it.

Nineteenth Sunday After Pentecost

Matthew 21:28–32 (A)

From Prattle to Practice

As we worship in our churches today, we utter very precious words. Through our singing and praying, confessions and creeds, we proclaim penitence and belief and pledge love and loyalty to our eternal God. Apart from this we could not continue as congregations and there would be no future for the church. Some of the most precious and significant words of the Bible are words of pledge and promise from the lips of those who committed their lives to God and Christ. "As for me and my house, we will serve the Lord," promised Joshua (24:15). "Deliver me from blood-guiltiness, O God . . . and my tongue will sing aloud of Thy deliverance," wrote the psalmist (51:14). "Here am I! Send me," exclaimed Isaiah (6:8). "I will follow You wherever You go," said an enthusiastic young man to Jesus (Luke 9:57). "I will lay down my life for You," proclaimed Peter (John 13:37).

The fact of the matter is, however, that words alone do not constitute a commitment, and there is a distinct precariousness in making such verbal commitments. We know this well by our innumerable failures to follow through on our commitments—failures to translate them into obedient activity in our everyday living.

Nor did Peter follow through on his heroic commitment, but after Christ's resurrection He was restored to a loving and obedient relationship to Jesus Christ. Perhaps this is the lesson of our text for today. Not only is it precarious to make verbal commitments—and they should not be made unless we are truly sincere—but there is the privilege of repentance and restoration when we fail to follow through. Even when we renege on our promises to follow Christ, He never ceases to reach out to us, seeking ever to restore us to a loving and obedient relationship with Himself.

May our worship today and every day include the restoration and recommittal of our lives to God and His purposes.

Living for Others

There is a way to test the authenticity of our relationship with God; it is by examining our relationships to our fellow beings. When we are short on compassion and concern for our brothers and sisters, it is probably because we haven't fully grasped or experienced God's infinite love for us. God is not holding back; His love is available. And so is His great wealth and power and all the other gifts needed to enrich our lives. They are, however, gifts that must be shared with others lest they turn to ashes in our hands.

There are, unfortunately, ambitious Christians who are more concerned about their own image than the needs of their fellow persons. They attempt to corral their God-given gifts for their own egocentric purposes. This was not true about Jesus Christ. Even though He was filled with the power of God, He never used it for His own glory or gratification. He became the servant of the very beings whom He and His Father created, using His divine power only to heal their hurts and free their spirits and reveal to them their rich inheritance as the children of God. As God-incarnate, Christ walked as man upon this earth— even through the experiences of torture and death—that He might touch human creatures with the love of their Father in heaven.

Now we are assigned to be Christs-incarnate—proclaiming, demonstrating, and communicating God's healing, reconciling love to one another and to His wandering, lonely, lost children around us. As Jesus "[took] the form of a servant," so we are to become the servants of God to people about us in order that "every tongue confess that Jesus Christ is Lord, to the glory of God the Father."

Confession or Camouflage?

It was stated in these meditations a couple of weeks ago that confession, if it is to be genuine, must result in cross-bearing. Now we may have to back up a step or two and recognize that before there can be genuine confession the camouflage, the window-dressing, the phony facades must be ripped off our lives and we must see ourselves as we really are.

Our Lord is not trying to frighten us; nevertheless, His words in our

271

lesson for today are radical and He invites us to take a radical stance, to make a radical decision, in the grand event of becoming His disciples. What He may be saying is that the business of following Him involves some pain. He first talks about the pain of amputation, the removal of hand or foot or eye, and is suggesting that life itself is more important than the individual members of the body. What Jesus is really getting at, of course, is the power of sin and death through invisible and spiritual appendages at work within us, and the necessity of removing these appendages, of suffering the pain of being separated from them and all that stands between us and God's will for our lives. Confession is very painful for a proud person, for this means the stripping away of the camouflage, the hypocrisy, the self-will that blocks God out of a person's life. It is spiritual surgery; it is radical surgery.

While our Lord's first illustration has to do with radical surgery, His second is medicinal and has to do with salt. The first has to do with the radical and sometimes painful separation of ourselves from those things that stand between us and God and are capable of destroying our relationship with Him. The "salt" illustration refers to the perpetual pain or discomfort of growing and maturing as God's children. However much it hurts when it is rubbed into fresh wounds, it is good, said Jesus. It helps to subdue and control the fire that rages within us. It sometimes burns like hell, but the burning is not forever, and it will help to keep us from going to hell, where the "worm does not die, and the fire is not quenched."

Suffer the amputations that are necessary! Let the salt do its work! It will change us; it will make us different people. It prepares for and perpetuates God's will and work in and through us. It will render us wholesome and happy as the sons and daughters, servants and ministers of God.

Wednesday   *James 4:7–12 (B)*

Lest We Throw Stones at Others

Sometimes we feel like nagging. Most often it takes the form of slicing, deprecating jibes, belittling, unappreciative attitudes towards other people's characters and contributions. What is so disconcerting is that it is usually not the incompetence of our victims that makes us critical toward them. It is often some disturbance or distortion within ourselves. It is a kind of projected form of self-deprecation. Because we feel small, inferior, invalid, inadequate, we find ourselves hacking away at somebody else until he or she is demoted to our assumed dimensions.

"Let him who is without sin among you be the first to throw a stone at her," said Jesus concerning a woman who was caught in a sinful act (John 8:7). When we recognize our own inner weaknesses, we are less likely to judge one another or to say things that may harm another person. Acknowledging our own humanity, we will not be so apt to play God with our own lives or toy with the emotions and affections of another.

God grant that we be truly human, acknowledging our frailties and failures, and yet authentic in our persistent search for and acceptance of God's control of our lives and destinies. May God's love and mercy for us cause us to drop our stones and be loving and merciful and tolerant in our attitudes toward others.

Thursday   *Luke 16:19–31 (C)*

"Get the Hell Out"

When the American Version of the Bible appeared over a century ago, a man came into an English book shop and asked for a copy of the "new Bible without any hell in it." The attitude expressed thereby has been characteristic of many people throughout the history of Christianity who are trying "to get the hell out" of theology and Christian teachings. Hell is indeed a repugnant doctrine—if one dare call it a doctrine. The fact that it does exist, however, is obvious all about us. Those who would like to "get the hell out" of the teachings of Christianity probably have little idea of the enormous price God has already paid to remove the fact of hell when He through Jesus Christ became man and died by torture in order to break the hold of sin and its consequences upon His creatures. Herein is the problem—and the tragedy: There is so much mercy, and still there is hell.

The good news of the Gospel is that there is deliverance from the hell that afflicts people today. It begins with the acknowledgment of sin, failures, mistakes in our lives. Having recognized with sorrow and confession our personal involvement in the hellish conditions that exist within and about us, we need no longer to brood over past errors but rather to accept God's acceptance of us as we are and to commit ourselves to His reign and control of our lives.

This means that we must dedicate ourselves to God's purposes as well, to be Christs-incarnate, channels and communicators of God's love and power into the hell that exists around us.

All those who trust in Christ as their Savior can eliminate forever any fear of hell in that glorious life eternal that Jesus guarantees through His death and resurrection on behalf of all God's creatures.

Friday   *1 Timothy 6:6–16 (C)*

The Curse of Accumulating

"While the affluent West's luxurious lifestyle continues to destroy the resources of this planet, 400 million starve and one half of the world's population exists in poverty." This is the cover statement of a recent book, and most of us brush it off with a "so what's new?" mumble and pass on to brighter thoughts. If we really dared ponder over it, we might have to admit that we as Christians are an integral part of that horrendous problem and are doing very little to respond to it.

As the children and servants of God, we are expected to renounce or remain detached from the things of this world and focus upon God and godliness, Christ and Christian service. This would demand concern for the poor and the suffering of our community and world. In the event that we are recipients of material wealth, we are charged with the responsibility to see to it that, as stewards of the gifts of God, His gifts to us do not dilute our devotion to Him but accentuate our commitment to the needs of our brothers and sisters on this planet.

May God help us to consider carefully what has been committed to us, not that we keep it for ourselves, for we will then lose it, but that we invest it wisely in meeting the physical needs of suffering people and in the blessed task of drawing them into the redeeming love of our great God.

Saturday   *Amos 6:1–7 (C)*

The Abrasive Truth

"Woe to those who are at ease . . . who feel secure. . . ."

Our week ends on a woe-filled note. There is much in Scripture that is not comfortable or comfort-giving. We would like to relegate the "woes" of Amos to the Old Testament, where we think they should stay. After all, the life of a Christian ought to be a life of peace and joy, and one needs a little of both after a week on the front lines of life's daily battle.

But do we dare, as concerned and conscientious Christians, to "rest easily," to be smugly secure in our kind of world? Unless we shut our eyes and clap our hands to our ears, or crawl into some dark cave to shut out the ugly sights and abrasive sounds of this world's suffering people, it is just about impossible to be at ease or to feel secure.

If we are to be healthy, maturing Christians, it seems that we will have to learn how to live in tension. It is an ongoing, never-ending tension between the peace and joy and comfort of a sin-forgiven, life-giving relationship with God through Christ and our tremendous, often frightening responsibility as His children and servants in our kind of world. For some Christians this has meant imprisonment; others have faced torture and death. We are all being challenged to change our affluent life-style in order to feed and house the millions who are hungry and unsheltered. How can any of us really be "at ease" or "feel secure" if we are awake and loving enough to be humane and Christian in this global village we call our world?

Maybe tomorrow's meditation will be more comfort-giving. For today, however, let us painfully consider the "woes" of Amos and muse on what they ought to mean to us.

Twentieth Sunday After Pentecost

Matthew 21:33–43 (A)

Our Involvement in the Crucifixion

Jesus had various reasons for doing so much of His teaching by way of parables. In some instances it was to hide the true meaning from those who were immature and undiscerning. In other instances it was to make unmistakably clear His message and purpose. He must have had the latter in mind when He told this parable. It was during His last week upon this earth. The ever-increasing hostility of the religious authorities was about to culminate in His execution. Our Lord, in very picturesque language, levels with them, and there is little doubt that some of them understood full well His meaning.

The parable points up the responsibility of our nation and our church before our Creator and God. Our greatest concern, however, is what He may be saying about us as individuals about our responsibility as His avowed followers. As the householder of the parable sent his son into the vineyard, so Christ is in our midst. And His presence demands a response. We are not as neglectful as were the tenants of this parable; we sing hymns, spell out our creeds, make the elaborate motions of worship, and are respectfully aware of altar and cross. But what does Jesus find in our hearts? He does not find the hatred of the parable-tenants, but He might find something just as insidious: preoccupation, procrastination, neglect to fully embrace Christ and His lifestyle, attempts to fit Him into our own formula or pattern, unwillingness to give Him prior devotion or to dedicate our lives to working within His vineyard and living out His purposes in our day-by-day activities because of the discomfort or inconvenience or personal sacrifice this may entail.

We remember the question Pilate put to the people during Christ's trial: "What shall I do with Jesus who is called Christ?" We know the answer. Every unconfessed sin and selfishly hoarded possession or gift in our lives cries out the same screaming answer: "Let Him be crucified" (Matthew 27:22). Until we commit ourselves totally to Christ, irrespective of the consequences, this is the answer of our lives. There is, however, another answer that we can make. It is that expressed by Paul when he said, "I have been crucified *with* Christ" (Galatians 2:20). Let us lay our sins, our guilt, our aims and ambitions, our very selves, at the foot of the cross. Let Him slay us and the dominion of sin and Satan and self-centeredness within us. Then our lives will become a vineyard yielding forth rich fruit to the glory of God, the salvation of others, and our own eternal joy.

Monday   *Philippians 3:12–21 (A)*

Let Us Press On

Jesus Christ is sufficient—and so is the righteousness He imparts to us. We don't earn or merit or gain it by following certain rules or rituals; we receive it as the gift of God's love. We possess this righteousness even now by faith in Christ. We have no need for any other.

This by no means indicates that we have arrived—that we have already reached a state of perfection. We do indeed belong to God; we are His possession. And yet we struggle constantly to surrender our beings to Him and let Him have His way with us. This does not come easily. It involves the crucible of conflict—even failure and defeat. But even when we fall, we fall only to rise again. Acknowledging but never nursing our failures, we claim God's gracious forgiveness and press on, knowing that our loving God understands and perpetually reaches out to draw us to Himself.

Even while we are God's sons and daughters, we are in the process of *becoming*. Our sanctification is not yet completed, and it won't be until we break through this mortal shell to become perfectly and eternally united with God. In the meantime our citizenship is in God's kingdom and we are here to advance that kingdom throughout our sorry world.

Tuesday   *Mark 10:2–16 (B)*

The Tragedy of Divorce

Some of us preachers, even those of us who stay married to the wife or husband of our youth, are reluctant about taking on this Gospel lesson. Some of you who have endured the tragedy of divorce are deeply disturbed every time you come across these words of Jesus. It is obvious that Jesus strongly disapproved of divorce.

All interpersonal relationships in the family of God, and marriage is a very special one, are to be treated as something sacred and permanent. Divorce or separation is always a tragedy, even when we acknowledge God's forgiveness for our errors and faults and the failure to make our relationships work.

We cannot make divorce acceptable as the world around us appears to be doing; it can't be painted over or garnished with respectability. We can, however, cling to the Gospel that proclaims sinners as eligible for God's loving forgiveness. Jesus came into the world to save sinners, and that includes the divorced. The forgiveness of God is total and eternal. And both the Word of God and the experiences of countless saints clearly testify to the power of God in picking up the broken pieces of human wreckage, and the broken relationships caused by such, to create new vessels of beauty and usefulness.

You are forgiven, you who have been shaken and flattened by this bitter experience. Claim that forgiveness, and go on with God. Your first allegiance is to Him and His will for your life. It is out of this kind of loyalty to God that you will discover your relationships to others becoming truly meaningful and joyful.

Wednesday   *Hebrews 2:9–11 (12–18) (B)*

What a Savior We Have!

God, through Jesus Christ, has come to us—assuming a status and a position that was inferior to the very angels that were His subordinates—becoming mortal, taking upon Himself our very nature, being born of a human mother, dying at the hands of His own creatures, all in order that we might live forever as His sons and daughters. And He continues to dwell with us—through His Spirit who inhabits our lives, reveals His purposes, and provides His grace for joyful and meaningful living and serving.

What a Savior we have! We are no longer strangers to God, aliens to His love and holiness, traitors to His purposes. Jesus actually became, in spiritual terms, our Brother. He participated in our humanity in order that we might become God's children. He identified with our sufferings, shared in our weaknesses, and called us His brothers and sisters.

We can't fathom this amazing truth; but we can become, with Christ, God's sons and daughters, by becoming identified with this Christ and His revelations of the Father. Through Christ we now have the same Father; with Christ we become His beloved children. It happens the very moment we by faith, claim and lay hold of and submit to what God through Christ has done on our behalf.

Can I Forgive Others?

Can I forgive others? a spouse who cannot respond to some of my childish needs? a son who shuns the moral values in which he and I have been brought up? a friend who turns his back when I need him? a husband who leaves his family without any support? a reckless driver who runs down a child? What about infidelity, addiction, cruelty? Can I—should I—forgive the perpetrators of such atrocities?

I can, and according to the words of our Lord, I must. This is what Jesus did and what He commanded His disciples in His earthly ministry. His love-your-enemy, do-not-resist, turn-the-other-cheek, go-the-second-mile style of life appears to be rather impractical, if not a little ridiculous, in our kind of world. It was His style of life, nonetheless, and His injunction to those whom He invited to follow Him.

This does not mean that we are to condone the failures and distortions of others any more than we are expected to condone our own. We may have to tolerate the weaknesses that others have not yet learned to transform into strength, or the liabilities they have not yet turned into assets. We need, for our sakes and theirs, to love them as valid, significant, worthwhile people even in the midst of their faults and failures.

Not only must we forgive others; our forgiveness must be genuine. It is so easy to assume a role, to put on a front, and to project a condescending, holier-than-thou sort of attitude. True forgiveness is not a degrading or demoting of the people to whom we are to relate. We must not, even unconsciously, seek to take away their stripes or reduce them in rank. We must accept them as our equals, our brothers and sisters in Christ. We can, with God's enabling grace, forgive others —and we must.

Lest We Be Ashamed

Some of us, in our timidity or our foolish feelings of inadequacy, almost give the appearance of being ashamed of our faith. Perhaps we are threatened by today's intellectuals or frightened by the hypotheses of our scientists or the theories of humanists and agnostics that appear to contradict the blessed truths of God's Word as we have been taught and have experienced them. We may have earned the scorn of secular scholars by our childlike clutch upon the traditional symbols or the ancient explanations of our faith, but our belief in the one true God as revealed by Jesus Christ is something of which we never need to be ashamed.

God is our Creator, our Redeemer, and the Source of all the grace and power we need to live happy, contributive lives. We can proclaim and demonstrate the grace and power of this great God by claiming our freedom from the fears and anxieties, the temporal and materialistic bondages of this world, to love and serve our fellow beings in joy. We know, not by the fallible tests and explorations of scientists, but by personal experience, that we are the sons and daughters of God and that we have been commissioned to be the ministers of His saving love to all who will listen and respond.

We have, in Christ, the answer to the aches and needs of people in our world; let us proclaim it and communicate it with boldness.

Saturday   *Habakkuk 1:1–3; 2:1–4*

Learning How to Wait

"If it seem slow, wait for it. . . ."

"I waited patiently for the Lord; He inclined to me and heard my cry" (Psalm 40:1).

The Israelites waited thousands of years for the kingdom that God through His prophets promised them. Not recognizing the revealing of that kingdom in the Messiah, Jesus Christ, many of them are still waiting. Christians have been waiting for the last two thousand years for Christ's second coming to fully reveal God's kingdom among the inhabitants of this planet—and they are still waiting, expecting that great Day to break in upon us at every turn in the road. We are learning that "faith is the assurance of things *hoped for*, the conviction of things *not seen*" (Hebrews 11:1).

The waiting goes on. Men and women have visions, real or imaginary, and because they are slow in becoming realities, they "wait for it" or abandon it. We become impatient in waiting for the visible return of Jesus to draw together God's eternal kingdom and enthrone Himself as King, so impatient that some of us are conned into latching on to the date-setting antics of self-styled prophets.

Most of us, in our personal and family lives, are always waiting for something. We tend to act a little like butterflies flitting from flower to flower in order to get all the honey we can out of life. We haven't learned how to wait gracefully. The life of faith is, in essence, a life of waiting and hoping, reaching out for the fulfillment that will not be completed or consummated until we leave this dimension to be totally and eternally with God.

Meanwhile we are enjoined to wait patiently. It is also possible to wait joyfully, to take each day as a gift from God and to serve Him by serving others about us—even while we wait for the response of God to some great need, some future direction for our lives, or the final revelation of His kingdom.

Twenty-First Sunday After Pentecost

Matthew 22:1–10 (11–14) (A)

Come to God's Party

Only those who accept the invitation will enjoy the party. There is no limit to the number who are invited to this ongoing event—the experience of eternal joy that God has prepared. Nor are there qualifications or standards to measure up to in order to attend. There is, however, no room for procrastinators.

It seems that most of the invitees are apparently involved in parties of their own. Or they are so busy about mundane matters that they have no time to embrace and celebrate the love and joy of God. They make all sorts of excuses: a family to rear, a paycheck to earn, a prize to win, a goal to attain, a life to live—even some religious exercise to perform. God's party can wait until some more convenient time, or after the other parties have proven dull and unsatisfying. God is indeed patient, but the opportunities to come to Him are not unlimited. And there are others who will respond to His invitation; they are the ones He will seek out and receive to Himself. They shall feast at God's banquet table forever.

We are invited. There is one requirement that must be met. Not only must we truly desire to come, we must come as we are—with no strings attached. It is not a costume ball. It is a celebration, a recognition of who we are and what we have become by the grace of God. Those who come under the disguise of their personal merits will find little joy at God's party. They will have little to celebrate, for they are incapable of receiving what the Host so graciously offers.

We have accepted the invitation. We have come as we are. We have met Jesus Christ and have accepted God's forgiving love through Him. We are even now seated at the great banquet table of God's unfathomable riches. Let us rejoice; this is God's party.

Let Us Be Happy

Let us be happy. It is not expected that we be constantly ecstatic or continually exuberant, but happy, full of joy, that deep-down inner contentment that persists even in the midst of trials and tribulations and difficult circumstances. As the very children of God, we really don't have a thing to worry about. Whatever our real needs, we know that God will fulfill them in His own time and in accordance with His will. We can well afford to celebrate, to live in thankfulness, and to allow the incomprehensible peace of God to mend the frayed edges of our troubled lives and make us serene and secure in our relationship to God.

Whether we are rich or poor, in the valley or on the mount, whether there be sorrow or pain, conflict or defeat, this need not threaten our relationship with God. It may not be easy, but worthy of every effort to cast out the troublesome demons that plague us. We don't have to allow these things to come between us and God. We belong to Him, and if we think and act as if we really belong to Him, nothing will alter that glorious relationship. We are His forever, and we can celebrate forever our adoption and our identity as His sons and daughters. He will provide us with the strength and courage that we need to confront and overcome anything that comes our way.

Embrace God's love anew today—and be happy.

God's Cure for One Man's Sickness

The man in question was well-heeled but in need of inner healing. He had kept all the rules of his religion, but there was a serious malady in his life that he couldn't account for. It is identical to that which all men and women carry about until they allow Christ to have His way within them. This rich young fellow was at least fortunate enough to recognize it and to question Jesus about it.

First came the *diagnosis:* "You lack one thing," said Jesus. It is the same diagnosis that our Lord would write upon every heart that does not harbor Him today. It is the sickness of our society and our world. "You have been weighed in the balances and found wanting"—lacking, said Daniel (5:27) to Belshazzar in interpreting the handwriting on the wall. It is this lack, this spiritual illness, that separates a person from his or her Creator and Redeemer regardless of that person's physical health or material worth.

Then came the *prescription:* "Go, sell what you have, and give to the poor, and you will have treasure in heaven; and come, follow Me." In this instance, at least, Jesus did not tell him to "believe" or "receive" Him, but came out with a fantastic statement that demanded a drastic alteration in the life of this man. It is a very disturbing statement to us as well, one we cannot accept without dramatically altering our lives. Our Lord's words, nevertheless, are plain and we ignore them at our peril. While we refuse to take them literally—as a necessary prerequisite for salvation—we may need to take them seriously as some sort of diagnosis and prescription for our inner sicknesses. The wealth of this individual who had come to Jesus for the cure to his inner sickness was the very thing that stood in the way of a cure, "and he went away sorrowful."

I wonder if our lives are as firmly entrenched in our material possessions as was the man of our Gospel lesson. We are probably wealthier by comparison today then he was in his day. Whereas we are saved by the grace of God—not by ridding ourselves of material baggage—is it possible that such baggage is preventing God from having His way in and through us? We cannot believe that Jesus would have us emulate St. Francis of Assisi, who was one of the few who did take our Lord's words literally, but we had better believe that our treasures on earth may well endanger our "treasure in heaven."

It is certainly something worth thinking about.

Wednesday   *Hebrews 3:1–6 (B)*

The Household of God

Jesus is truly our Brother, but He is much more. Whereas we love and share as siblings in God's household, we glorify our Brother Jesus as God's beloved Son, Our Redeemer and Lord, as one with God in the very creation of our universe, and as far more important to us than any gifted teacher or eloquent preacher of this or any other century. Therefore when we hear His voice, as we have heard and hope to continue hearing it, we had better take notice. Our salvation is dependent upon a true faith in what Christ has done on our behalf, the kind of faith that expresses itself not only in vocal expression but also in loving obedience to His proclamations and commands.

We know what happened to our forebears who deliberately or carelessly fell short of God's commandments and standards. God speaks to us through Jesus Christ and His ever-present Spirit in our lives. It is quite possible that we, too, may fail to hear His Word or may foolishly ignore His will for our lives. Our relationship with God, our inclusion in His household, is effected and sustained by faith. That faith is demonstrated in our ever-deepening commitment to God and His purposes.

It is very difficult to go solo in respect to our daily relationship with God. Not only do we continue to rely on God's grace, we need each other's help, and we need to love, share, learn together, rejoice together, and support one another in our walk with God.

Thursday   *Luke 17:11–19 (C)*

The Necessity of Gratitude

Concerning ungodly people, Paul once wrote: "For although they knew God they did not honor Him as God or give thanks to Him." And then he added, "they became futile in their thinking and their senseless minds were darkened" (Romans 1:21). Failure in thanking contributes to failure in thinking; it is no wonder that God has become to many people a fuzzy, opaque, indistinct blob.

What about genuine gratitude? In the first place, it must be *prefaced with penitence.* Someone once prayed: "Forgive us, our great God, for giving nothing more than surpluses toward the fulfillment of human need and accomplishment of divine purposes." "Leftover" giving may mark us as decent, civilized human beings, but there is hardly anything Christian, saintly, or even commendable about this kind of giving or sharing.

Second, our gratitude must be *manifested by faith.* Gratitude is, in essence, the confidence that, whatever may come our way, God is lovingly and perpetually present. To be grateful, to give thanks, in spite of or in the midst of the tragic things that befall us, is to manifest the healthy conviction that God can bring beauty out of ashes, redeem and reconstruct, heal and hallow, give meaning and purpose, hope and happiness, and transform the very elements designed for our destruction into the agents of our salvation.

Third, our gratitude must be *expressed in worship.* It is recognizing God for what He is worth, seeing something of His splendor and glory, His love and grace, His rich provision for us in our needs.

Finally, it must be *demonstrated through love.* Having been made eternally rich through Christ, we are now enjoined to offer our sac-

285

rifices of gratitude on the altar of humanity's needs—particularly the needs of our fellow persons all around us.

It is this kind of thanksgiving that pleases the heart of God today.

Friday   *2 Timothy 2:8–13 (C)*

Expect to Suffer

Suffering is to be expected in the course of Christian living and ministering. It is, in fact, an integral part of any course of life in our world. Laborers, professional people, dedicated artists—all must endure times of suffering and hardship if they are truly dedicated to their respective callings. Even the ordinary but highly important task of rearing a family involves suffering. Is it so unusual or unthinkable that the ministers of God be expected to endure suffering as they serve among suffering people in a suffering world?

We are to be reminded of Jesus Christ and what He suffered on our behalf. We are also to remember His promise that, as we suffer and endure for His sake, we shall discover the joy of living, that out of the ashes of our suffering and dying comes the beauty of life everlasting. We have nothing to lose but everything to gain as we suffer in our walk with God and in our service to humanity. God will grant to us the grace to endure and even to grow and mature through our suffering.

We are engaged in the grandest vocation granted to God's creatures —that of serving Him through our loving service to our fellow creatures. It is worth everything we have to give to it. Even the sufferings, the conflicts, the crucible experiences that prepare us to be God's ministers of love, are worth enduring if they better equip us for His assignment for us. We need not pray that God remove our painful experiences, but that He transform them into cleansing fires that renew and refresh us for His purposes, and that we always remain faithful to Him.

Saturday   *Isaiah 25:6–9 (A)*

A Place of Joy Forever

I have often wondered what Isaiah would say to us in our hours of despair over what is going on in our world about us. Maybe it would go something like this:

"God has not forsaken His children. He continues to be concerned about the poor and about those who suffer under the oppression of wicked rulers. Earthly fortunes will crumble, cities will fall into ruin, nations will be dissolved.

"But God's promises will be fulfilled, when the pride of egocentric men and women will be brought low, and our Creator's plans will be consummated for those who are faithful to Him!

"It shall come to pass; it shall come to pass!"

Twenty-Second Sunday After Pentecost

Matthew 22:15–21 (A)

The Matter of Loyalties

Men and women willingly or unwillingly "render . . . to Caesar the things that are Caesar's." They sweat and toil, risk and sacrifice, to keep on good terms with the visible world about them. They make their primary investments in this brief earthly interlude. It is hardly surprising that people encounter disorder and disharmony in their lives. They have their wires crossed; they are living in a wrong relationships with creation about them; they give their foremost allegiance to the wrong values and forces.

Jesus emphatically underscores the existence of our responsibility to another world, another loyalty: "Render . . . to God the things that are God's." He does not deny or ignore the existence of the physical and temporal world nor the dues humanity must pay to it. Jesus full well recognizes our humanness. He endured it; He understands it. But never does He for one minute lose sight of the eternal and ultimate world of the spiritual and the divine. And never does He cease to exhort His disciples as to the necessity of making this their primary and foremost loyalty.

We live in this world; there are certain dues we must render to it. If we are to find genuine meaning and purpose for our lives, however, our primary focus must be upon the eternal world which is ours through faith in Jesus Christ, the Savior sent by God the Father. As did the coin that bore the imprint of Caesar thus belong to Caesar, so every man, woman, and child created by God, redeemed through Jesus Christ, and infilled by the Holy Spirit bears in his or her very nature and upon his or her immortal soul the stamp of God's ownership. We owe our lives, and all that may include, first and foremost to God. Our primary loyalty is to Him.

For Those on the Front Lines

We are grateful for the family of God, the followers of Christ who are laboring faithfully within His purposes. Our gratitude and concern are especially directed toward those who are on the front lines in positions of great risk to health and life. Many of them have endured torture and imprisonment as a consequence of their faith and arduous service. Some have joined the martyrs of ancient times in their efforts to advance the kingdom of God. Thousands of our colleagues are enduring suffering and material loss because they persist in proclaiming and witnessing to Christ in difficult places.

We are, of course, grateful for those who are quietly and profoundly pursuing God's objectives in places and in ways unknown to us. We applaud our brothers and sisters and pray that God will grant them much joy and fill them with His power as they faithfully witness in word and deed to people about them.

It is important that we commend one another and that we encourage and support our co-laborers in whatever ways we can. The task is difficult, the road is rough at times. We all need the feeling of strong, undergirding arms to enable us to bear the burdens of our respective ministries.

May God grant to each of us the sensitivity to comprehend something of what others are going through, those known to us as well as those unknown, and the urgency to hold one another up before God in prayer. God bless our great family!

How to Become Great

It is probably that most of us, at some time in our lives, aspire to greatness, or at least to some prominence or preeminence in life. It is this top-of-the-pile compulsion that dominates so many of the frenzied and bizarre activities that characterize our religious, social, entertainment, and political worlds today.

The disciples of Jesus were no exception. They had listened to Jesus talk about the kingdom of God that was to come. It was probably out of love for the Christ that they made their request of Jesus. They were fond of their Lord and wanted to stay close to Him. It was also, in part, self-concern. They were looking for positions of prominence and responsibility in this new kingdom that was about to emerge. "Grant us," they requested of Jesus, "to sit, one at Your right hand and one at Your left, in Your glory."

Jesus didn't put them down, but He put them off for the time being. They would soon enough learn the price of greatness. James and John did eventually become great—even in the eyes of the world—but it was far different from what they had anticipated.

Jesus set before His disciples and before the world the example of true greatness in suffering for the sins of all humanity. "Though He was in the form of God . . . [He] emptied Himself, taking the form of a servant. . . . He humbled Himself and became obedient unto death . . . on a cross" (Philippians 2:6–8). It doesn't make any sense to the world, but in the eyes of God, this is how to become great. "Whoever would be great among you must be your servant," He said to His disciples. It is this that puts us all within the range of greatness. It is a call not to personal esteem or worldly acclaim, but to servanthood.

You and I are candidates for this kind of greatness.

Wednesday   *Hebrews 4:9–16 (B)*

Serenity in the Midst of Struggle

Those who, by faith, enter into the life and grace granted by God are introduced to a life of joy and peace and rest. They can cease their fruitless struggles to please or win the favor of their Creator and rest in what God through Christ has already done for them. There are other kinds of struggles and conflicts for the redeemed children of God, but they never need to grapple for God's love and grace, or wrestle with guilt feelings, or deliberate over doubts as to their status and identity as God's children.

They enter, as well, a whole new vocation for their lives, for while they rest in God's loving-kindness, they begin to labor in a new dimension as children and servants of God to introduce others to the life of eternal joy and rest that is available to them through Jesus Christ.

We need to renew, to charge up our faith from time to time, to make sure we keep the faith, lest we regress in our relationship with God and fall once more into that fruitless struggle to exist apart from Him.

Nevertheless, we have in our Lord, Jesus Christ, not only a Savior but a Keeper, a Guardian over our souls, One who knows well our failings and hang-ups, who understands the trials and conflicts that come our way, and who will grant us the grace to come through them unscathed. There will be wounds, even scars to remind us of those wounds, but victory is assured if we stay close to that One who is the dispenser of divine grace.

Thursday   *Luke 18:1–8a (C)*

Some Thoughts About Prayer

". . . they ought always to pray and not lose heart."

The privilege of prayer: Because Jesus Christ has entered through the veil into the Holy of Holies before us, we through faith have direct access to the very mercy seat of God. "Let us then with confidence draw near to the throne of grace," writes the author of the Letter to the Hebrews, "that we may receive mercy and find grace to help in time of need" (Heb. 4:16).

The purpose of prayer: Prayer is not simply petition and repetition, feeling and sentiment; nor is it a sanctified form of begging, a convincing God of something He already knows and thereby compelling Him to some sort of action. It is primarily an action of devotion whereby Christians dedicate, submit, consecrate themselves to God and can be brought to the place where God through them can accomplish the very things for which they have prayed.

The power of prayer: It lies not in its particular method or exercise, nor in the number of hours spent in that exercise. It lies in God. To pray in power means to pray in faith, to pray Spirit-guided prayers. The only prayers that He does not respond to are those prayers that He does not inspire.

The persistency of prayer: It is this that is so aptly illustrated in our Gospel lesson. The premise is this: If an unjust judge, who has regard for neither God nor man, would yield to the persistency of an unknown widow because he was afraid that she would annoy him by her repetitious requests, *how much more* will a just and merciful God respond to and reward the persevering petitions of His own loved ones who cry to Him and relate to Him.

Let us pray. . . .

Preach the Word—Be the Word

"Preach the Word . . ." Paul exhorted Timothy.

"Go therefore and make disciples of all nations," Jesus commanded His disciples.

This is our commission and our responsibility as 20th-century disciples of Jesus Christ. We are to preach, to verbalize, to proclaim. But we are to do more than that; we are to *be* the Word of God. In a sense, God is incarnate in us. His loving Spirit indwells us. We are not only channels or conduits of His life and salvation, of the saving, redeeming, liberating grace of God; we are preaching and communicating that which is a part of ourselves. We are to be the sacrament of the glorious message of salvation, broken bread and poured-out wine among the lost, lonely, broken, sin-bound inhabitants of this planet. Pentecost has made us the incarnation of what we preach. There are times when verbal proclamation is secondary; the first requisite is to be what God has empowered us to be—loving, concerned, caring, Spirit-filled servants of God. Then we may be inspired to verbalize what we are by God's grace and to make our words the living Word of God to heart-hungry people about us.

Most of the people we relate to have heard the words of the Gospel before. Some of us are especially called and trained to proclaim that Gospel—to put it into words that can be heard and understood. All of us responsible for living that Word, fleshing out the proclaimed Word, and thereby communicating God's liberating grace to those around us.

While there are some people who need only to hear the proclamation, there are many others who will know God's love only through our God-inspired, Spirit-filled love that demonstrates and proclaims the eternal, forgiving, saving, liberating love of God through Jesus Christ.

Wrestling with God

"For I have seen God . . . and yet my life is preserved."

It appears to be ridiculous and of questionable value, but people have wrestled with God from the beginning of time. Most wrestle in rebellion, seeking and all too often succeeding in keeping Him from occupying and controlling their lives. It may appear to be paradoxical, but one aspect of God's graciousness and loving-kindness is His willingness to wrestle with us. He refuses to step over the threshold of a person's rebel will. No one is forced to submit to the purposes of the Creator. Yet God continues to wrestle with His stubborn, recalcitrant creatures. Some of them will appear to win only to lose forever their battle with God, nevermore to experience the love and joy of His blessed will and purposes for their lives. Only those who lose their battle with God and submit to His will and purposes discover the joy and beauty for which they were created.

Yet we continue to wrestle with God even as we grow in wisdom and understanding of who He is and what He proposes to do in and through us. Sometimes it has to do with guilt and doubt, at other times with our sin-stained will that continues to offer resistance to our Creator and Redeemer as long as we are shackled by the mortality of this existence. God will always, we pray and confidently hope, be the ultimate winner in these frequent conflicts that envelope us. We submit, we must submit to that divine love that can overpower our self-centeredness and live victoriously in and through us.

God does not deny us the wrestling of doubt or guilt or self-will any more than He did the struggles of the psalmist, who in his hours of despair and depression often questioned God. Even if it results in His touch upon our thighs and a painful limp, He will lovingly draw us into submission to His blessed will and make our feet strong again to carry out our commission as His beloved servants; and we will proclaim with the psalmist: "O give thanks to the Lord, for He is good; for His steadfast love endures forever" (Psalm 118:29).

Twenty-Third Sunday After Pentecost

Matthew 22:34-40 (41-46) (A)

What Do You Think of Christ?

We know what the Pharisees thought of Christ. We understand something of the disciples' early comprehension of their Master, the Lord Jesus. The question that Jesus put to the Pharisees is fully as pertinent today: "What do you think of the Christ?"

Some people look upon Him as a mere historic figure and profess no faith whatsoever in Him. There are others who regard Him and even worship Him as He was often presented in their past experiences, a sort of meek, mild, gentle, comforting, problem-solving Christ to whom they can turn when the road gets rough. There are those who see Him today as a radical, revolutionary figure who hacked at the establishment of His day and gave validity to the sinner and the slave, the poor and the outcast of society. Many in our generation attempt to find in Him a refuge or escape from all that afflicts our world today; others use Him strictly as a means for personal gain or pleasure. Then there are those, of course, who discover in Him and His teachings meaning for life and purpose for living.

God's Word and our doctrines based on that Word define Him as Son of God and Son of Man, human and divine, Savior and Lord. But what do *you* think of Him? He is not truly real to so many people, but just a picture on the wall, a lovely memory from the past, a symbol or a name to pray to when they are desperate enough to pray. What is He to us?

When we accept Him as He is, our Savior and Lord, and all that He wants and intends to be in us and through us, then our lives become total and complete. God grant that we may grow in our comprehension of Him and His purposes for our lives and that we become ever more deeply committed to Him and His will for us and His objectives in our world today. And God grant to us the willingness and the ability to be detached from the things that clutter up our lives, even these earthly securities we so desperately cling to, in order that we may truly follow after Him.

When Our Witness Bears Fruit

"For you received the Word in much affliction, with joy inspired by the Holy Spirit . . . you became an example to all the believers . . . your faith in God has gone forth everywhere. . . ."

The letter of Paul to the church at Thessalonica begins on the high note of joy and enthusiasm. His arduous ministry, which often took him through towns where he was stoned for his preaching and driven out, was finally beginning to pay off. According to Luke's narrative in the Book of Acts, the church in Thessalonica began amidst much affliction. Paul began by preaching in the synagogues of the Jews and won a few converts, but a larger number of Greeks were attracted to Paul's preaching and converted to Paul's Christ, which resulted in a riot, and Paul had to flee the city. Now the church that was established there had grown and the Christians welcomed this contact with Paul, with whom it all began; and Paul was overjoyed at what had transpired among the Thessalonian Christians.

It is a beautiful example of what happens when the seed that is sown finally takes root, blossoms forth, and eventually bears fruit. The church of Jesus Christ is not totally dependent upon Paul or any single person to keep it going and growing. The Spirit of God through dedicated people will work the wonders of God in the most difficult situations. Affliction there will be, but there is likewise "joy inspired by the Holy Spirit," and the wonders that God works through His children make the church live, not only in Thessalonica but everywhere.

Do things like this happen in our churches? Indeed they do. Are we the kind of Christians through whom God's Spirit can inspire and bless others in our congregations—and other congregations in our community?

Tuesday   *Mark 10:46–52 (B)*

Serving People Where They Are

I remember how past attempts to formulate sermons on this particular Gospel lesson usually turned this episode in the life of Jesus into a sort of analogy to point up our Lord's ability and purpose in healing spiritual blindness. Jesus has indeed come to break into such blindness with the Gospel of light and salvation, to tear the scales off our eyes that we may see our need for Him, God's love and grace that can fill that need, and His will for our lives as His servants.

Other interpreters of the Gospel look upon this incident as indicative of Christ's power to perform miracles, thereby revealing His divine origins and ultimate objectives.

Both of these interpretations are valid, but perhaps we would do well to take this healing-the-blind incident at face value. It may give us some direction in respect to the ministry of the church today. Implied and demonstrated is the real meaning of Christian discipleship and servant-hood. The time is past when we can simply hold forth with weekly preaching services and center our activities around the sacred few who gather regularly in our sanctuaries. We got by with a modified concept of discipleship in years past that all but ignored the needy, the blind and the lame, the hungry and the unsheltered, the dispossessed and disinherited multitudes about us. We left this task, for most part, to secular agencies and pacified our consciences by supporting our denominational efforts to build a few schools, hospitals, and homes for the aged.

Jesus did not preach to the blind man. He healed him, enabling him to see again, and thus enabling him to be a whole man again. This is, as far as we know, all that He did at this time. He met and lovingly dealt with this man at the point of his obvious and immediate need. The net result, as told in Luke's version of this incident, was that this man glorified God for the restoration of his sight and subsequently became a follower of Jesus Christ.

Maybe this says something to us about how to carry out our servant-hood as the disciples of Jesus.

Wednesday   *Hebrews 5:1–10 (B)*

Growing Up as God's Children

In the days of old, high priests were appointed to stand between a sinful people and a holy God, to act on behalf of the people. These priests were themselves sinners and could therefore understand the frailties and weaknesses of the children of Israel for whom, through sacrifices and ceremonies, they sought God's forgiveness.

In Christ we honor the Priest of priests, who has been assigned by God Himself to present the Sacrifice of sacrifices—His own body on the cross—as sufficient to atone for all the sins of all people in all the world. Knowing our weaknesses without succumbing to weakness, tempted without yielding to temptation, Jesus is our worthy Advocate in reconciling sinners with a forgiving God.

And yet some of us act at times as if the price Jesus paid is insufficient to cover our guilt. If we as God's children are assigned to be the ministers of God, how dare we be content with the Pablum of work-righteousness, or the sweet honey of subjective ecstasy, the milk of cloud-hopping experiences, when we ought by now to be feeding on the solid meat of Christ's radical, risk-fraught, joy-giving teachings and activities?

God help us to grow up in the Christian life, to mature, to develop some sensitivity to the needs of people and some skill in terms of applying the life and doctrines of Christ to those needs. We are God's ministers; may He make us worthy of our appointment.

Thursday   *Luke 18:9–14 (C)*

King of the Hill

There is one vice of which no person is free. It is one which we loathe when we see it in someone else and yet are reluctant to admit in ourselves. We know of those who admit to being bad-tempered or are weak when it comes to sex or drink or money, but hardly do we ever hear anyone accusing himself or herself of this vice. It is the vice of pride, the temptation and endeavor to be "king of the hill." This is the central and basic evil within a person's nature. It was through pride that the devil became the devil. It is pride that leads to every other vice.

It is represented and presented in today's lesson in the character of the Pharisee in the temple. Here is a picture of a man who was satisfied with himself and, as such, could never meet God. He was decent, law-abiding, religious—and he knew it. He was self-confident and sufficient unto himself, a sort of "king of the hill," a winner in the game of life. He had prestige, ample wealth, and some power. What else could he want? And he was thankful to God for what he was—or so his prayer seems to indicate. Do you know any church members like that? Are you one of them?

Our lesson draws another picture, a picture of a loser. He was one who had little thought about anybody else at this moment, no criticism of others, but was utterly dissatisfied with himself. He couldn't even lift his eyes, but in his sorrow over his sins, his failures and flaws, with despair in his soul, smote his breast and prayed: "God, be merciful to me a sinner."

Two men came to church that day, but only one met God. It was the one who came in humility, seeing nobody's failures but his own, with no axes to grind, and his only desire was to get right in his own heart with God. According to Jesus, he did; he "went down to his house justified."

Friday   *2 Timothy 4:6–8, 16–18 (C)*

A Superb Testimony and Stirring Challenge

"I am already on the point of being sacrificed," said Paul. In another version it reads: ". . . my life is being poured out on the altar" (NEB).

I suspect that few of us can identify with Paul as to the content and depth of his commitment. We find it difficult to believe that Jesus expects this of any of us. Yet He did of His original disciples. "The cup that I drink you will drink," He once said to them (Mark 10:39).

The truth is, however, He is expecting and getting this kind of response from many of His disciples throughout our world today. Christians are risking their lives to be "little Christs" in the most difficult situations in which they find themselves. They are not seeking martyrdom any more than we are, but they are compelled by the love of God to risk their lives and whatever they possess to bring the love of God into the lives of people about them. "Present your bodies as a living sacrifice," wrote Paul to the Christians at Rome (Romans 12:1). Paul followed his own injunction and exemplified the kind of response Christians ought to be making to their God. He was constantly "being poured out on the altar"; it appears that he was even expecting to be a martyr for the sake of God's kingdom.

A good question to ponder today: "Am I ready to be offered?" We may be doing fairly well, as Paul did, to "keep the faith," but are we ready to be a sacrificial offering for Jesus' sake and the sake of the kingdom? How about "being poured out" for the sake of others? It is a good deal to ask of us, and God alone has the right to ask this of those He has created and redeemed. He does ask it; but He demands nothing. Our answer must be a response to His love, not to His commands.

God may not expect us to measure up to the intensity and courage of Paul's life and witness. He may, however, look for our willingness to be "poured out" in our love for others and in the accomplishment of His purposes. Would He really be our loving God if He expected anything less?

A Song of Hope

We are likely to remember Jeremiah for his lamentations over the infidelities of Israel. In this Old Testament lesson we hear a new song, a song of God's love for His children. It is not the words of judgment, but the music of hope that we hear through the lips of the great prophet: "The Lord has saved His people, the remnant of Israel. . . . With weeping they shall come, and with consolations I will lead them back. . . . Proclaim, give praise, and say, 'The Lord has saved His people. . . .'" And with hope there comes joy: "Sing aloud with gladness for Jacob."

It was hope indeed—kept alive in the hearts of a remnant until the time that God sent forth His Son to make that promise valid not only for the Jews but for all people on this planet. The promise has been fulfilled in the coming of Christ. With His coming, God came to His people, His creatures upon this earth. With His sacrifice on the cross, His resurrection from the dead, God's judgment upon sin was overturned and His love poured out upon all who believe. Gathered from "the farthest parts of the earth," we have come to know our great God as a God of love who came to us and who now abides within us through His Spirit.

The new kingdom has still not been fully revealed, but Christ has strengthened our hope with the assurance that the great Day will soon break in upon us and that we are the children of God forever.

Let us "sing aloud with gladness!"

Twenty-Fourth Sunday After Pentecost

Matthew 25:1–13 (A)

While We Sleep

Our Lord is not entertaining children with fairy tales; He is forewarning and forearming His faithful followers for a future event of tremendous significance. It is an event so dazzling in its importance that it outshines every other event the world has ever known.

There are lessons we can profit from in the parable before us. For one thing, the final advent of Christ will find His church a mixed body, including genuine as well as not-so-genuine professors of religion. There were ten maidens. They all possessed lamps. They had one objective in view. Yet only five of them were admitted to the marriage feast activities.

The final advent of our Lord, whenever it happens, will take men and women by surprise. This was true about Christ's first advent. Though our Lord's final advent must ultimately be accepted, it is not really expected by the masses of our world.

The final advent of Jesus Christ will find many within the institutional church and the average congregation who are not ready for His coming. All of the maidens had burning lamps; five of those lamps burned out. Some of us may be holding lamps which are burning very low, a faith that is about to burn out. This lack or defect did not divide the wise maidens from the foolish until it was too late to do anything about it. Could this happen to us?

The final advent of Christ will be a time of rich reward for those who have surrendered their lives to Him and have labored faithfully in His vineyard. This has been promised and is awaiting those who truly "keep the faith" and are constantly working and watching in view of the final advent.

"Watch therefore, for you know neither the day nor the hour," said Jesus. We are called and empowered by God's Spirit to be loving, serving, devoted children in our world today. By being such we are thereby hastening the day of His final coming and are ready for that great Day, whenever it may be.

It Will All Be Worthwhile

Whereas we need never to strive for our salvation, for God's forgiving love and acceptance, we need constantly to struggle and strive within the process of Christian growth. It is the struggle to allow God to have His way with us: to cast off the shackles of self-concern, the appendages of fear and worry, our dependence upon the things of this earth, our fleshly desires for material security and recognition, the gnawing need to be successful in this life. It is in the process of doing this that we become open and pliable, loose and flexible, to the Spirit's indwelling and outpouring. If we could truly abide in the Vine, we would grow and bear fruit. Our problem lies in learning how to abide, to let go and let God, to rest in what He has done for us and be totally committed to Him and what He wants to do through us.

It is all worthwhile, for our earthly conflicts will one day resolve in an eternal life and experience that is more glorious than anything we can imagine. Our dear ones who are no longer with us, who were wrenched from us through suffering and pain, have already entered into that experience. It awaits every one of us who remains faithful to our Lord and to His commission for us in our remaining days upon this earth.

Remember, Jesus died—and rose again. So we shall rise again and, with those who have preceded us, be joined totally and eternally to our God and Christ.

Morality—Jesus' Style

In the first years of the Christian church there were many struggles on the part of those first believers between the Old Testament and New Testament moralities, or between those who were still hung up on the ancient Law and those who had gained some insight into the meaning of the Gospel. Paul was probably the most enlightened and avid interpreter of Jesus' Gospel, and he emphatically declared that Christians are set free from the Law in order to accept God's love as revealed in Christ and His redemption and are enabled by His Spirit to relate in love to their fellow beings. People must go back to the basic absolutes of love-God-love-your-neighbor, which can be understood and fulfilled only as a consequence of faith in and obedience to Jesus Christ and His teachings.

According to New Testament morality, when we accept Jesus Christ as Savior and crown Him Lord of life and living, we will recognize and confess our utter inability to please God by way of rules and regulations and accept that One sent by God who kept the Law in our stead and who sets us free from the demands and judgments of the Old Testament law to receive God's forgiving love and to relate in divinely impelled human love to our fellow creatures.

Immorality, then, as we need to understand it, is the failure to love God and our neighbor, even to love others in the measure that Jesus loves us. It is, as well, our failure to stand up against those inhuman institutions and laws that come between us and our love for God and between us and our love for our fellow beings—that divide races, perpetuate bigotry, favor the rich over against the poor, or that promote wars of violence that destroy the souls, if not the bodies, of our fellow citizens.

God will forgive us for our immoralities, but God forbid that we fail to recognize them and, by His grace, seek to overcome them.

Wednesday   *Hebrews 7:23–28 (B)*

Jesus Christ, the One and Only

The ancient Israelites needed priests to mediate between them and God. Jesus Christ is the one and only High Priest who broke through every barrier between human beings and God and revealed Him as a forgiving, loving, grace-giving God. We need no longer lean on symbols or rely on priests to make God real and available to us. He has been revealed through Jesus Christ. The act of reconciliation has been effected through His sacrificial death and supernatural resurrection on our behalf. God continues to reveal Himself through His Spirit and through the activities and proclamations of those who follow Christ.

Jesus did what no mortal priest or religious leader can ever do—He obliterated the darkness, the uncertainty, and the inscrutability that once existed between God and His creatures, and restored us forever to an intimate relationship with Him. Everything that happened before Christ was but a shadow of what was to come, even the ancient worship that prepared the way for the coming Christ. Christ is the Truth that has come, and He is here with us to draw men and women to the truth.

He is the Way to God—directly and eternally. He is the Life that sustains us and compels us to dedicate our lives to broadcasting this truth to those who are still in darkness. He is the Fulfillment of our deepest longings, the Answer to our most complex problems. He is Christ, our Lord, our God, and our Way to God.

Thursday   *Luke 19:1–10 (C)*

When Conversion Is Genuine

Our lesson for today is not a parable, but an actual incident which happened in the ministry of Christ. It teaches us as well as any parable that Jesus used in His teaching. For one thing, it is an excellent portrayal of the *significance of circumstances* and the part that such circumstances about us, be they joyful or tragic, ordinary or extraordinary, have to play in the process of bringing us to God. In the manner that hunting dogs "tree" a raccoon, so a self-centered and self-sufficient person often has to be "chased up a tree" before he or she is somewhat prepared for God's message of eternal life and hope.

The incident before us also presents a beautiful picture of the *outflow of divine grace.* The character of Zacchaeus was less than remarkable. He was, as a tax collector, very unpopular, and unscrupulous as well. And yet this was the individual who was about to become the object of divine grace and, as a result of such grace, to undergo a remarkable transformation. Whatever Zacchaeus may have understood about himself, Jesus saw a man who was "up a tree" in his life, in need of divine grace, the grace He had come to grant to humanity. "Zacchaeus, make haste and come down; for I must stay at your house today," said Jesus.

The final picture emerging from our lesson is that of the *necessary response.* Zacchaeus, our lesson informs us, "made haste and came down, and received Him joyfully." Then he said to this Jesus, as the grace of God took hold of his life: "Behold, Lord, the half of my goods I give to the poor; and if I have defrauded anyone of anything, I restore it fourfold." There was hard-core, agonizing reality in that little speech, but it was a necessary response for Zacchaeus, and our Lord regarded this confession and commitment as evidence of a genuine conversion: "Today salvation has come to this house."

That is all God needs from us, our glad and unlimited response, before He can translate and transform us as God's beloved children. God forbid that such a response be halfhearted.

Thanksgiving and Giving

While we thank our God for His loving patience in the face of our reluctance to grow, our slowness in maturing and developing into the kind of instruments that would be useful to Him, and praise Him for the comfort and security we find in Him even in the midst of this world's conflicts and calamities, we are disturbed by the cries of pain, the sounds of suffering, that break through into our hallowed little circle.

There are some people we cannot help at this moment—and we prayerfully commit them to the loving-kindness of God. There are others that we can aid and support. If we neglect to do all that we can to hold them up or share in their suffering, we ourselves may be subject to God's judgment.

Our thanksgiving must be thanks accompanied by giving—the giving of ourselves to others in need—or it may be little more than mockery. It is relatively easy to condemn our world's oppressors and relegate them to whatever hell God may have prepared for them. It is more difficult, and far more important, that we lovingly and sacrificially identify with the oppressed, that we share their afflictions and stand with them against the monsters who use and abuse them, and that we discover together the joy and freedom of living for God. We are, thanks be to God, His servants.

"Let Justice Roll"

The words of Amos, or the words of God through Amos, are a severe indictment against the worship activities of the Israelites. We wouldn't expect such an indictment over our beautiful and impressive worship services. They are Word-centered, faith-strengthing celebrations that turn us on and send us out into our Monday-through-Saturday world with joy and enthusiasm. Yet God may have something to say about our religious celebrations as well. It might go something like this: "Your robed choirs and great organs may stimulate congregations, but such is not music to My heart. Your proper liturgies and impressive pageantry will probably make people feel devout and religious without doing much to extend My kingdom or accomplish My purposes. Even the

Word that is preached, the sacraments administered, may be little more than hollow mockery if they do not proceed from and result in hearts and lives that are committed to My Word and My will as revealed through My Son. If the people who gather to make their confessions and sing My praises do not feel lovingly compelled to carry out My obectives, to stand with the oppressed against their oppressors, to work for the dignity of every human being, to share their goods and gifts with those who are deprived, to accept and love their fellow persons even as they accept and love themselves, and to proclaim the love of God to those who will listen, then their worship is farcical and their relationship to Me very much in question."

God would never speak words like these to us—or would He?

Twenty-Fifth Sunday After Pentecost

Matthew 25:14–30 (A)

The Case of the Missing Talents

A decade or so ago many of us had some misgivings about the church. Membership was lagging. Lay people were leaving. Seminarians were refusing ordination. Young people laughed at the church as irrelevant. Philosophers and even theologians were announcing the death of God. Today there appears to be an upsurge in religious interest and activity, but not necessarily in spiritual vitality and validity. Hungry people still view the church as uncaring. Politicians scoff at the church as incompetent. Businessmen spurn the church as unrealistic. Military officers scorn it as idealistic. The church is peripheral when it should be central. It is on the edge when it should be at the heart. It is silent when it should speak. It dallies when it should act. And Malcolm Muggeridge, a devout Christian, has boldly announced or predicted "the end of Christendom" even while he "feels a renewed confidence in the light of the Christian revelation in which it first began."

Maybe it all adds up to a case of missing talents. Our great God has through His Spirit equipped His redeemed children with all that is needed to make the church a powerful, effective instrument in a power-mad but powerless world today. God is always out to do the impossible: to bring order into disorder, purpose into purposelessness, fullness into emptiness, healing into sickness, and to restore aching, hungry hearts to Himself. He can do this, however, only through His faithful children as individuals and as members of the institutional church. Unfortunately, the church has not recovered all the missing talents, or has invested God's gifts to His children in ways and matters that serve its institutional programs and purposes rather than human need in the world about it.

Can we change? Are we changing? Or are we, by our neglect to lovingly invest our talents and gifts in the needs of people, contributing to "the end of Christendom"?

Are We Ready?

Over against those far-fetched attempts by self-appointed prophets to predict the time of the visible return of our Lord are our Lord's own words informing us that His return or reappearance will be sudden and unexpected. And yet the final coming of Christ, whenever it happens, should be no surprise to His faithful disciples. We ought to be ready to meet our Lord whatever the appointed day or hour. It really makes little difference whether we are alive or have already passed on to life everlasting; when He comes we shall see Him and with Him judge the world.

While we live upon this planet, we should live as if He were already here. Indeed, He is here! His disappearance after His resurrection was followed by Pentecost. And Pentecost marked, by a wonderful event, His return to invisibly infill and indwell the hearts of His disciples. The way in which we can always be ready for the final and ultimate reappearance of Christ is not to gather on some hill in pious meditation. It is to recognize and rely upon the Spirit of God within us and to extend His kingdom through witnessing to and serving humanity about us. We are to walk in faith, to serve in joy, and to praise God whatever the circumstances that surround us. God grant that we remain totally dedicated to Him and His purposes. Then we are ever ready for His visible reappearance.

Empty Hands

A verse out of the Book of Deuteronomy pictures the manner in which the Old Testament worshipers were to come to God: "They shall not appear before the Lord empty-handed; every man shall give as he is able, according to the blessing of the Lord your God which He has given you" (Deuteronomy 16:16–17).

All of us, as we come to God, come with "dirty hands." They have been soiled with the deeds of self-centered living. We come, however, sincerely and in faith believing that in Christ there is cleansing and atonement. Something that continues to cause sorrow to the heart of our Lord is that so many who have found cleansing and forgiveness at

307

the divine Fountainhead are still coming to God with "empty hands," or with fists clenched tightly in miserliness and selfishness. They fail to bring with them the sacrificial offerings of love and gratitude, of praise and thanksgiving. They know not the experience of Luther who said: "I have had many things in my hands, and I have lost them all; but whatever I have placed in God's hands, that I still possess."

Jesus noted in an act of temple worship, "putting money into the treasury," people's real attitudes toward their Creator God. He first saw the kind of giving we might call *surplus giving:* "Many rich people put in large sums." He did not scorn their gifts and made no comment whatsoever concerning their actions, except to say, "Many rich people put in large sums." The second thing our Lord noted was an example of *sacrificial giving:* a little figure of a woman making her cautious, timid, almost ashamed approach to the temple treasury to deposit her two copper coins. Listen to His evaluation: "This poor widow has put in more than all those who are contributing to the treasury. For they all contributed out of their abundance; but she out of her poverty has put in everything she had, her whole living."

May God's love for each of us be so overwhelmingly obvious that we will gladly and sacrificially commit ourselves and the gifts and goods that come our way to spreading the Gospel and helping others.

Wednesday   *Hebrews 9:24–28 (B)*

In Our Stead—On Our Behalf

Jesus, our great High Priest, entered the Holy of Holies, the inner sanctum of God, to make the one-for-all and once-for-all sacrifice, giving His life as the one, sufficient, perfect sacrifice to end all sacrifices, in order to make men and women holy, righteous, and totally acceptable to His heavenly Father. What the ancient law and religion could not do, and what we cannot do for ourselves, God did on our behalf through His Son, Jesus Christ. The forgiveness of God is complete, canceling out the necessity of any future offerings or sacrifices.

It is for this reason, because of what Christ has done for us, that we have the assurance and confidence we need in order to boldly approach our loving God. We can come before God with untroubled consciences, knowing that our past sins will no longer be held against us. We are now truly the people of God, His children and servants forever.

How important it is that we who have by faith entered with Christ into the Holy of Holies keep that faith and allow nothing to deter us in our walk of faith and obedience! It is worth whatever cost we may have to pay—loss of jobs, reputations, material possessions, even the sacrifice of our lives—to hold fast our salvation and follow closely behind our Lord.

This we will do with the help of God.

After This—Then What?

An Indian chief named Crowfoot is reported to have said, "A little while and I will be gone from among you, whither I cannot tell. From nowhere we come, into nowhere we go. What is life? It is a flash of a firefly in the night. It is a breath of buffalo in the wintertime. It is a little shadow that runs across the grass and loses itself in the sunset." "It is appointed for men to die once," the Scriptures declare (Hebrews 9:27). "What man can live and never see death?" queried the psalmist (89:48).

Despite the exquisite and dignified words of the Indian chief, or even the words of Scripture, we cannot entirely reduce the ugliness or minimize the horror of death. We cannot forget our first childhood contact with it, nor the shock and pain of its brutal invasion of our family circle. We cannot completely rid ourselves of its insidious threat to our being. As surely as comes the end of summer, the yellow grass and the fallen leaves, so surely must we face up to the fact of death, its parting of the ways, its incomprehensible darkness.

But faith does have an answer for this ultimate anxiety. Our Christ not only faced it, bluntly and biologically; He was victorious over it. He transformed it from an enemy bent on our destruction into a friend that promises to usher us into eternal glory. The Christian faith says that we bear the mark of the eternal. Thus death is *not* final; it does *not* have the last word. It is a necessary incident in the journey to our full enjoyment of eternal life.

Our concern, then, is not that we shall die, for that is certain. It is that we live the days still remaining to us on this planet in God's life and purposes and for the benefit of our brothers and sisters about us.

While We Wait

It is not surprising, in the darkness of this world's chaotic struggles, that we hope intensely for the very special intervention of God through the promised return of our Lord Jesus Christ. We feel at times so unnerved, frightened, bowled over with frustration and despair, that we look desperately for some sign in the sky, some miracle out of heaven, and even wish for the final day of this dispensation, the culmination of God's purposes upon this world that will put an end to the misery that abounds about us. Nor is it surprising that some of us will grab at any straw in the wind, latch on to any strange happening that may suggest the possibility of this taking place in our lifetime. Christians have been doing this for centuries, and yet time marches on, and with it the sorrows and joys of this world's inhabitants.

Maybe God is telling us to mind our own business, to tend to those matters which He would have us be concerned about, to leave these cosmic, still unknown and unrevealed things in His hands. While we accept and anticipate His promises concerning the great day of our deliverance, when we shall blissfully go to be with Him for all eternity, He would have us occupy ourselves with the task at hand—that of laboring within our suffering world to reveal and communicate His love to all His human creatures.

Let us remember that the Lord is faithful, even when our faith falters. He will sustain us and watch over us whatever the difficult times or the circumstances that press in upon us.

The Incomparable Love of God

Should God speak to us through Hosea today, it might go like this: "How profoundly I love My children whom I have created. I continue to reveal to them My compassion; I help to bear their burdens and accompany them through the adversities that afflict them; I heal many of their sicknesses and demonstrate My loving concern in the midst of their deep sorrows and excruciating sufferings; I hold out to them My salvation and invite them to partake of My saving and redeeming grace. Yet they turn from Me to pursue their own objectives. They expend their energy upon the fleeting things about them. Even those who honor Me with their lips persist in investing their lives in the foolishness of the world.

"What more can I do for My beloved children than I am already doing? It is even as I love them and because I love them that I must allow them to go their own way, to satisfy their desires upon the husks of their temporary existence, to fill their emptiness with things that rust and decay and will pass away. When they refuse to follow Me, I will follow them—even into the dark, cold caves of nothingness or the pits of despair—seeking always to draw them back to My redeeming love, to restore them to My will for their lives. How much I love My children whom I have created!"

Return, you who have strayed from God's blessed will for your life; return to that One who created you, who loves you, and who patiently waits for you to come back to Him!

Third-Last Sunday in the Church Year

Matthew 23:1–12 (A)

Every Christian a Leader

Some of you are leaders in your church or some community organization, and this is fine.

It is well to remember, though, that those who are led by the Spirit of God will often be considered "losers" by the world at large. This is because they follow Jesus Christ, and His leadership is synonymous with servanthood. It is because they, rather than resolving the conflicts and problems of the world, point to the new kingdom and to their God who alone can resolve the conflicts and struggles of humanity. Rather than promoting themselves and their own glory, they lead people in glorifying God. Instead of promising people success, they challenge them to make sacrifices; instead of comforting them in their self-centeredness and apathy, they provoke them into accepting responsibility for the poor and the less fortunate about them. Instead of being leaders of people, they take the lead in being servants to people, seeking to lead them into spiritual fulfillment, as well as responding to their physical needs. This is because they are lovers of people rather than masters over people, and they dedicate themselves to communicating and demonstrating, in word and deed, God's saving love and grace to His creatures about them.

All this refers not only to leaders, but to every one of us, for we are all called to be servants of our heavenly Father and of our fellow beings among whom we live and work. In a very real sense we are all leaders of one sort or another, at least in the measure that we seek to "lead" others to Christ. We can't drive people to the Lord; we must lead them. We can do this only through servanthood, not through domination or mastery.

The Extent of Servanthood

"We were ready to share with you not only the Gospel of God, but also our own selves."

Paul and his co-workers responded to Jesus' injunction very seriously. While their initial and primary task in promoting the God-movement and advancing the new kingdom was proclamation, it is probable that they would have had little success with the church at Thessalonica if their responsibility there had been limited to proclamation alone. Paul was a leader in every sense of the word, but he was successful in that role because he came to serve these people, to share himself with them. A successful pastor is one who serves, who shares himself, gives of himself to his co-ministers, the members of his congregation. And that congregation will be successful, in God's eyes, only inasmuch as its members share themselves with others in the community.

The Christians who are most effective in their person-to-person attempts at soul-winning are not those who go door to door in their efforts to spread the Gospel and win converts. God can use such methods even if they are confined to handing out tracts or Bible portions, but the most effective witness is generally the result of cultivated relationships with individuals, sometimes over a long period of time, during which loving, caring, and sharing are involved. Such loving involves a measure of pain, being a "little Christ" to others, self-denial and cross-bearing on behalf of others. This is what servanthood is all about. It is difficult to see how one can channel the love of God without being a loving person. Proclamation is essential; it needs to be accompanied by and generally preceded by loving and sharing.

"Make love your aim," Paul once said (1 Corinthians 14:1). That is the crux of and motivation for servanthood.

A Matter of Endurance

"He who endures to the end will be saved."

It's not the sort of thing we enjoy preaching or hearing sermons about, but Christ's ominous warnings of what might happen to His followers were anything but encouraging. If we were actually exposed to what Jesus and His original disciples had to face, it is probable that few of us would be very enthusiastic or aggressive about the Christian faith.

It is, nevertheless, the same Lord and the same faith that we are celebrating today and, in several areas of our world, God's children are experiencing these very things that Jesus talks about in our Gospel lesson.

It is distinctly possible that something of this sort—call it persecution or cross-bearing or whatever—could happen to us before our course in life runs out. It is rather noble of us to say, as said Peter to his Lord, "I will lay down my life for you" (John 13:37). What would we say or do if we actually faced up to that necessity?

Cheer up! It may never happen; and if it does happen somewhere along life's journey, God will give us the courage and grace to cope with it. The point is, if some "Christ" or self-styled prophet or apostle peddles a primrose-path kind of gospel that excludes the cost and pain of discipleship, hold that person suspect. He or she is not telling the whole truth.

"He who endures to the end will be saved," said our Lord. We are not saved by enduring, but by the grace of our loving God as revealed in Jesus Christ. The faith that accepts and appropriates that forgiving and sustaining grace must, however, endure to the end—and this must be by the grace of God.

Wednesday   *Hebrews 10:11–18 (B)*

Again, We Are Forgiven!

"Christ . . . offered for all time a single sacrifice for sins. . . . By a single offering He has perfected for all time those who are sanctified."

We are forgiven all our sin, past, present, and future, because "Christ . . . offered for all time a single sacrifice for sins," because He died on the cross on our behalf. The proclamation of the Word, the administration of the sacraments, confession and absolution—these repeatedly bring us back to the center and core of our faith, our recognition of and commitment to this blessed gift, this grace, that draws us, cleansed, redeemed, and perfected, into the very heart of God.

We are forgiven! Even as we sin, we are forgiven. We need not seek forgiveness, we *are* forgiven. Yet with profound grief and sorrow we come daily to the cross to unload our grievous burdens and claim anew this superlative gift, this release from sin's guilt. We don't offer sacrifices, but we offer our gratitude. This will, if we are truly sincere and understanding of the meaning of forgiveness, resolve in sacrifices of another sort—our lives and all that we are and have in loving service to God and to our fellow beings.

Praise be to God who "remembers [our] sins and [our] misdeeds no more."

Thursday   *Luke 21:5–19 (C)*

Hang in There; the End Is Near

Jesus is telling His disciples just how it is in this world—and what it will be like as we approach the final round of this dispensation. When His followers pressed upon Him for some sign that would indicate that the end is near, His response was, "Take heed that you are not led astray" that we should "not go after" those who confuse people with their foolhardy, premature predictions. The time of this dialog with the disciples was some two thousand years ago. In a sense, our modern prophets who are constantly announcing, "The time is at hand!" are correct in that the time has always been "at hand" from the day of Pentecost until this very day. "But the end will not be at once," said Jesus. It is indeed possible that the end will be another two thousand years or more into the future. The point is, we exist in the midst of all these things that "must first take place."

It is not a pleasant scene that Jesus portrays as a prelude to that final event. Whereas we may not yet be personally involved in these horrendous happenings, we are through the media alerted to the fact that these very things are taking place throughout our world. The odds are that it will become much worse as the end draws near. His injunction to us is not to run and hide, or to thumb-twiddle on some mountaintop waiting for His coming, but to endure, to keep the faith, to be His loyal servants in the midst of all this.

The word of comfort He passes on to us is, "not a hair of your head will perish." It is a figurative statement, of course, but indicates God's loving concern for His children and promises that if we endure, and this by His grace, the wisdom and strength that He provides, then, in the words of Paul, "the sufferings of this present time are not worth comparing with the glory that is to be revealed to us" (Romans 8:18).

For Such Times as These

We ought to be thankful that He saved, appointed, and commissioned us for just such a time as this. This world at this moment is exactly where He wants us to be. He has entrusted us with the commission to represent Him and reveal Him to this kind of world. He is the only hope for humankind, and we are the harbingers of that hope. He is, and this is beyond our comprehension, dependent upon His redeemed children to prepare this world for the day of His appearing. We obviously have not completed that important assignment. Let us be about it—and leave those things that need not be our ultimate concern up to Him.

The conditions of our world, the apostasy, the corruption, the utter disregard for God and His will, the atrocities and tragedies, and our failures in attempting to change the course of our world's mad rush to destruction, drive us back to our God to be renewed and recharged, to be reassured and encouraged. This is good; but God forbid that we crawl into some dark cave or become engrossed in some self-concocted ecstasy that numbs us to the world about us while we wait for His appearing. If we do, we may be caught short; for He would thrust us out, again and again, into the frightful tempests of our world to earn our living with the talents He has given us and to bring His light and love and salvation to the impoverished souls of fear-stricken men and women.

Our Family in God

"Have we not all one Father? Has not one God created us? Why then are we faithless to one another . . . ?"

There is probably no religion on earth as divided as is the Christian religion. Hundreds of sects and denominations are spread throughout our world, all of them claiming allegiance to the one God, many of them incapable of or unwilling to relate to other Christian groups.

Today there are attempts to heal some of the breaches and bridge some of the gaps between Christ-honoring groups—particularly among Catholics, Lutherans, Episcopalians, Presbyterians. In recognizing that we worship the same God as He is revealed through Christ, we are discovering a refreshing kind of unity; and we may even learn how to love one another. This kind of unity may be especially relevant in these end times when we may have to learn how to do things together in our hell-bent world and, when persecution does come our way, to hang together lest we hang all by ourselves. It is important, as Christians, that while we respect one another's differences and diversities, we be faithful to God and to His Word. As always, let His Word be our guide.

Second-Last Sunday in the Church Year

Matthew 24:1–14 (A)

When Faith Endures

It is Jesus' profound concern that not one of us abdicate the kingdom into which we have been received. There will be many temptations in these end-times. Siren voices will reach out, seducing, deluding, deceiving, seeking to lead God's children astray. The world will be wracked by cataclysmic events. Governments will fail; traditions will be nullified; customs and mores will change. There are catastrophes affecting the lives of millions of this world's inhabitants at this very moment; persecution, torture, imprisonment, even death, is the lot of God's children even now. It is not surprising that many who follow Jesus are betrayed by false promises of temporal peace and comfort, even of material security and boundless health, that are handed out by leaders Christ has not chosen who are twisting His teachings into claims He never intended.

This world will never be transformed into the kingdom of God. Nor will it become an eternal oasis of glory and light. It is subject to death, and is even now dying in its iniquity. Only those of us who faithfully follow Christ will live forever. Yet even we will suffer within this suffering world. This was Jesus' lot when He lived as a man in this world. It is and will be, in some measure, our lot too.

It is those whose faith endures to the end who can be assured of salvation. We don't have to be afraid of whatever will happen to us or to our world. Christ guarantees, though He does not reveal the day or the hour, that these terrible things that transpire about us will come to an end, and we shall live forever in the joy and glory of God's eternal kingdom.

Monday   *1 Thessalonians 3:7–13 (A)*

Let Us Thank God

We ought to spend much time in thanksgiving—for what God has done for us and for what He is doing through His beloved servants.

And we ought to rejoice and to praise our God for what He will continue to do through His sons and daughters throughout the world about us.

A bit of hindsight should help us to understand that the afflictions that plagued us and the conflicts that beset us brought many of us closer to God and became the crucible that purified and fortified us for loving servanthood. If we recognize God's dealings in the past—and this in spite of our failings and faithlessness—we should be encouraged to put our future in His hands and believe that God blesses through the storm and the static as well as through the sublime and the ecstatic.

Whatever our God allows in our lives can be utilized to enable us to increase and abound in love for one another and for our colleagues all over our world, to establish, to sink deep our faith, and to be ready for our Lord's return or for that hour when we shall separate from our mortal shells to return to Him. Thanks be to God!

Tuesday   *Mark 13:24–31 (B)*

Something That Is Secure

"Heaven and earth will pass away, but My words will not pass away."

The judgment of God falls not only upon His creatures who inhabit this world, but upon the institutions they create. Every nation upon this planet will be judged even as ancient Babylon was judged. All authorities, corporations, bureaucracies, ideologies, traditions, and institutions shall be called to account before the judgment of God. Whatever their motives for existence, whatever their contributions to humanity's existence and benefit, they bear the stamp of depravity; they become, for the most part, the very enemies of God's kingdom. While many of them are necessary to our present existence and have been useful in furthering God's purposes, they will never become a part of His kingdom in that great day when He shall be revealed.

Yet over against the wickedness of Babylon is the righteousness of Jerusalem—the remnant, redeemed by Jesus Christ, who persist, even within the institutions that seek to control them, to follow and serve their Redeemer and King. God knows who they are, this remnant, and while the institutions which men create fall under His judgment and are destined to "pass away," there shall come out of these institutions those who bear upon them the brand of God's redeeming grace, and they shall live forever as the citizens of His eternal kingdom.

319

We Are Equipped

Peter once wrote: "God's divine power has given us everything we need to live a truly religious life through our knowledge of the One who called us to share in His own glory and goodness" (2 Peter 1:3 TEV).

We are assigned to live and serve in the end-times. We cannot run and hide as the world crumbles about us; we can stand up and be counted. We are equipped for this very thing. We need to acknowledge and learn how to use our equipment. The New Testament writers wrote to people who had suffered much and who expected to suffer much more in the world they encountered. Now it is our world; the end-times are upon us. We are to expect suffering; we are also expected to serve in the midst of suffering.

We, of course, seriously question our capabilities in respect to our assignment in these end-times. In a world of computers and space shuttles and laser beams, of atheistic ideologies and totalitarian political philosophies, a world that could be destroyed instantly by a push-button war or gradually become extinct through the continued misuse and abuse of its natural resources, a world that appears to be on the brink of great and violent conflict, our first inclination may be to burrow into some deep, dark hole and pull it in after us. Our natural faculties simply do not enable us to face this kind of world. But we are credentialed, appointed, and commissioned for just such a time as this. "God's divine power has given us everything we need. . . ." It is now time to go about accepting it, laying claim to it, and making it work in and through our lives.

You and Your Talents

As God's children and His ministers and servants in a rebellious and disjointed world, we are the recipients of God-imparted gifts to be used toward the accomplishment of His objectives in our world. It is true that some of us appear to have more than others, but all of us are of equal importance to God and have been entrusted with talents to be used to glorify and serve Him. The value or significance of these gifts is not to be determined by the accolades of our peers, but the manner in which they are accepted and utilized for the glory of God. The disturbing thing is that even some of God's children use them for self-service and self-gratification and stagnate their lives by neglecting to invest them in the needs of their fellow beings. What is worse is that they thereby grieve their loving God and become obstacles to the advancement of His kingdom.

These talents are many and varied. Not all of them are acknowledged and respected by our fellow persons. The most profound ones may be the most invisible—the gifts, for instance, of love, faith, patience, understanding, sensitivity, courage, and the like. They are all given because they are needed for the accomplishment of God's objectives. We are, by the enlightment and empowerment of God's Spirit, to discern and acknowledge and stir up the talents that have been committed to us. Then we are to utilize them, be they the abilities to make music or make money, to preach or write or teach or paint pictures or solve problems or whatever, to serve the needs of those who lack such abilities and, ultimately, to extend God's kingdom throughout our world.

Let us glorify God with our lives and talents!

Friday   *1 Corinthians 15:54–58 (C)*

We Are Motivated

There are some people who can discover motivation for good works apart from the commands and promises of the Christian faith. For most of us it is the fact that death in this world is followed by everlasting life in the next that gives us the courage to go on—even to the point of risking our lives on behalf of others.

We shall indeed be raised from the dead. Our God has not given to us the explanation of just how it shall be done. Our three-dimensional insights would not be capable of comprehending it even if He had. But this we know: The perishable shall become imperishable and the mortal will become immortal on that great day. And this is really all we need to know; it provides all the motivation we need to labor committedly and sacrificially in the purposes of our Lord.

Let us be awake and aware—always! Even as we rest in what God has done on our behalf, let us be on the tiptoe of expectancy, working, serving, giving, loving, keeping the faith and demonstrating that faith to the world of men and women about us. The time will come soon enough when we shall experience together the eternal wonders of the next dimension. As for now, let us praise God for the assurance of our salvation, our citizenship in His kingdom about to be revealed, and the glorious truth that our death in this world will be followed by our resurrection into the next. Let us hold on to one another in love and dedicate ourselves in loving service to God and humanity.

Saturday   *Isaiah 52:1-6 (C)*

We Are Blessed!

How blessed are those who are chosen to be the servants of God! What a message they have to proclaim concerning God's love for the human family! Not only do they speak of God's judgment, but imbued with His Spirit and authorized and empowered by His saving grace, they are to make known His salvation, to spread the glad tidings of His redeeming and reconciling love to all who will listen to His gracious Word. As it says in poetic language in the verses just after today's reading, they are "beautiful."

It is true that God will judge and condemn to eternal darkness all who persist in opposing Him and His purposes. It is equally true that those who deserve nothing less—who have rebelled against their Creator-God and broken His law and have worshiped and lived for the things of this world—that they can be redeemed from the pits of darkness and be reconciled to God. We who are now God's children and servants were once the children of darkness and disobedience. God sought us, found us, and took us back to Himself. Now we are enjoined and assigned to live out and proclaim boldly the redeeming, reconciling love of our God to our fallen, lost, suffering brothers and sisters throughout this planet.

It's a joyous task, a tremendous responsibility, an exciting adventure, a difficult and pain-filled struggle.

We plunge ahead with confidence—and with the assurance that our great God has circumscribed us with His love and care, and that we are His precious vessels, His children and servants forever.

We are indeed blest!

Last Sunday After Pentecost

Matthew 25:31–46 (A)

Ministry and Servanthood

Our salvation is a gift of God, not a consequence of our efforts to please Him or to serve others. It has the result, however, of making us willing to live in obedience to His Word and to help our neighbor. The good deeds we do as God's dear children, in response to His love, are very precious in His sight. In today's reading Christ praises them highly. We notice that He does not mention the believers' sins. These, as well as any imperfections that cling to their good deeds, are washed away by His blood.

What an incentive to once more pledge our lives to ministry and servanthood and, empowered by the Holy Spirit, to minister in love to our brothers and sisters about us! God grant us the grace to be His ministers and servants in our broken world.

Monday   *1 Corinthians 15:20–28 (A)*

We Are Alive!

It is the resurrection of Jesus Christ that assures us of our own personal resurrection. It begins even now when we are born again through faith in Christ. It is culminated in the life and experience that follows our exodus from this world. Among the great freedoms that we celebrate is our freedom from the fear of death. There need be no apprehension concerning that ultimate event in the life of a Christian. Death is not the end but really the beginning. It is not termination, but promotion. And this we know—because Jesus arose from the dead.

If, indeed, Christ had not been raised from the dead, our faith would most certainly be "futile," our sins not forgiven, as St. Paul writes in the verses just before our reading. We would have no hope and little joy save for the few precious hours we come upon in our earthly course. There would be, no doubt, little motivation for good works. We would probably be as involved in the dog-eat-dog, get-what-you-can, do-your-own-thing kind of existence as are the millions who know not the Christ or who refuse to entrust their lives to Him.

"But in fact Christ has been raised from the dead. . . ." This changes the whole picture. Life has been transformed from a dull, lifeless gray into a whole collage of colors. There is hope and joy and love and meaning to life, not only for the short journey we travel on this globe, but for all eternity. "As in Adam all die, so also in Christ [we] shall all be . . . alive." This life is "now"; it shall be forever. We are alive! Let us rise up and live and love and serve!

Tuesday   *John 18:33–37 (B)*

Christ Is Our King

"So you are a king?" Pilate asked of the shackled prisoner standing submissively before him. "You say that I am a king," responded Jesus. "For this I was born, and for this I have come into the world, to bear witness to the truth."

The announcement was greeted with laughs and sneers. He said He was a king, so they dressed Him like one, placing a robe about His shoulders, a crown of thorns upon His head, a reed into His hand. "Hail, King of the Jews," they mocked (19:3). Then they replaced the reed with the heavy cross which Jesus bore up Calvary's hill, where it bore Him in excruciating agony. Fastened to the cross appeared the title: "Jesus of Nazareth, the King of the Jews" (19:19).

They thought they were rid of Him forever. Less than three hundred years later the powerful Roman eagle took a tumble. The despised cross of the humble Galilean took precedence. The tables had been turned. The empire that had crucified Christ now bent the knee before His representatives.

This was the Christ whose coming we recognize anew as we approach the season of Advent. He came as a *Prophet* to teach God's human creatures the grand truth of God's infinite love for them and the salvation that is offered to them. He came as a *Priest* to offer Himself as a mediator and a sacrifice for all the sins of all the people. He kept God's law, which the human creatures could not keep, and took upon Himself the guilt and eternal consequences of humanity's law-breaking. He became our Substitute and suffered vicariously on our behalf. His sacrifice was efficacious because He was and is, God's Son. He came as *King.* He continues to govern the universe through His almighty power and majesty. He fosters, protects, defends, and reigns as the Head and Cornerstone of the church, pointing perpetually to that eternal kingdom which has been provided for and is promised to His faithful followers and servants.

Christ is our King. He has come; He is here; He will soon reveal Himself openly. Let us renew our allegiance to Him and truly crown Him as King of our lives and living.

Wednesday   *Revelation 1:4b–8 (B)*

Our King Is Coming

"Behold, He is coming with the clouds, and every eye shall see Him, everyone who pierced Him; and all the tribes of the earth will wail on account of Him."

One can perceive an excited writer in these words of John. It is almost as if he had just received a message from the great beyond and could hardly wait to pass it on to the suffering, persecuted Christians throughout the then-known world. There are, no doubt, some staid, lethargic, apathetic Christians who need to be awakened and shaken up from time to time, but for most of Christendom the message is being proclaimed loudly today: "He is coming; our King is coming!"

Unfortunately, the concentration of many Christians upon the coming King does not appear to inspire and motivate them for loving service to this world's inhabitants on behalf of their King. Rather it seems to numb them to the suffering round about and to their responsibility in the midst of it.

May Christ the King be the King of our lives even now as He shall be forever in that kingdom to be revealed, and may the truth of His kingship spur us on to living our lives for Him and for our fellow human beings.

Thursday   *Luke 23:35–43 (C)*

Crown Him as King

"He saved others; let Him save Himself," scoffed the rulers of the people. "If You are the King of the Jews, save Yourself," the soldiers mocked.

It was precisely because He did come to "save others" that He could not save Himself. It was necessary that He die for the sins of the people. It is not so surprising that the religious leaders of His day could not understand all this and had to revert to mocking and scoffing. We cannot fully understand it. Yet this was the manner in which the kingdom of God was initiated among God's creatures. "Therefore," said the writer of the Letter to the Hebrews, "let us be grateful for receiving a kingdom that cannot be shaken. . . ." (12:28). And Luther wrote in his famous hymn: "The Word they still shall let remain nor any thanks have for it; He's by our side upon the plain with his good gifts and Spirit. And take they our life, Goods, fame, child, and wife. Though these all be gone, Our victory has been won; The Kingdom ours remaineth." This is the certainty that encompasses the true followers of Jesus Christ, to whom He said: "Fear not, little flock, for it is your Father's good pleasure to give you the kingdom" (Luke 12:32).

We crown Jesus as King; but if we crown Him King at all, we must crown Him King of all. He is with us today, leading us to high adventure, self-denial, danger, sacrifice, for nothing is too great to risk or to lose for the sake of the kingdom. He will be with us through all eternity in the kingdom of God, where He truly will be King of all and over all forevermore.

Friday   *Colossians 1:13–20 (C)*

This Is Christ—Let Him Love You

"[God] has delivered us from the dominion of darkness and transferred us to the kingdom of His beloved Son, in whom we have redemption, the forgiveness of sins."

We have been transferred to the kingdom of Jesus Christ. Jesus did not make Himself King. He did what no king is ever expected to do. "[He] emptied Himself, taking the form of a servant, being born in the likeness of men. . . . He humbled Himself and became obedient unto death, even death on a cross" (Philippians 2:7–8). It was God, His Father, who made Him King. And what a King we have! How gracious is our loving God to place us in His hands and under His domain! "Image of . . . God . . . first-born of all creation. . . . In (Him) all the fulness of God was pleased to dwell, and through (Him) to reconcile to Himself all things . . . making peace by the blood of His cross." This is the Christ whom millions of people refuse to accept as the King of their lives, whom men and women scorn or ignore or crucify afresh in their unbelief and rebelliousness, whom many of us often hold back from or fail to trust and obey.

It is He who is our King. Do we dare to do any less than crown Him

Lord of all? How can we ever withhold our love, our loyalty, our lives, and all we possess from the King of kings?

This is the end of the season of Pentecost in the church year. Next week brings in the season of Advent and we begin all over again to adore and celebrate the Christ of the Gospel, the Son of God, that One who has come to save us from our sins and who will come again to gather us into His kingdom. This is the Christ; let Him love us, comfort us, reign over us, sustain us, advance His kingdom on earth through us. This is Christ, our Savior and Lord and King, and we are His forever.

Saturday   *Jeremiah 23:2–6 (C)*

"The Lord Is Our Righteousness"

What a glorious song with which to end the church year!

Sing it again; sing it often: "The Lord is our righteousness." Only the righteous can be citizens of God's kingdom. No one else need apply. Only those who recognize their bankruptcy, their utter inability to do anything to please God, who realize that there is nothing righteous within them, that they are among the lost, will be eligible for citizenship in the kingdom and prepared to receive as a divine gift the righteousness of God. It is only because Jesus, the Righteous One, has become our righteousness that we can account ourselves among the accepted and redeemed children of God. There is no other way to enter the kingdom—to regard Jesus as our King rather than our Judge—than to approach the kingdom as undeserving sinners who through faith in Jesus are accepting that One who took God's judgment upon Himself and covered us with His own righteousness.

The Lord continues to be our righteousness. No matter how devoted and successful we are in our service assignments, or how defeated and failure-fraught we may feel in the depressing hours of our lives, "The Lord is our righteousness." Nothing else matters—successes or failures—in respect to our relationship to God. Nothing changes in respect to God's regard for us. We are righteous in His eyes and eternally His sons and daughters.

Begin the new year with the song; continue through the year singing the song. Take heart, rejoice, for "The Lord is our righteousness!"